THE POLITICIZED
ECONOMY

SECOND EDITION

THE POLITICIZED ECONOMY

MICHAEL H. BEST
University of Massachusetts, Amherst
Department of Economics

WILLIAM E. CONNOLLY
University of Massachusetts, Amherst
Department of Political Science

D. C. HEATH AND COMPANY
Lexington, Massachusetts   Toronto

PREFACE

Our purpose in this text is to introduce students of political economy and American politics to a radical interpretation of the American system. In the first edition we argued that injustices lodged inside the American political economy could not be rectified reliably and humanely through the policies of the welfare state; attempts to do so, we thought, would help to drive traditional liberal constituencies to the Right. We retain and extend this perspective in the second edition, adding new evidence and arguments to support it. Several chapters have been extensively revised, and some of the initial themes have been developed in more detail. To be specific, we have

1. written a new introduction, which condenses and summarizes the major themes that find expression in later chapters and calls attention to the ways in which each thesis is connected to the others;

2. rewritten and relocated the chapter on stagflation (now Chapter 5) to connect it more closely to the argument in preceding chapters and to bring out more fully how it provides a critique of the interpretations of unemployment and inflation now debated publicly;

3. extended the discussion of the political economy of ecology (Chapter 3) to incorporate a wider range of issues;

4. included an analysis of the distributive effects of the welfare state budget and of the politics of reindustrialization in the chapter on the crisis of the state (Chapter 6);

5. developed more fully in several chapters the discussion of how the organization of private consumption that prevails in the American political economy contributes to inflation, to the pressures to extend inequality, to the assault on the environment, to the crisis of the welfare state, and to the drift to the Right in American politics.

The text is continuous with the first edition in its emphasis on the ways in which our economy has been politicized, on the need to reconstitute the economic priorities of liberals and conservatives, and on the conviction that radical interpretations organized around the labor theory of value lack the categories needed to explain the political dimensions of economic life.

We have accumulated new debts to colleagues and students in developing this second edition. We would like to thank Catherine Best, Michael Gibbons, Jane Humphries, Joseph Martin, Leonard Rapping, Cadwell Ray, Herbert G. Reid, and Charles Sackrey for their ideas and help.

Michael H. Best
William E. Connolly

CONTENTS

THE POLITICIZED
ECONOMY

INTRODUCTION

Our civilization, broadly speaking, is defined by two fundamental sets of priorities. It seeks an economy of growth so that each generation will be more prosperous, secure, and comfortable than its predecessor, and it seeks to sustain a democratic relationship between the state and its citizens. The first priority is embodied in the standards of efficiency, cost effectiveness, and productivity found in the economic order, and it finds expression in the organization of property, profit, management, work, and consumption that typifies our society. The second priority is reflected in our concern with human rights, the quality of human relationships, the political prerogatives of citizenship, and the accountability of the state to its citizens through contested elections.

This text explores changes in the relationship between the priority of productivity and the priority of democracy. Its concerns, therefore, cut across the traditional academic boundaries among political science, sociology, and economics. It is a study in political economy—a study of how political and economic relations now intersect and merge in America.

■ Productivity and Democracy

The civilization of productivity is a very recent historical achievement. The medieval society of only a few hundred years ago, for instance, revolved around quite different standards and practices. Commerce was considered a lowly activity, and profit beyond a minimum level was condemned as a form of avarice. *Usury*—a loan offered at a high rate of interest—was a sin. Innovation in tools and techniques was restricted to prevent individuals from acquiring an unfair advantage over others and to protect those with traditional skills and crafts from obsolescence. Advertising one's wares was considered deception. The legitimate goal of economic activity was to provide the material means for more worthy or noble pursuits; affluence was not a legitimate goal in itself.

Along with the distinctive orientation to economic life went a type of person very unlike the modern individual. The peasant, for instance, was more impulsive, more direct in personal relations, less concerned about cleanliness and control of the public display of bodily functions. Punctuality, self-discipline, planning for the future, and close calculation of private gain played a smaller role in the life of the peasant.

> Much of what appears contradictory to us—the intensity of their piety, the violence of their fear of hell, their guilt feelings, their penitence, the immense outbursts of joy and gaiety, the sudden flaring and the uncontrollable force of their hatred and belligerence —all these, like the rapid changes in mood, are in reality symptoms of the same social and personality structure. The instincts, the emotions were vented more freely, more directly, more openly, than later. It is only to us, in whom everything is more subdued, moderate and calculated, and in whom social taboos are built much more deeply into the fabric of social life, that this unveiled intensity of piety, belligerence, or cruelty appears as contradictory.[1]

We recall some of these differences between two civilizations neither to urge a return to the feudal era nor to lament a world lost forever. The recollection serves first as a reminder that many studies of political economy tend to construe motives and purposes prevailing in our order to be universal traits that every order must acknowledge. Second, we are reminded that just as the personal orientations of one age were "symptoms" of a particular social order, so too our identities are bound up with the order we inhabit. It is difficult enough to examine the foundations of an order that has shaped the kinds of people we have become. But the quest is doomed from the start if, following the lead of many contemporary theories of political economy, we pretend that the character structure typical of our society is typical of human nature as such. Such an orientation forfeits the opportunity to examine reflectively the complex relations among the organization of the economy, the organization of the state, and the organization of the self that prevail in contemporary life.

Debates persist over the sources of the transition from feudal to capitalist society. But one theme, central to the concerns that occupy us, seems clear enough. By the seventeenth century, when this transition was already proceeding, a notable group of political economists became hopeful that the new organization of economic life would carry benign consequences for political life. These theorists are properly defined as political economists because they paid close attention to the way economic life and political life intersect—to the bearing each has on the other. The early justifications of capitalism, then, constructed during a period of social instability and political unrest, were tied to the hope that the new economic order would prevent tyranny and foster a stable and just political order.

The expansion of commerce was thought to be a key ingredient. First, commerce helps shape and regulate human passions in socially desirable ways. It supplements the traditional maintenance of order through the threat of punishment by the sovereign or the fear of eternal damnation; it does so by allowing one set of passions—those of greed and avarice—to find a harmless outlet in the pursuit of economic gain.... The rules of commerce ensure that those engaged in it will either exercise self-restraint or else fail in their objectives. Passions like "greed, avarice, or love of lucre" that had been previously condemned could now be "usefully employed to oppose and bridle such other passions as ambition, lust for power, or sexual lust." [2] The vision of a new person created by new economic arrangements thus did not originate with Karl Marx. It found a previous expression in the political speculations of the early defenders of capitalism.

The competitive market and later the pursuit of economic growth were celebrated not primarily because of the material prosperity they would bring but because of the political consequences they would produce. Montesquieu, the eighteenth-century social philosopher, believed that commerce and democracy went together because commerce encouraged the development of social civility:

> The spirit of commerce brings with it the spirit of frugality, of economy, of moderation, of work, of wisdom, of tranquility, of order and of regularity. In this manner, as long as this spirit prevails, the riches it creates do not have any bad effect.[3]

Montesquieu was impressed with the beneficent political consequences of the new form of property; for it could be transferred across state lines with ease by its owner. In a society with free commerce, he believed, the state would thus have to treat its subjects justly or see a portion of private wealth transferred to other states. With the perfection of commerce, "rulers have been compelled to govern with greater wisdom than they themselves might have intended; for, owing to these events, the great and sudden arbitrary actions of the sovereign have been proven to be ineffective and only good government brings prosperity to the prince."[4] With the extension of commerce the self-interest of the ruler becomes synonymous with the best interests of the population.

Sir James Steuart, the Scottish political economist who preceded Adam Smith, echoed these sentiments. When foreign commerce is highly developed, the statesman, tempted to seize the wealth of his subjects, confronts a form of wealth "which avoids his grasp when he attempts to seize it." Governing becomes a more subtle art of persuasion and negotiation; "he must now avail himself of art and address as well as of power and authority."[5]

These theorists anticipated a reciprocal relationship between democratic politics and a free-enterprise economy. The relationship has proved to be inconstant (there are capitalist economies that are not at all democratic); it has proved to be volatile even in some states where it has gained a foothold (some capitalist states with democratic political forms have become fascist regimes). Furthermore, even in the most favorable instances, the relationship has been more precarious and restrictive than had been anticipated (democratic states have tolerated slavery, have selectively excluded minorities from effective participation, and have periodically intimidated dissident movements). But the affinity between democracy and capitalism has been *comparatively* close. To state the comparison in negative terms: no other form of economic life has supported democratic politics as often and as securely.

And yet, we will argue that the relationship is becoming more tenuous and problematic in the United States today. Most social scientists hesitate to explore this issue, perhaps because they fear that if the relationship between political democracy and the system of private productivity is precarious, the future prospects for democracy are too bleak to contemplate. If this economy becomes inhospitable to democracy, what form of economic organization could serve as its host? Certainly the record of socialist states in the twentieth century is not reassuring in this respect. While this question is indeed important, the devotees of democracy must not use it as an excuse to avoid questions about the future compatibility of democracy and private productivity. If democracy's current host does turn out to be sickly, the supporters of democracy must be ready to look elsewhere for sustenance.

But why do we express concern about the future durability of this relationship? Our complete answer constitutes the body of this text, but we can here introduce some of the themes to be developed.

Let us consider one index of the global shifts in the structure of the American political economy. By comparison, for instance, to seventy years ago, a larger portion of the American population today is either *employed* by institutions whose primary purpose is to control, observe, confine, reform, discipline, or regulate other people (for example, the police, the military, and private security agencies; advertising agencies; mental hospitals; prisons; reform schools; parole boards; welfare agencies; nursing homes) or is the *object* of these operations (for example, illegal aliens; prisoners, dissidents; welfare recipients; mental hospital and nursing home patients; delinquents).

There is, of course, a particular series of causes for this trend. But, we contend, a common thread can be discerned within them: it reflects a disparity between the patterns of conduct the civilization of productivity must today spawn to foster its ends and the willingness or ability of many people to conform to these patterns. The *predispositions* to conduct inside the family, the workplace, the locality, and the school are often at odds with the *requirements* imposed by the order. The process produces two effects upon the state. It impels the state to assume more tasks of subsidization, enforcement, and discipline in the economy, and it restricts the means by which the state can play its role effectively. Consider some of the forms this process takes.

1. *The Consumption Bind.* The legitimacy of the political economy of growth, including the willingness of people to put in a

full day's work for a full day's pay, flows largely from its promise to bring more and more people into the charmed circle of affluence. And the legitimacy of the pursuit of private affluence flows from its promise to make people content once they move into the charmed circle. But that legitimacy weakens as people become aware that the pursuit itself incorporates a self-defeating dynamic, and it becomes increasingly difficult and expensive to manage, discipline, and subsidize those persistently closed out of the circle of affluence.

The self-defeating character of the pursuit resides first in the fact that many private goods decline in value as their availability is extended to everyone, and second in the fact that changes in the social conditions of private consumption progressively convert goods from luxuries consumed for enjoyment into necessities people must obtain to work or participate in community life.[6] Thus, quiet resorts lose their value as they get crowded; technical education becomes a prerequisite of employment when many have acquired it; the automobile, once a vehicle for leisure, becomes an expensive necessity when the world of work, consumption, and culture is built around the expectation of its use.

Only a shift in emphasis away from *exclusive goods* for private consumption toward *inclusive goods* for collective consumption (such as mass-transit systems, preventive health care, and public parks) could reverse the self-defeating logic built into the society-wide pursuit of private affluence. But that shift, as we shall show, would require corollary changes in the role of profit, the organization of work, and the structure of our social life.

2. *The Mobility Trap.* In an economy governed by the pursuit of private profit, companies constantly shift to endeavors in which profit margins are higher. The economy therefore requires a mobile labor force. To secure a good job, a worker must be ready to move to wherever good jobs are located. But the mobility that promotes growth and profits also operates over the long run to weaken family, neighborhood, and community bonds and ultimately citizen concern for the interests of future generations. The erosion in these areas takes a toll in divorce rates, delinquency, isolation of the elderly, and deterioration of the public will to deal with such issues as urban affairs and environmental problems. When established social institutions no longer absorb these community burdens, they become new expenditures passed on to the state. The new expenditures in turn reduce the disposable income available to working people. People become increasingly

resentful of the state and increasingly insistent that the false promises made on behalf of the life of mobility be fulfilled.

3. *The Regimentation of Work.* The political economy that generates corporate concentration and discontented workers impels private and public bureaucracies to devise new means to subject workers to more effective disciplinary control. An increasing percentage of the work force is hired to supervise, control, observe, and penalize other workers. But the extension of disciplinary controls further accentuates worker discontent, taking a further toll in productivity, product quality, and corporate/state expenditures.

4. *The Extension of Adolescence and Obsolescence.* The frantic pace of technological and occupational change required by the civilization of productivity operates, on one side of the life cycle, to extend the period of adolescence, and, on the other, to hasten the point at which middle-aged employees become obsolete. The skills acquired by young employees tend to lose their market value and social importance just at the point in the life cycle when people are most in need of stability, social ties, and a sense of self-respect. The old are often cast off in the name of progress. But when each new generation anticipates that it too will face this fate, the questions become, who benefits from this ceaseless process, and when during the life cycle are the benefits enjoyed?

5. *Economic Dependence and Global Insecurity.* The pursuit of perpetual growth requires the exploitation of a constantly expanding portion of the earth's resources. Indeed, more and more components of nature progressively become "resources" to be exploited. The effects include not only the deterioration of the soil, water, and air but also the destruction of vegetation, animal life, and the natural landscape. The economy becomes increasingly dependent on crucial resources located in foreign countries. The state is thus compelled to build a massive military machine to protect these essential supplies, and it becomes increasingly obvious that this combination of awesome military strength, foreign hostility, and dependence on foreign resources enhances the prospect of nuclear war. The historical trajectory of the civilization of productivity poses a threat to civilization itself.

The evolution of the civilization of productivity makes it more difficult today to think of the economy as a harmless outlet for passions, the market as the benign regulator of economic transactions, and the state's dependence on the private economy as naturally conducive to democratic politics. Today it seems more likely that democracy is maintained in the face of economic pressures to confine and subdue it.

Today the state does not merely allow commerce to follow its own beneficent course; it joins private institutions in striving to *mobilize* broad segments of the populace to accept the imperatives of work, consumption, styles of living, and tax payments dictated by the system of productivity. And as public recognition of the consumption bind becomes more widespread; as recognition grows of the mobility trap, the regimentation of work, the dynamics of personal obsolescence, and the global insecurities fostered by the civilization of productivity, it also becomes more difficult for new generations of Americans to identify with the future they are building. New disciplinary strategies are required to bring individual conduct in line with the imperatives of the economy. And these strategies strain even further the fragile relationship between the politics of democracy and the economy of productivity.

■ The Politicized Economy

Social relations can assume a variety of forms, and a particular social relation can shift from one type to another before the participants have become closely aware of the change. Consider, by way of illustration, a simplified version of a social tie, a market transaction, and a political connection—as each might find expression in marriage.

In a simple social relation, each partner is connected to the other through a set of traditions unreflectively followed by both. Each accepts an established division of labor and adopts a set of duties and rights attached to that division. If either breaks one of the norms, both agree that an unjustifiable transgression has occurred. The obligations of each, moreover, extend well beyond specific assignments. If one mate should, say, become seriously ill or deformed, the responsibilities of the other are not thereby erased. Love, tradition, and duty are the defining characteristics of this relation.

If the marriage connection were a simple market relation, the obligations of each partner would be quite limited; perhaps they would be specified in a contract. The terms of exchange would not be settled autonomously by the couple, but a competitive market in wives and husbands would establish the going prices.

The wife might perform six units of housework in exchange for four units of yardwork. Sexual acts might be classified into types and placed on a preference scale by each partner so that a market rate of exchange could be established. If one partner became ill or ugly, the other would search in the open market for a better deal. Contracts limiting obligations and exchange rates established in a competitive situation would define the market marriage.

Finally, the connection would be political if the parties were interdependent or shared some commitments but were also locked into a continuing struggle over how to constitute aspects of the relation. Perhaps the wife, repudiating the traditional division of labor, would press for a relation in which each would serve as breadwinner and homemaker. Or perhaps the husband, responding to pressures from friends, children, and parents to whom the wife has appealed for support, would adjust the old assignments somewhat but then launch a love affair with a younger person to undermine the confidence and power position of his mate. The possibilities are endless. Struggle and maneuvering within a setting of interdependence, but a setting interpreted rather differently by each party, would mark a politicized marriage.

So far our attention has been fixed on the marriage relation as interpreted by the participants themselves. We have pretended that appearance and reality always mesh in marriage. But it might turn out, certainly, that a power relation actually underlies the market connection, rendering the terms of exchange quite uneven. Or the traditions embedded in the social tie might treat one party as naturally inferior to the other when in fact nothing in the parties themselves requires this treatment. Or the political relation might be informed by aspirations that are in fact unattainable, thereby introducing conflict into a situation for no good reason. When a power relation that is unrecognized by one or both parties distorts a social or market relation, we will say that the relation is partially (or imperfectly) politicized. The relation becomes more fully politicized to the extent that both parties, though generally not in the same way, define it as a conflict over the shape of the relation itself, planning their strategies and responses accordingly.

With these distinctions in mind, we can now summarize the political dimension of our thesis more closely. Each of the italicized concepts is defined and elaborated in the main body of the text.

1. *Markets and Power.* Underlying *market transactions* in the American economy are *power relations that* subordinate the

worker to the owner, workers in the *competitive sector* of the economy to those in the *corporate sector,* the *small owner* to the *large corporation,* consumers to producers, and the *public interest* to the *private interest.* As the adverse effects of *uneven economic development, labor mobility, regimented work, irrational product priorities, ecological destruction, inflation,* and *underemployment* accumulate, they progressively unravel the fabric of established social relations. As these social ties deteriorate and as the priorities of the order decline in their ability to gain the reflective allegiance of many citizens, the power dimension of market relations becomes magnified.

2. *The Politicized Economy.* As the power dimension of economic relations is explicitly recognized by increasing numbers of people, these practices themselves tend to become more explicitly and thoroughly *politicized.* Since the state is the only legitimate forum of *public accountability,* many of the political struggles are transferred to it for resolution. State involvement in a large array of economic transactions renders the political dimension of economic life even more visible to participants, and each organized interest presses its economic claims as vigorously as possible upon the state.

3. *The Welfare-State Dilemma.* The state, as the legitimate forum for defining and resolving public issues, becomes the site for a widening range of struggles. But even where responsive officials occupy the most important state positions, the welfare state typically lacks the resources to cope with the dislocations in humane and rational ways. The very *dependence* of the state on the performance of the privately incorporated economy ensures that the order will be *imperfectly politicized* in one basic respect: the institution legally accountable to the public cannot promote public purposes effectively, while the private institutions that avoid public accountability consistently pursue policies at odds with public needs. The responses available to the welfare state increase its size, its regulatory functions, and the tax burden it imposes on its citizens; but its limited effectiveness generates growing public hostility to the welfare functions it adopts. The state is held accountable for failures *located in the very nature of the relationship between it and the privately incorporated economy.* It becomes the visible target of a public resentment that is rooted more deeply in the priorities and imperatives of the system of productivity.

4. *The Repressive Potentialities.* The accumulation of these failures and hostilities fosters a political movement from the right

to reduce the size of the state, to curtail its regulation of business, and to cast off those constituencies closed out of the productive system. This response, intended to allow the market to flourish once again, will actually enable the strong to prey upon the weak more ruthlessly. The reduction in state welfare functions will be matched by an escalation in its punitive control over those unwilling or unable to adapt to the priorities of the system of productivity. The welfare state becomes at once a catalyst and a casualty of irrational practices lodged in the historical development of the civilization of productivity.

This account includes an *interpretation* of existing practices and an *extrapolation* to future possibilities. The extrapolation does not represent an iron law of development. In fact, public recognition of these ominous possibilities might lead to reforms that would democratize economic relationships and revise prevailing modes of work, ownership, and consumption. There are dangers and uncertainties in moving in such a direction. For instance, there is no contemporary model to draw upon in exploring these reforms, just as there was no operative model for the adherents of capitalist democracy in an earlier period. But if the interpretation offered in this text is on the right track, it is the most viable path open to the American political economy today.

■ Explanation and Prescription

The study of political economy embodies a perspective that American social scientists have sought to avoid, at least until quite recently. Political economists explain in order to arrive at prescriptive judgments. They bridge that artificial split between *is* and *ought* that has led to so much mystification in contemporary social science. We have already disavowed that split, for instance, by suggesting that if our interpretation is correct, the case for a redefinition of our basic economic priorities has been advanced considerably.

Any theory of political economy sets the terms within which prescriptions are formulated and ideals developed. The interpretation contains the ideal within it. It would be strange indeed for someone to accept the free-market interpretation of the American system as represented, for instance, by the work of Milton Friedman and then to opt for socialism as an ideal. For the free-market account contains assumptions that, if true, show socialism to be inefficient, coercive, and self-defeating. Socialism simply runs against the grain of human nature as understood by market theorists. It is not by caprice that classical and neoclassical economists celebrate capitalism and condemn socialism: their own theories make it irrational for them to do otherwise.[7] The task of the student of political economy is to ascertain which assumptions in an interpretation support a particular set of ethical conclusions and then to ask, To what extent are those assumptions justified? How does one decide between these assumptions and other sets embedded in alternative theories?

The assumptions and concepts we employ to comprehend corporate capitalism are most congenial to an ideal of democratic socialism. Where others see disconnected problems susceptible to piecemeal solutions, we see an interlocking set of institutions in need of more radical reconstitution. Where others identify necessary limits set by the dynamics of industrial society per se, we often see unnecessary constraints imposed by the historical arrangements of corporate capitalism. Where they would counsel personal adjustment and collective patience, we would urge impatience and opposition. Our political commitments, like theirs, arise out of our understanding of the established order, and thus it is differences at this level that must be illuminated and debated.

The study of political economy, then, unavoidably connects explanatory theories to evaluative judgments. Because of this inner connection, one who seeks to repudiate a set of economic ideals will be required to undermine the explanatory theory that sustains them.

■ The Holistic Approach

In identifying structural defects in corporate capitalism, we employ a holistic approach. This approach, unfamiliar to many students of social science, has become familiar to students of ecology. It is the opposite of the reductionist approach, which has been criticized by ecologist Barry Commoner as follows:

> [There is] a specific fault in our system of science . . . which . . . helps to explain the ecological failures of technology. This fault is reductionism, *the view that effective understanding of a complex system can be achieved by investigating the properties of its isolated parts.* The reductionist methodology . . . is not an effective means of analyzing the vast natural systems that are threatened by degradation. . . . Reductionism tends to isolate scientific disciplines from each other and all of them from the real world.[8]

Holists see inner connections where reductionists see separate phenomena. Holists suspect that trying to account for, say, inflation in terms of one or two independent factors wrenches it out of the systemic context in which it is shaped. Reductionists ignore a complex web of internal relations in the name of precision. Finally, holists perceive that interwoven institutions can slowly redefine one another without much noticeable effect and then suddenly generate significant qualitative changes in the entire system.

Ecologists have learned, for instance, that a new parasite introduced into a lake slowly alters the balance between the various species of fish; the new balance increases the vegetation content of the lake, affecting in turn the oxygen content of the water; and these changes together diminish the self-purification capacity of the water. As the changes accumulate, with each accentuating changes in the others, a minor change in the weather, previously without effect on aquatic life, might now kill a whole species of fish. If so, as the dead fish pile up in the water and on the shore, the water becomes more putrid, threatening other species; algae growth flourishes, further reducing the oxygen level in the lake and threatening to kill off all the fish. The relations among the various elements shift, and the system itself undergoes perceptible changes. Reductionists would ask, if the parasite was so important, why did its effects not show up earlier? How come the lake still stinks now that we have eliminated the parasite? Hoping to hold the basic environment constant while experimentally varying specific factors to isolate the casual influence of each, the reductionist misses the point: A new ecological system, quite unlike the one operative when the parasite was introduced, now maintains itself despite the parasite's departure. The whole new system must be understood in order to reestablish the self purification capacity.

So too with political economy. For example, in this text we explore the connections between the instrumental, routinized mode of work that prevails in our society and a variety of other dimensions of the system. The structure of work life, we argue, is internally connected to inequality, environmental degradation, inflation, and irrational product priorities, as well as being an affront to the dignity of the worker. Work-life arrangements partly shape and are partly shaped by each of these other institutions, and none of them is adequately comprehended until its connections to the others are understood. Moreover, work routines that were interpreted in one way by workers in an earlier period might take on a different appearance in a later period, even though the structure of the work itself has not noticeably changed. Thus, routinized, authoritarian patterns of work were once legitimated by the promise that they would contribute to the material affluence of future generations. But the future has now arrived. For many Americans, the promise has not been fulfilled, making them cynical about still more promises for a new future. And the progeny of the affluent, having tasted the benefits of affluence, have found it unrewarding. Thus, justifications accepted by an earlier generation become less convincing to a later one. And in the new context, the old modes of work, still required by the system of political economy, generate new obstacles to the smooth operation of that system.

This example merely introduces the methodological principle of this text: since each institution is interwoven into a larger complex, to understand any one part of the system, it is necessary to grasp the whole.

■ Political Economy and Political Controversy

A text widely held to be unbiased generally recapitulates the views that happen to prevail at the time it is written. It reproduces conventional assumptions without subjecting them to critical scrutiny. We hope, in this sense, that our text will be thought of as biased and controversial. For in examining inflation, unemployment, inequality, environmental control, the structure of work life, and the crisis of the state, our overriding purpose is to challenge the prevailing accounts of these topics. We do give some attention to the established interpretations. We explore the Keynesian approach to inflation and unemployment, the functionalist theory of inequality, the classic theory of "scientific management" of workers, the market model of environmental management. But our purpose is to expose underlying assumptions that are susceptible to criticism, to show weaknesses in the interpretations, to introduce alternative interpretations that seem to us to account better for the phenomena in question.

Learning a new theory is like learning a new language: one stumbles at first; constant practice is necessary; long discussions with others similarly involved are indispensable. When journalists, television commentators, educators, and politicians persist in interpreting the issues of political economy through conventional categories, the task is even more difficult. Then it is like learning a foreign language with no one else to talk to and no certainty of ever reaching the country where people do talk that way.

We know of no neat way out of this bind. It afflicts the study of every dissenting interpretation. But since a growing number of people suspect that the established ideas do not adequately explain the established system, we trust our ideas will be given attention. We are not certain that our interpretation is entirely true, but we think it is on the right track. And we know that no one can assess the worth of prevailing ideas without seriously exploring at least one theory that challenges the assumptions hidden inside those established beliefs and ideals.

NOTES

1. Norbert Elias, *The Civilizing Process: The Development of Manners* (New York: Urizen Books, 1978), p. 200.
2. A. O. Hirschman, *The Passions and the Interests: Political Arguments for Capitalism before Its Triumph* (Princeton: Princeton University Press, 1971), p. 41.
3. Quoted in Hirschman, p. 71.
4. Ibid., p. 72.
5. Ibid., p. 82.
6. We discuss the consumption bind in Chapters 3 and 5. Between the first and second editions of this text, Fred Hirsch developed a theory of consumption that both complements and improves the formulations we were striving to develop. The discussion of the consumption bind now incorporates his account. See Fred Hirsch, *The Social Limits to Growth* (London: Routledge & Kegan Paul, 1977).
7. Many social scientists now acknowledge that their biases influence the outcomes of inquiry. Although this is true, it is not the problem we are now addressing. Our point is actually a more basic one: explanatory theories sustain norms. For development of the pertinent arguments, see Charles Taylor, "Neutrality in Political Science," and William Connolly, "Theoretical Self-Consciousness," both in *Social Structure and Political Theory,* edited by William Connolly and Glen Gordon (Lexington, Mass.: D. C. Heath, 1974), pp. 16–66.
8. Barry Commoner, *The Closing Circle* (New York: Alfred A. Knopf, 1971), pp. 189, 191 (italics added).

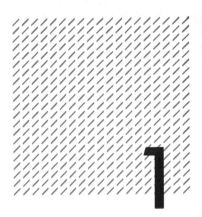

PERSPECTIVES ON POLITICAL ECONOMY

Not all perspectives on corporate capitalism in America are equally illuminating. We will examine four models, exemplified in the works of Milton Friedman, Arthur Okun and Paul Samuelson, John Kenneth Galbraith, and André Gorz, and argue that each successive view is an improvement over the preceding one. To set the stage for this examination, we must first ask, what is there about the idea of a free market regulating economic transactions that exerts such a powerful grip on so many students of political economy?

■ The Idea of a Market

The president of Exxon, responding in 1974 to widespread criticism of the high price, low supply, and high profit margin of oil, invoked in the traditional manner the image of the market to ward off "punitive" government policy:

But time and again it has been demonstrated that the free market mechanism is the most efficient allocator of the nation's resources. The basic laws of supply and demand will bring price into equilibrium and will establish the proper level of production. The consumer is best served by free competition in terms of the lowest price of goods consistent with long term availability. Government attempts to mandate the functioning of the marketplace succeed only in frustrating the efficient distribution of productive resources and products.[1]

Consumers today are skeptical of such views of a self-balancing market. Many believe that imagery of this kind only veils corporate power in the economy and deflects public efforts to render that power more accountable. But since few public officials are willing to replace this old image of the market with a more realistic picture of the American political economy, the image itself continues to prevail by default. It influences our thought and action more than we care to admit. It is, for example, the image of the self-balancing market that sustains the widely held distinction between a *polity* properly subject to democratic control and an *economy* where such public accountability is unnecessary and illegitimate.

The idea of a national market economy is abstracted from the more specific concept of a local marketplace where a large number of independent producers and consumers meet to buy and sell goods. By examining briefly this more specific concept, we can, first, derive some of the conditions that must prevail before we can properly transfer the idea from a local setting to the transactions of an entire national economy and, second, come to understand why the image of the self-balancing market continues to be so attractive.

Consider a hypothetical community of family farms situated, say, in the lush plains of Illinois at some time well before 1900. Each family raises crops and livestock, partly for its own subsistence and partly to sell to others for cash. Most of the cattle are shipped to Chicago, but a portion of the farmer's vegetables, fruit, eggs, chickens, and milk is offered for sale at the local farmers' market. Each farmer comes every Saturday during the harvest season to sell some goods and to buy others. Other members of the community (the blacksmith, minister, barkeeper, sheriff, banker, schoolteacher, and so on) also come to the market to buy goods.

We can reasonably assume that each individual will arrive with a solid idea of what he or she needs; with the intention to sell at the highest available price or buy at the lowest available price; with some awareness of the cost involved for other farmers in producing this year's crop; and with a knowledge of the range of prices and product quality in the local market. Finally, most of the buyers and sellers are permanent residents of the community. Their self-respect depends on their neighbors' and friends' respect for them, so dishonest practices like false representation, collusion, sabotage of competitors' crops, and bribery of the sheriff or banker are minimized in this market. The farmers' market, though competitive, is situated within a community characterized by persisting ties of mutual knowledge, trust, and respect.

When such conditions prevail, the market clearly produces benefits for each of its participants and for the community as a whole. The sellers are usually able to get a price that covers slightly more than their costs of production. The buyers are able to compare competing products for quality and price, purchasing those they need at the lowest available prices. The price for any product itself reflects the choices made by the multitude of individual buyers and sellers. And sellers are both encouraged by profits to produce more crops for sale next year and informed by this year's sales as to which items are most likely to be in greatest demand then. The market thus allocates goods efficiently. It also allows individuals freedom to choose among competing goods and sellers. And it does all this without having to draw upon any central authority with sufficient coercive power to set product quotas, determine prices, establish wage levels, or ration goods. Since the need for a central authority is minimal—it enforces contracts and punishes criminals—there is very little chance that the local government will acquire enough power to tyrannize the community. Limited power is not open to corruption to the degree that unlimited power is.

We can now understand why the idea of a private-enterprise market economy is so attractive to libertarians who seek above all to protect the liberty of each individual to own, work, sell, buy, and speak without fear of sanctions imposed by a central power. Such libertarians will find it comforting to view a complex national economy as a market system. But they may overlook features of the larger system that do not fit neatly within the frame of a market system, and thus their policy prescriptions could intensify rather than relieve dislocations in the national economy.

A compelling image, then, can sharpen perception in some settings and distort it in others. But which effect does the market image produce today? This is exactly the question that proponents and critics of market theory of political economy answer differently. To extend the market beyond the boundaries of a local community to the parameters of a nation-state is, in the eyes of classical liberals, to expand the area where economic efficiency and individual liberty can flourish with minimal threat of governmental tyranny. According to critics, though, such an extension must fail: it creates coercive relations between owners and workers; it blinds market economists to those inefficiencies and exploitative tendencies that do not fit into their model; and it encourages public policies that neglect the most pressing needs of subordinate groups. Just as, in an earlier age, social control over mature citizens was sometimes seen as if it were merely a form of parental authority over children, so, critics claim, the attempt to treat the national economy as if it were merely a large local market wrongly legitimizes a system of exploitative production and unjust distribution.

■ The Market Theory of Political Economy

Perhaps the most persuasive and uncompromising attempt to apply the market image to the political economy of contemporary America is found in the work of Milton Friedman. Friedman has led the attack against those who contend that the Great Depression demonstrated the need for massive state intervention into the economy. We can state in summary form the preconditions that Friedman assumes are present in the American system, preconditions that provide the foundation for a viable market system.

1. In each product area there are enough privately owned firms to ensure that no single firm can set prices or otherwise subvert impersonal market controls; as a result prices reflect the pressures of market competition.

2. Barriers to entry, such as capital requirements, economies of scale, one firm's monopoly over key natural resources or distribution channels, are not so great as to prohibit the entry of new firms into the market. Prospective price rises induced by barriers to entry into any specific product line are limited by competition from substitute products (for instance, coal for oil).

3. While each producer seeks to maximize profits within the limits of market constraints, each consumer seeks to maximize private satisfaction through market purchases.

4. Consumers have sufficient knowledge about the quality and durability of available products, the authority of competing advertising claims, price differentials among comparable products, and the relative dependability of firms with respect to servicing products to enable them to make rational consumption choices within the marketplace.

5. Owners, workers, and consumers sufficiently support market principles and outcomes (the structure of work, nature of products available, distribution of wealth and income) to allow market mechanisms to function with a minimum of resistance and subversion. Mutual consent to most market transactions lubricates the system and minimizes the necessary support role of the state in enforcing contracts and maintaining law and order.

Point 5 is an implicit requirement of Friedman's theory; the others are explicitly avowed in his major study, *Capitalism and Freedom*.[2]

According to this theory, when the preconditions of private property and market competition are met, several benefits emerge: the parties to commodity and employment contracts are "effectively free to enter or not to enter into any particular exchange, so that every transaction is strictly voluntary."[3] Consumers are free to choose among products and sellers; sellers are free to choose which product markets to enter; and the potential "employee is protected from coercion by the employer because of other employers for whom he can work."[4] The market thus coordinates transactions while it protects individuals against undue coercion by other individuals or organizations.

The market economy, which promotes freedom in economic transactions, also provides the necessary condition for political freedom in the modern state. First, the market removes the need for direct government intervention into economic arrangements. Second, it provides the base from which many autonomous and distinct interest groups can emerge to ensure the "dispersal and distribution" of government power. Third, it provides relatively secure places of employment beyond the reach of government authority for political dissidents. Finally, it enables "patrons" with market resources to finance unpopular political programs and ideas. Indeed, the market system helps to ensure that diverse political and economic ideas will be disseminated, for if the demand for radical ideas is high, competitive publishers will strive to produce a supply.[5]

Friedman's contrast model—the system against which he compares the operation of the market economy—is the form of coercive state socialism generally associated with the Soviet Union. This selection is no coincidence, for Friedman believes that any form of collective control over the means of production must destroy the preconditions for individual economic choice and political freedom. The point, then, is not that individuals are perfectly free in a market system but that they are tolerably free in the areas that count in comparison with individuals living under any other system. Many idealistic socialists, Friedman acknowledges, have said that socialism can promote freedom and equality, but "none of the people who have been in favor of socialism and also in favor of freedom have ... made even a respectable attempt at developing the institutional arrangements that would permit freedom under socialism." [6]

There are, Friedman concedes, coercive pressures in contemporary American capitalism, but these threats do not come from within the market system itself. They flow out of government intervention into the self-balancing market. The government typically seeks to implement economic "reforms" through public policy, but its intervention invariably undermines individual freedoms while creating economic effects quite at odds with those intended.

Thus minimum-wage laws, designed to shore up the income of wage earners at the bottom end of the scale, actually force employers to lay off workers earning less than the minimum wage, thereby worsening the plight of such marginal employees. Public-housing programs designed to improve living conditions of the poor lead to the destruction of many old housing units, to a rise in the number of occupants per dwelling, and to a number of negative side effects associated with subsidized housing. Thus the lives of most of the poor are made worse while urban property and business interests benefit by the removal of poor people and slum housing from the urban core. The graduated income tax, designed to reduce income inequality, encourages the reinvestment of corporate earnings (as opposed to paying dividends taxable at a high rate to stockholders), which favors the growth of the large corporation over the development of new, competitive enterprises. The income tax also generates a huge government bureaucracy to monitor tax returns and to catch those who would evade payments they find unjust. Similarly, the capital-gains tax, set lower than the income tax to foster investment, actually channels investment into the largest corporations by encouraging them to reinvest retained earnings rather than distribute earnings to stockholders as dividends taxable at a higher rate. This tax policy reduces the efficiency of the economic system by fostering a concentration of investment funds in established firms.

Friedman supplies other examples, but there is an inner logic that unites most of them:

> The central defect of these measures is that they seek through government to force people to act against their own immediate interest in order to support a supposedly general interest. These measures are therefore countered by one of the strongest and most creative forces known to man—the attempt by millions of individuals to promote their own interest, to live lives by their own values.[7]

His conclusion is quite clear. Government must increasingly withdraw from economic life so that the self-balancing market system can reassert itself. And this will occur only if more people come to understand Friedman's theory of the market and his analysis of how government intervention systematically distorts and disrupts the market system. A reduction of its economic activities would allow government to return to its proper functions: defense of the nation, maintenance of law and order, enforcement of contracts, and provision of a stable monetary framework for market transactions.[8]

The most challenging critiques of Friedman's theory of political economy will emerge later as we explore alternative theories, but perhaps some preliminary points can be raised now.

Friedman labels himself a positivist who believes, among other things, that each concept in a scientific theory should be defined precisely and that the conditions of its use should be spelled out carefully so that any investigator can tell when the concept may be used in describing and explaining the economic world. But the idea of freedom, even though it serves as the keystone of Friedman's theory, is nowhere carefully defined by him, nor are we given impersonal means of deciding when it may be applied to economic or political relations. Despite Friedman's casual treatment of the idea, it is in fact a controversial notion: fundamental differences in political philosophy are reflected in differences in the ways it is understood.[9] It is thus not enough to say that "political freedom means the absence of coercion of a man by his fellow men,"[10] because we must first find out what coercion means to the theorist and whether his meaning sufficiently covers the pertinent area. For instance, does the failure to act to eliminate poverty, when such public action is possible, constitute a restraint on the freedom of the poor? Does failure to act when I am in a position to help another constitute a restraint on his freedom? How do these judgments about the meaning of freedom square with Friedman's view that the market promotes, while the government restricts, economic freedom?

Moreover, different ideals of freedom are linked to different conceptions of human nature—why people behave as they do and what is most fulfilling to them. But Friedman does not really confront these issues either. For example, he equates the ability of the consumer to choose between alternative products with the ability of the wage earner to choose a job from those offered by alternative employers. In each case, he says, the consumer and the worker are free from coercion because there are alternatives available. But a socialist, with a quite different view of human nature, would never equate these two choices. For although the worker is (sometimes) free from coercion by one employer because he can work for another, the market system makes him unfree to get a fulfilling job in which he is not subject to the authority of the employer alone but participates with other workers in shaping the conditions of work. For the socialist the private-enterprise market system can itself be coercive in the way it restricts the range of work alternatives for those who do not own productive resources. The socialist will draw a sharp line between owners and workers because, he thinks, owners systematically limit the freedom of workers.

Moreover, even if one accepts his idea of freedom and his view of human motivation, an internal defect of some importance in Friedman's theory renders his ideal of the self-balancing market utopian in the sense that, by his own assumptions, no political system can be devised that would both protect freedom and minimize state intervention in the market economy over the long run. That is our charge. Let's see if it can be sustained.

Short-term government intervention in the market, in Friedman's view, is systematically counterproductive. Why, then, does the government intervene? Is its intervention endemic to market capitalism and democratic government, or is it simply the result of bad policy decisions by unintelligent liberals in office? Friedman does not say. Rather than analyzing the causes of intervention, he simply casts blame on the government for its action. For example, explaining the government's recurrent temptation to introduce wage and price regulations as part of its effort to hide its own responsibility for inflation, he says, "Governments ask for the self-restraint of business and labor because of their inability to manage their own affairs." [11] But this avoids rather than answers the important question, why are governments unable to manage their own affairs?

Let us examine a bit more closely the view of political activity and government decision making implied by Friedman's market theory of economic transactions. One important virtue of the market is that it provides the economic base from which a variety of interest groups can organize and press their claims upon government. And we can expect each group that is able to organize to do so because its members will want to mobilize political resources to protect or advance interests they share. The market theory of the economy implies, in short, a *pluralist* theory of the polity, in which many groups advance their claims upon government, each group receiving some of what it wants and no group receiving everything. The pluralist image of democratic politics is in fact very much like the market image of economic transactions.[12]

Suppose under these general conditions a company gains a temporary market advantage; perhaps a key resource of its competitors is depleted, or its own managers are more efficient, or it gains a lucrative government defense contract. We must expect the company to consolidate its temporary advantage, perhaps by seeking to influence government policy in its favor. It will convert part of its economic advantage into political resources (contributing to key congressional campaigns, bribing officials, promising bureaucrats future jobs in its company, and so on) and then use those resources to gain policies that shore up its market position (for instance, favorable tariffs, long-term government contracts, access to inside information on diplomatic initiatives, credit policies, highway programs). In this way it may well convert its temporary advantage into a permanent position of market superiority. And this behavior would be quite rational, according to Friedman, because it promotes the firm's self-interest.

Similarly, we can expect that if a large number of citizens are jointly disadvantaged by market processes, they will use their voting power to influence public policy in their favor. They might seek unemployment compensation, public health insurance, social security, and so on, to relieve pressures and risks imposed by the market. To press in such directions might be irrational (given Friedman's assumptions) from the vantage point of the long-range public interest, but it is quite rational from the vantage point of the short-term private interest of those who suffer losses from the market system.

Now it is demonstrably easier in a pluralist democracy for a group to secure a public policy to its advantage than it is for other groups to reverse that policy once its wider disadvantages become clear. For the group intensely committed to the prevailing policy usually has to defeat counterproposals at only one point in the complex legislative-executive-bureaucratic process, while the more diffuse opposition must be successful at every stage in order to get its policy through. Thus we can see that the continuing pressure of each group to manipulate the market in its favor accumulates into a pattern of government intervention into the market. The predictable result is a large set of policies supporting the most powerful corporations and a smaller pile of welfare policies supporting citizens trying to protect themselves against unemployment, indigency in old age, high medical costs, and so on.

If these tendencies are, according to Friedman's assumptions, built into the very pattern of interaction between a private market economy and a pluralist polity, how could he seek to forestall them? He might opt for limitations on the freedom of groups to organize and to press for public policies that would give them a short-run advantage. But Friedman could hardly accept this response. It would undercut his basic justification for the market system itself. For that justification rests on the claim that the market system, more than any other system, protects the freedom of individuals to organize and to press claims upon the government.

Another response, more congenial to Friedman's orientation, is to persuade private citizens, business managers, and government officials that continued intervention in the market system is against the public interest in the long run, however tempting it might be to particular interests in the short run. This is the note upon which Friedman ends *Capitalism and Freedom*. We must warn citizens, he asserts, of "the threat that we face"; and we can only hope to reverse established trends "if we persuade our fellow men that free institutions offer a surer, if perhaps at times a slower, route to the ends they seek than the coercive power of the state." [13]

But given Friedman's assumptions about the springs of human behavior when people are free, we must expect his plea to be accepted by many groups rhetorically, only to be ignored when each group pursues its self-interest through government. Friedman has accounted for the failure of government intervention, remember, on the grounds that it seeks to persuade people to forgo their immediate interests in the name of the public interest. But his own call to restrain government intervention into the economy falls into the same trap. It calls upon people "to act against their own immediate interests" by refusing to seek market advantages through government policy "in order to promote a supposedly general interest"—maintenance of the market system.

When its political and economic tendencies are explored in conjunction with Friedman's assumptions, the system of market capitalism and pluralist politics emerges as an inherently unstable system. It tends to evolve into the very corporate capitalism and welfare state that Friedman decries. Only if he were ready to give up a key premise of his theory would this undesired implication be avoided. But if he were to drop the premise that only a system in which people are free to follow their short-run self-interests can operate noncoercively and effectively, one of the central reasons for adopting the theory in the first place would disappear. His failure to confront these issues results, we think, from a tendency in classical and neoclassical economic theory that the perspective of political economy seeks to avoid: the failure to explore carefully the dialectical relation between economic transactions and political practices.[14]

■ The Mixed Economy in the Welfare State

The main body of contemporary economic thought, neoclassical theory, treats the economy as a mixed system in which, as Paul Samuelson expressed it, "both public and private institutions exercise economic control."[15]

In many areas of the economy, such as agricultural production and service industries, the market rather efficiently regulates wages, prices, and production levels in the interests of consumers. In other areas, such as steel and automobile production, a few producers dominate the market; together constituting an oligopoly, they exercise some control over prices. In a very few areas, such as telephone and electric utilities, one producer dominates the market. In the last two sectors large, highly capitalized firms are efficient in fulfilling consumer demand, but the controlling firms' large share of the market requires that the government intervene to some degree in order to compensate for reduced influence of the market. According to neoclassical theory, then, the government should and does operate as a regulator of monopolies, an enforcer of antitrust laws against oligopolistic firms possessing discretionary market power, a provider of public funds where market competition and government regulation place certain groups at serious disadvantage or fail to fulfill important needs of the entire population; and a stabilizer of the business cycle through fiscal policies (such as rates of taxation and levels of government expenditure) and monetary policies (such as adjusting the supply of money) to sustain growth without high inflation, high unemployment, or balance-of-payment difficulties.

In this revisionist theory government plays a crucial role in the economy. If the system is to work equitably, government must often intervene for particular disadvantaged groups (members of depressed areas, victims of discrimination, the elderly) and collective interests not adequately protected by the private economy (pollution control, education, defense). It is therefore absolutely essential that the government itself be responsive to democratic controls. The mixed economy, in short, requires the politics of democratic pluralism, through which public elections keep the state accountable to the people; and strong lobbying by private interests, shortchanged by the market, generates the needed government response.

Neoclassical political economists are generally optimistic about the extent to which the state can meet these conditions. Thus Samuelson, in the first reference to government intervention found in his classic text, says that "the citizenry, through their government, step in with expenditures to supplement the real or money income of some individuals . . ." [16] providing, for instance, old-age insurance and hospital beds. But to emphasize that there are proper limits to government intervention, he, like Friedman, states that "public benefits through taxes are more coercive than private purchases in the market." [17] Where possible, the market should be left to itself.

During the early and middle 1960s, the theorists of the mixed economy were generally euphoric. Their theory seemed to have high predictive power; it was increasingly accepted by the Congress, Presidents Kennedy and Johnson, and the public; and policies based on it promoted growth with high levels of employment and modest inflation. But even before the later increases in unemployment and inflation (an unexpected combination for neoclassicists), critics raised questions that are not easily answered within the confines of the neoclassical model:

1. Why do inequalities in income and wealth, approximately the same today as in 1910, remain so marked in the face of the tendencies toward equality inherent in "natural market forces" and tax policies and welfare programs designed to narrow them?

2. Why does the system of production for private profits produce such disastrous effects on the environment, threatening the clean air, pure water, energy supplies, plentiful minerals, and fertile soil that sustain human life and economic productivity?

3. Why does discrimination persist between whites and blacks, men and women, in spite of competitive forces that should presumably reward the nondiscriminating, lower-cost firms with higher profits and threaten the discriminating, higher-cost firms with market failure?

4. Why do the greatest and most direct benefits of government programs in defense, police service, highways and air terminals, higher education, research, slum clearance, and housing subsidies flow disproportionately to the most affluent when the ostensible point of the welfare state is public action in support of the most needy? [18]

5. Why does the mixed economy promote so uneven a development that large cities face continual crisis while suburban areas flourish, the Southwest booms while Appalachia languishes, and some suffer from malnutrition while others seek new and exotic luxury goods?

6. Why does the United States maintain such a huge military and intelligence presence in the nonindustrial countries with which it trades? Since the imminent threat of Soviet invasion in most of those countries is minimal, is there some connection between our system of political economy and the United States' international militarist posture?

7. Why do so many of the children of affluent parents, who have experienced at first hand the benefits of consumption, demonstrate in one way or another that they have little confidence in the order that they have inherited?

To pose these questions is to reveal that while neoclassical economists have a theory of what motivates consumers and firms and a view of what role the government ought to play in the economy, they do not in fact have a developed theory of political economy. With the exception of questions 1 and 2, which we will explore later, neoclassical theorists typically ignore these issues or treat them as if they were "political" or "social" issues somehow separable from the autonomous system and discipline of economics.[19] They show little awareness in their writings that changes in the organization of economic life have penetrated into the very structure of political life and have rendered economic life itself indelibly political.

Arthur M. Okun, chairman of the Council of Economic Advisors under President Johnson and author of *The Political Economy of Prosperity,* typifies this perspective.[20] He devotes most of his book to an exposition of how economic advisors under Kennedy and Johnson were able to promote prosperity (sustained increase in aggregative output and income) through the subtle use of tax policies, selective government expenditures, and regulation of the money supply. He closes on a plaintive note, maintaining that an unpopular war generated economic activities and government policy that disrupted the best-laid plans.

After concluding his analysis of the economics of prosperity, Okun acknowledges that even during the peak years of success, the policies supporting prosperity did not make the cities safer or more attractive or ease industrial pressure on the purification capacities of the air and waterways or make mass transit available for low-income citizens or reduce military spending to free funds for other purposes. "In retrospect," he says, "I wish more of the fruits of growth had been devoted to the public sector than to the mere expansion of private affluence." [21]

But why hasn't the public benefited more? Why are currently popular recommendations for sustained growth (outlined in the last chapter) remarkably like those that produced the results Okun now regrets? Why have the public expenditures of the past been more favorable to the wealthy than to the poor? Okun does not pair his expressions of regret with new answers to these pertinent questions. He seems content to assert that today, as yesterday, the policy proposals of the advisor must work within the constraints of a "pluralistic political process" in which organized groups "present their views and press their cases." [22] The key constraint in the political system "is not primarily wealth or class; small businesses are as powerful in this respect as the mighty giants of the petroleum industry." [23] The key, apparently, is that organized interest groups always have an advantage in a pluralist system over the unorganized public interest. Legislators will respond, for example, to the strong pressure from milk producers for a price increase because while the benefits to the producer will be great, the cost to each consumer will be minimal, and the legislator prefers diffused discontent that he can avoid to intense discontent focused upon himself. This is offered as a sufficient analysis of how political constraints can limit the economic advisor's ability to generate rational economic policy.

Okun's failure is this: in office he works as a technician promoting economic growth through policies limited by political constraints that he does not really comprehend. Out of office he moralizes over the need for more equitable growth policies but fails to suggest how such policies could be constructed and why they remain outside the range of political dialogue. Operating first as economic technician, then as economic moralist, he never really speaks as a political economist.

■ The Planning System in the New Industrial State

John Kenneth Galbraith makes an effort to explain phenomena that other economists have taken for granted or treated as being outside of economics. Individual freedom through market competition is the keystone of Friedman's theory, and sustained economic growth through a mix of market and government controls is the core of the Samuelson-Okun position. Understanding and taming the power of the large corporation is the central theme of Galbraith's work.

In an early book, *American Capitalism: The Concept of Countervailing Power,*[24] Galbraith argued that the rapid growth of oligopolies in many product areas rendered the market less and less effective in regulating corporate behavior. The corporation, through its ability to set prices, bargain for wage rates, plow back retained earnings, and locate in the most favorable labor market and political climate, has accumulated great power. But, Galbraith then argued, its power is restrained by countervailing power, by the ability of other large organizations to apply pressure to it when its policies infringe upon their interests. General Motors' power to set wages is limited by the countervailing power of organized labor to strike; its ability to set prices is limited by the bargaining power of other large firms that furnish it with needed materials; its ability to exploit consumers through exorbitant prices or shoddy products is limited by the government, which in turn is responsive to the general population through elections and interest-group pressure. In Galbraith's early system the government is an umpire, stepping in to aid those groups and interests that lose out in the system of countervailing power operative in the economy. The entire system of political economy emerges as a delicate set of balances among corporations, labor, and consumers in which no organization gets its way completely and few are left out entirely.[25]

But in his more recent studies, particularly *The New Industrial State* and *Economics and the Public Purpose,*[26] Galbraith has modified his initial theory: power remains the cornerstone of the system, but the emphasis has shifted to the corporate sector, or as Galbraith describes it, to the planning system.

Galbraith's revised theory consists of a complex set of claims, nicely stated but vaguely formulated. We will summarize his central ideas by considering his views about the economist as apologist, the nature of the planning system, the determinants of consumption, the relations between the planning system and the market system, and the relation between the state and the economic system.

THE ECONOMIST AS APOLOGIST

The market model of economic transactions was initially applied to a system of many small firms competing for consumers in a setting where the barriers to entry for new firms were minimal. Why does the market model still attract academic economists, Galbraith asks, in the radically different conditions of today? First, because the intellectual framework with which a profession is familiar exerts a powerful hold over the minds of its members, even when changed conditions make it less applicable. It provides them with familiar concepts and assumptions to bring to bear on contemporary issues. Second, in the age of technology and technique, the simplifying assumptions of the market model provide a base from which mathematical models can be constructed and refined; the form of the model is nicely adapted to the style of thought preferred by contemporary social scientists.[27] Finally, Galbraith suggests, to explain corporate behavior in terms of its power is to invite citizens and governments to try to tame that power, to render it accountable to those affected by it. Since this is true, "perhaps the oldest and certainly the wisest strategy for the exercise of power is to deny that it is possessed."[28] Economists who join the chorus of such denials retain in this way the respect and support of the planning system. They serve, half unwittingly, as the apologists for that system. Habit, adaptation to a preferred style of thought, and self-interest converge in this way to sustain a system of thought that is not supported by the evidence. This is a harsh charge; its validity depends upon the truth of Galbraith's claim that the images projected by market theorists do not fit the new system of political economy.[29]

THE PLANNING SYSTEM

The planning system, one of two systems that together constitute the American economy, consists of a few hundred of the largest corporations. In 1971, 333 industrial corporations controlled

70 percent of all assets employed in manufacturing; and in transportation, communications, banking, and finance, a similar if less extreme concentration can be discerned.[30] In Galbraith's view, the owners of these large corporations have less and less power over the firms' policies.[31] Control is typically dispersed among a rather large group of managers and technicians in the contemporary corporation, and the owners themselves are less and less able to understand the complexity of the institution that pays them dividends. Power has shifted to the corporate technocracy, to the administrative officers, budget analysts, engineers, and other technicians who work in committees inside the corporate bureaucracy.

That segment of society controlling the factor of production most scarce and most strategic to the production process will invariably play a pivotal role in shaping the economic life of its period. In agricultural society, land was the strategic resource; the owners of land were therefore powerful men. Control of capital was a prime source of power in an earlier phase of accumulation in the capitalist system. But today possession of technical, specialized knowledge has become crucial; it is central to the planning system. And those who possess these skills—the technocrats—have therefore become the pivotal power brokers of our age.

Technology involves the application of scientific knowledge to practical tasks. In a large, highly technical productive enterprise, several conditions must be met if production and marketing are to proceed smoothly: a large amount of capital must be available; human production assignments must be narrowly and precisely defined; the lead time from the inception of a product idea to the beginning of mass production is necessarily long; specialists in organization and coordination, none of whom can alone understand the entire process in detail, must together plan research, production, marketing, and sales so that the entire operation proceeds coherently. These are the conditions of modern production that make planning imperative.

The technocracy, to plan effectively, needs a reliable source of capital, usually to be found in the retained earnings of the large firm. It must have a reliable work force trained in the production skills needed. It should have some control over the raw materials and primary products it will use in production so that these items will be available in the right amounts at the right prices at the right time. It needs to know that the product it is designing today will be demanded by consumers some years later when the product is finally made. And it must know that the state will continue to pursue policies compatible with its capital, labor, materials, and market requirements. Thus the advanced technology of the modern corporation requires extensive planning, and the planning can be effective only to the extent that the environments inside and outside the corporation are subordinated to the plan. Such reliability is best maintained through technocratic control over those factors. Galbraith clearly believes that these conditions are approximated in the new industrial state:

> But much of our life, and nearly all of it that involves the procurement and use of income, is subject to the decisions of the technostructure. It sets our prices, persuades us on our purchases, and distributes the resulting income to those who participate in production.[32]

The technocracy, according to Galbraith, is not guided solely by the profit motive. It does seek enough profit to finance expansion and to pay reasonable dividends to nonresident stockholders. But it is primarily concerned with retaining its autonomy in decision making, increasing the size of the corporation it runs, and expanding the frontiers of technological research and its application to production. Fulfilling these objectives enhances the status and prerogatives of the technocracy: new positions are created for more technocrats; their skills become indispensable to the corporation; and outsiders (including owners and government bureaucrats) must rely more and more on the technocrats' judgment to appraise corporate objectives and performance.

But if the technocracy increasingly controls the market instead of being controlled by it, and if it is not motivated simply by higher profits, two basic tenets of classical and neoclassical economic analysis have lost their validity. To what extent, then, is the planning system controlled by or accountable to new forces? Galbraith clearly thinks that the state, organized labor, and the market each exercise some degree of control over the planning system, but he also thinks that the balance has shifted in favor of the planning system itself. It controls much more than it is controlled. As the corporation grows, "the goals of the corporation will be a reflection of the goals of the technostructure. And the goals of the society will tend to be those of the corporation." [33]

THE DETERMINANTS OF CONSUMPTION

In the theories considered earlier, the individuals are seen as the authors of their own demand for consumer goods. Those firms survive, in the long run, that serve the desires of autonomous consumers; and if the consumers' desires are sometimes frivolous or if fulfilling them requires the destruction of scarce resources, the pollution of waterways, or sacrifices in the production of public goods such as health care and education, the ultimate fault lies not with the productive system but with the sovereign consumers who impose such demands. Galbraith challenges the doctrine of consumer sovereignty and the tendency of its exponents to exempt the corporate system from responsibility for its production priorities.

Two factors converge to compromise consumer sovereignty. First, the planning system requires a reliable demand for its expanding supply of products; and second, once the system has satisfied the basic needs for food, shelter, and clothing, at least of the affluent, it can rather easily manipulate the less basic desires of the affluent. "The further a man is removed from physical need the more he is open to persuasion—or management—as to what he buys. This is perhaps the most important consequence for economics of increasing affluence." [34]

The firm influences demand through advertising, packaging, and frequent style changes. Advertising is the most important factor, and Galbraith insists that his theory explains what remains a mystery to neoclassicists—why the advertising budget of the corporation is so huge. Increasing consumer demand by linking style changes and exotic designs to happiness and status, the planning system helps to create the conditions for its own expansion. It brings consumers, to some extent, under the control of the plan. And if production priorities of the planning system turn out to be irrational in some respects, if the system produces private affluence for some while public programs in transportation, health, poverty, and environmental purification languish, the fault shifts from the sovereign consumers to the planning system itself. Consumers' awareness of the extent to which their own purchases reflect faulty corporate priorities is a precondition, Galbraith maintains, of their emancipation from corporate control.

THE PLANNING AND THE MARKET SYSTEMS

Auto, steel, oil, and banking companies are prototype members of the planning system, but there are still 12 million smaller firms that fall outside its orbit. Farmers, small retail establishments, construction firms, small manufacturers, restaurants, and garages constitute the core of the market system. The firms in this system remain responsive to the impersonal regulation of the market.

But they are not subject to market constraints alone; they must operate in an environment also populated by members of the planning system. Corporations in the planning system can set a price for goods they will receive from companies in the market system by going to the lowest bidder. They can respond to the demands of their own workers for higher wages by setting a higher price for their goods, thereby increasing the costs to firms in the market sector. They can gain some control of organized labor in the corporate sector by using the surplus labor in the market sector as a potential replacement for unskilled laborers in the corporate system. In most respects, Galbraith asserts, both employers and employees in the planning system dominate and exploit employers and employees in the market system. This uneven struggle between systems, he says, comes to overshadow the more classic conflict between the owning and working classes in a single market system.

THE ROLE OF THE STATE

In *The Affluent Society*, Galbraith argued that the United States was marked by private affluence and public squalor: public needs such as health care and urban renewal, which could best be met through public expenditures, were subordinated to private expenditures for private consumer goods. But he now holds that the national government, especially the executive branch, accommodates its policies to the needs of the planning system in a more subtle way, which cannot be captured by a crude distinction between private purchases and public expenditures. Public expenditures for the military establishment, space and corporate research, highways and air terminals are oversubscribed, while public expenditures for health care, mass transportation, housing for the poor, and education are undersubscribed. The state, in short, employs its resources to provide services and support for the planning system. Other public needs are left in the lurch. Workers and employers in the market system must go to Congress for their support because congressmen from smaller constituencies, where local business is important, are most likely to be responsive to them. But Congress is the place where political debate is the loudest and political power the most dispersed. The identification of the planning system with the executive branch gives it yet another advantage in promoting its objectives. Since the success of its policies are now central to the vitality of the economic system, it is easy to argue that the protection of the national interest by regulatory agencies, foreign policy, monetary and fiscal policies requires most of all the protection of corporate interests. If unemployment is high in the planning system, the government must help to spur the sale of automobiles even if the predominance of the car itself is a crucial ingredient in the energy crisis.

The giant corporation, then, exercises power directly over consumers and over employees and employers in the market system through its ability to set prices, control costs, and regulate demand. It then indirectly exerts power over these same constituencies as citizens by its ability to secure government policies in line with its priorities. Consumers, market employees, and market entrepreneurs are forced to seek whatever remedies they can through Congress, the weakest branch of the national government. The imbalance between the corporate and market systems is extended in this way through the state's identification with the priorities of the corporate system.

That is, in rough outline, Galbraith's theory. It discards the classical separation between a political system marked by power and an economic system regulated by impersonal markets. It challenges the doctrine of the consumer as the sovereign director of the economic system. It repudiates the view that profit maximization is the overriding objective of the firm. It traces many of the structural defects in the American political economy to the unequal terms of trade between the planning and market systems. And it sees the state as the all-too-willing partner of the planning system, extending rather than rectifying the imbalances created by that system.

We believe that Galbraith's theory represents an improvement over the Friedman and the Samuelson-Okun theories of political economy, but several defects and omissions remain. First, in his eagerness to emphasize the role of the technocracy, he underestimates the owners of capital as a powerful source of resistance to the socialism he recommends. Second, he views the technocracy as the inevitable beneficiary of a line of technological advances that could not have taken any other form. But there is good reason to believe that the direction American technological development has taken is not the direction all technological development must take. If that is true, then Galbraith's theory of technological determinism would have to be modified, and we would have to ask why the United States pattern of technological development did foster the large private corporation, the minute division of labor, the great dependence of workers, and so on. Third, while moving helpfully beyond the simple theory of consumer sovereignty, he still fails to expose the most basic determinants of consumer choice in the political economy of corporate capitalism. Fourth, Galbraith shares with adherents of the first two theories a tendency to focus on relations of exchange between buyers and sellers of goods and to ignore the relations of production between owners and workers in the work place itself. He has introduced political ideas into the relations of exchange, but it is even more important to show how they enter into the relations of production as well. These four areas of criticism are best explored through a theory of political economy that takes them explicitly into account.

■ The Politicization of Production Relations

André Gorz, a radical political economist and activist in France, has developed a theory of political economy that reflects the influence of Marx's early writings on alienation. In Marx's view, when work life is repetitive and routinized, when workers have little or no chance to interact creatively with other workers in shaping the productive process, when the product of work serves no important social function attributable to the workers, the workers come to experience themselves as passive, isolated beings naturally subordinated to forces beyond their control. They internalize the judgments others make of them as "workers," and their activities and relationships outside of work tend to duplicate those within work. They take on the very characteristics that classical economists assume to be natural to the wage laborer and the private consumer while feeling deep resentment and dissatisfaction with the form of life they are required to live. Building upon this theory, Gorz contends that alienated work and alienated consumption within the corporate system oppress people in their capacities as workers and consumers while generating a potential base of effective opposition to that oppression.

Consider, first, Gorz's view of the determinants of consumption in the contemporary system. He surely agrees with Galbraith's critique of the image of sovereign consumers. But Galbraith's own explanation of consumption pictures consumers as far more gullible and less rational than they in fact are. More important than advertising, or rather, a factor that allows advertising to make such an impact, is the narrow set of options facing potential consumers. They must choose from a small range of available alternatives in order to satisfy their needs for food, recreation, sociability, transportation, and shelter.

As the automobile becomes society's principal mode of transportation, highway systems are constructed by the state to facilitate its extensive use, housing patterns, manufacturing centers, and shopping plazas are organized around the expectation of its use. While the state's support services for the automobile are expanded, those for mass transit are allowed to decline. It does not, in such a setting, take slick advertisers to convince people to buy cars. "The possession of an automobile becomes a basic necessity because the universe is organized in terms of private transportation." [35]

The corporate system organized around private profit creates new consumer needs at the same time it serves established ones. When industrial production pollutes the air, urban dwellers come to equate the need for air with a vacation, air conditioning, or a more expensive home in the suburbs. When people hustled off to the suburbs lack public transportation to visit relatives and friends, the need for social life becomes a need for a second car. When the inequality and unstable employment associated with private enterprise produce high levels of crime, the middle class equates the need for security with the expenditures for private schools, household security, insurance, and expanded police protection to protect life and property under these historically specific conditions. When food packaging, processing, and distribution create tasteless food fortified with potentially dangerous preservatives, consumers identify the need for nutrition with expensive organic foods and natural vitamin pills. In these ways the system of production and distribution itself helps to produce new consumption imperatives. The "sovereign consumer" is then forced to choose among a rather narrow range of options to serve these artificially induced needs.

But a viable theory of political economy must not view people simply as consumers. They are also citizens, students, workers, lovers, and parents, and the lives they live in each of these roles affects their involvement in the others. People are not the ahistorical agents of neoclassical economic theory but social beings constituted in part by the complex web of relationships into which they enter. If, for instance, my work is debilitating and its pace is controlled by others, if it leaves me with little sense of purpose or fulfillment, if it requires me to relate to others only as functionaries, then during my leisure hours I will seek to escape this oppressive reality. The form of my escape will reflect in part the image of myself formed at work and in part the means of escape available in the system. If private consumption is the main game in town, it is the game I will play. As Gorz puts it, the productive system offers private consumption as the "means of evading this intolerable social reality; and the implementation on a grand scale of these individual means of escape (automobiles, private houses, camping, passive leisure) thereby creates a new anarchic social process, new miseries, inverted priorities, and new alienation." [36]

Many needs are collective. Their fulfillment would involve people in persisting relationships of mutual understanding and reciprocity at work, in neighborhoods, and in larger communities. But if work life lacks such richness, then the production system ostensibly designed to serve human beings in fact meets our material requirements in ways that frustrate our needs. People may adjust to these conditions; we may even construe the conditions themselves as part of the human condition. But that is because we fail to explore the possibility of a work process organized with human needs in mind; a production system that provides collective goods such as public transportation, neighborhood laundry centers, day care centers, recreation areas, health stations, and cooperative stores; and a social system that organizes the production and use of goods so as to foster extended relationships in neighborhoods and communities.

Gorz contends that needed and possible changes in work life, product forms, consumption patterns, and community relationships could foster a social atmosphere more fulfilling than that we now have. Structural change in these institutions would also relieve some of the pressures on the nuclear family. That embattled institution is today called upon to absorb the pressures and injuries imposed upon it from the outside, while its traditional means of performing its functions are being progressively stripped away.

The Galbraithian interpretation of the technocracy is also defective from the vantage point of this alternative model. The technocracy is not quite the power group Galbraith imagines. Linking power to the most strategic or most indispensable factor of production is questionable. Every factor is indispensable to some degree; the fact that slaves were the most indispensable factor to a slave system certainly did not lodge power in their hands.[37] It is true that technocrats do assume an importance in day-to-day decisions not previously noted by neoclassical economists. But technocrats, taken as individuals, often suffer, if less blatantly, from the alienation that plagues other dependent employees. They are typically overtrained for the work they do, and no amount of tinkering with household hobbies can compensate for the "permanent underemployment of abilities in passive and monotonous work." [38] But their technical training is in another respect too narrow. To retain an active presence in an industrial sector marked by rapid change requires a broad, theoretical training, but the technicians' training is often quite specific and sharply defined. As a result technocrats find that they often depreciate rapidly in the eyes of their employers. Many individual technocrats find that the status and the influence of the technocracy in general touches them only during the prime of their productive lives.

When there is a large supply of technicians, owners can select those who are eager to adapt to their purposes. When the economy is under pressure, "technicians, engineers, student researchers discover that they are wage earners like the others"[39] since technocrats, like other dependent employees, can be laid off when their services are no longer needed.

The technocracy sees itself as mediating between groups of owners and workers, who each seek to politicize the productive process by struggling over wages, pensions, work rates, and so on. But the technocracy, Gorz insists, falsely believes that these issues can be settled by reference to extrapolitical criteria, by reference to the rational imperatives of productivity and efficient economic growth. It tries to expose both groups to the facts of economic productivity and to gain their mutual consent to these imperatives. But this self-imposed role is largely illusory, says Gorz. The technocracy in fact gears its assessments to the expectations owners have for profit and control. This is to be expected when one group of employees in the industrial sector—the technocrats—strives to "keep a balance between a bourgeoisie which is in power and a working class which is not." Its effort must play mostly "into the hands of the former."[40] Failing to understand that the form technological advance has taken under modern capitalism and the relations of production attached to that form do not represent the only pattern of development possible, the technocracy deceives itself ideologically as it accommodates to the employers. It is in this sense that "depoliticization is the ideology of the technocracy itself."[41] And that ideology justifies the role of the technocracy to itself and to other segments of society.

Gorz also endorses a view of the relation between the state and the corporate system that goes well beyond Galbraith's position. In the short run, corporate capitalists, disagreeing among themselves in many respects, will often find their own priorities at odds with those adopted by the state. For instance, owners would often like to convert public resources funneled into education, health, welfare, and retirement programs into disposable income available for consumers to buy the goods of private producers. And when some or all owners act on these preferences, they will often find themselves ranged against the public priorities sanctioned by the democratic state. These differences, in fact, typically dominate the politics of party contests, election campaigns, and legislative struggles.

But the corporate system and the state are allies when the more basic, long-range interests of private capital are taken into consideration. "Precisely what distinguishes neocapitalism from traditional capitalism is that the former recognizes the necessity of the mediating role of the state; its efforts no longer aim at restraining public initiative, but at orienting it for the benefit of monopoly accumulation." [42] Public support for the educational system provides trained manpower for each occupational level in the corporate system. Welfare and unemployment programs moderate the boom and bust cycles plaguing early capitalism and dampen potential militancy within the working class. Defense expenditures provide direct profits for many corporations and the means by which other corporate interests are protected abroad. The expansion of the state's role in the economy is accepted, then, as long as its involvement and expenditures support corporate accumulation and expansion without challenging the system of production for profit.[43]

Gorz, though a socialist, is also more wary of nationalization of the means of production than Galbraith is. To nationalize *before* dependent employees have established a more powerful position within the corporate system may well extend the corporate-state alliance to the disadvantage of the lower class. The prior requirement, Gorz contends, is to improve the workers' power position within the firm itself. By pressing militantly for structural reforms —the kind of reform that reconstitutes power relations and creates resources for new advances at a later date—workers can help to ensure that nationalization, when it comes, will come on terms more congenial to worker interests. By establishing a foothold now, they have a better chance to participate in management if and when nationalization occurs.

There is no foolproof strategy for progressive change in the political economy of corporate capitalism. The system's ability to divert, deflect, suppress, and destroy dissident movements is well established. But a socialist strategy that proceeds, so to speak, from the bottom up is most likely to promote the desired momentum. It is also most likely to generate a humane socialism oriented to a less alienating system of work.

Gorz goes well beyond Galbraith's break with neoclassical theory in his interpretation of the determinants of consumption and the relations between the state and the corporate sysem. He also explores the internal dynamics of the production process itself—an important topic almost completely ignored by Galbraith. In fact, Gorz would argue, Galbraith's failure to confront this last area contributes to the defects in his analysis of other areas.

There are deficiencies and omissions in the Gorz argument as well. Thus while he identifies the ways in which the prevailing system generates needs it does not fulfill, he tends to assume that the system can continue to operate successfully on its own terms. If labor does not challenge it, it will continue along the same track. But the capitalist system is in many ways a fragile system, even without a political challenge from labor. The United States, for instance, is a high energy user; its system of production and consumption is predicated upon a steady flow of oil. If oil-producing nations should cut off that supply, the system would face a severe crisis. There is also the fact of nuclear proliferation and the increasing chance that some Third World country will employ nuclear blackmail against the system it views as its oppressor. These and other conditions make the United States vulnerable to repressive police-state reactions to such threats at home and abroad. These circumstances, we will argue, provide an additional case for a reconstitution of our political economy that complements the affirmative oaoo developed by Gorz. Unless we reorganize our system of production, distribution, and consumption, the established system of political economy may crack in dangerous ways.

Also, when Gorz examines the prospects for worker control and the reorganization of work processes, he is thinking of a French work force more firmly anchored in a socialist movement than is any segment of the American work force. While his analysis of worker alienation fits the American situation, his strategic program does not now speak to an active movement in the United States. The relations within the blue-collar work force, moreover, do not parallel those in the French blue-collar force. The United States has an underclass of marginally employed blacks, Puerto Ricans, and Mexicans whose struggle for secure employment and adequate income sometimes brings them into conflict with workers in the corporate sector who seek to protect themselves from a similar plight. This intraclass conflict, not really duplicated in France, introduces a defensive conservative potential into the American working class. It may be possible to moderate these tendencies, but this is just one example of the many differences between the two societies that suggest caution in the application of the Gorz model to the American setting.

These specific limitations of the Gorzian theory are linked to a larger defect: his theory of the state in capitalist society is underdeveloped. He tends to assume that the state can successfully maintain conditions favorable to capitalist accumulation. But it may be that the cumulative effect of necessary state expansion into inflation and employment regulation, public education, public employment, corporate research subsidies, military expenditures, public welfare, and highway programs itself contributes to a crisis of state performance and legitimacy. (We shall argue that it does in the last chapter.) Gorz believes that the repressive apparatus of the state—its use of police, military, surveillance, tax, and employment powers to intimidate and isolate dissidents—will be unleashed when workers challenge the system of private ownership and profit. But he does not thoroughly probe the possibility that the state's failure to deliver on its own promises for material affluence, full employment, job security, inflation control, and equal opportunity will generate a similar response. Gorz sees the state primarily as the protector of capitalist interests. It is perhaps more correct to see it as sometimes representing capital and sometimes representing the public's best efforts within the prevailing order to cope with dislocations created by the system of productivity. Operating within narrow limits of the permissible, the state's best efforts often inadvertently create new dislocations while responding to established ones.

When that is said, though, we believe that the Gorzian model illuminates features of the American political economy overlooked or obscured by the alternative models considered. Sometimes in conjunction with Galbraith's analysis of the terms of trade between the corporate and market systems, more often on its own, Gorz's model deepens our comprehension of structural deficiencies in the American system. We will employ his work as a touchstone for our own assessment of inflation, inequality, economic growth, ecology, work life, and state crisis.

American students are not often exposed to the perspective Gorz represents. Lacking exposure to this framework, they lack an opportunity to appraise its strengths and weaknesses. Gorz thinks that this educational deficiency too can be explained:

> The domination of one class over another is not exercised solely by means of political and economic power, but also through its evaluation of the possible and impossible, the future and the past, the useful and the useless, the rational and the irrational, the good and the bad.[44]

If some find the initial charge, with its image of class domination, too stark (compare the impact of this picture to that of the market image), they may nonetheless appreciate the challenge of considering a competing view. The best way to reappraise prevailing ideas is to compare them with a theory that locates the possible and the impossible, the rational and the irrational, differently. Only then can one judge reflectively whether the established interpretation or its alternative identify and explain contemporary problems most effectively.

NOTES

1. M. A. Wright, "The Assault on Private Enterprise." Address to the Twenty-sixth Annual Business Conference, Rutgers University, May 31, 1974.
2. (Chicago: University of Chicago Press, 1962). Point 5 is emphasized by some other economists. See Kenneth Arrow, *The Limits of Organization* (New York: W. W. Norton, 1974).
3. Friedman, p. 14.
4. Ibid., pp. 14–15.
5. Ibid., p. 18.
6. Ibid., p. 19.
7. Ibid., p. 200.
8. Ibid., p. 27.
9. See, for example, Isaiah Berlin, Two Concepts of Liberty" (Oxford: Clarendon Press, 1958); Gerald MacCallum, "Negative and Positive Liberty," in *Contemporary Political Theory,* edited by A. de Crespigny and A. Wertheimer (New York: Atherton Press, 1970); Steven Lukes, *Individualism* (New York: Oxford University Press, 1973); and William E. Connolly, *The Terms of Political Discourse* (Lexington: D. C. Heath, 1974), Ch. 4.
10. Friedman, p. 15.
11. Ibid., p. 135.
12. One of the important modern formulations of pluralist theory is advanced by an economist: Joseph Schumpeter, *Capitalism, Socialism, and Democracy* (New York: Harper and Row, 1947). For a striking example of the use of economic categories in political explanation, see Anthony Downs, *An Economic Theory of Democracy* (New York: Harper and Row, 1957).
13. Friedman, p. 202.
14. This critique rests on Friedman's own assumptions. Our explanation of the growth and import of corporate capitalism is not identical with this, although some points will be the same.
15. Samuelson, *Economics,* 8th ed. (New York: McGraw-Hill, 1970), p. 37.
16. Ibid., p. 44.

17. Ibid., p. 45.
18. For documentation of these points, see Gerhard Lenski, *Power and Privilege* (New York: McGraw-Hill, 1966), Ch. 10, and Michael Harrington, *Socialism* (New York: Bantam Books, 1970), Ch. 12 Lenski, a conservative sociologist, estimates that "one third to two thirds of the value of all governmental services redound to the benefit of the most privileged 2 percent" (p. 311).
19. A series of studies that have treated discrimination (question 3) as an economic problem began with Gary Becker, *Economics of Discrimination* (Chicago: University of Chicago Press, 1957). Although it is the classic in its field, it sold fewer than 2,000 copies in its first nine years of publication. The studies generally either fall back on outside sociological and psychological factors or, like Becker's, argue that employers with a "taste for discrimination" pay a tax in the form of higher-cost employees. Thus policies designed to increase competition would force such employers to abandon their "taste" or be driven out of business. However, the origins of a "taste for discrimination" are not examined. See David M. Gordon, *Theories of Poverty and Underemployment* (Lexington, Mass.: D. C. Heath, 1972), and Orley Ashenfelter and Albert Rees, eds., *Discrimination in Labor Markets* (Princeton, N.J.: Princeton University Press, 1973).
20. (New York: W. W. Norton, 1970).
21. Ibid., p. 124.
22. Ibid., p. 7.
23. Ibid., p. 8.
24. (Boston: Houghton Mifflin, 1952).
25. For a more detailed summary and critique of the umpire theory of pluralism, see William E. Connolly, "The Challenge to Pluralist Theory," in *The Bias of Pluralism* (New York: Atherton Press, 1969).
26. (Boston: Houghton Mifflin, 1967 and 1973, respectively).
27. The way in which a style of thought appropriate to some highly successful field (say, mechanistic physics in the nineteenth century) tends to be appropriated uncritically by practitioners in other fields where it may not be so appropriate is explored by Stephen Toulmin, *Foresight and Understanding* (New York: Harper and Row, 1961), Ch. 5.
28. Galbraith, *Economics and the Public Purpose,* p. 5.
29. Assuming that Galbraith is right about the discrepancy between image and reality, Thomas Kuhn sheds light on the importance of Galbraith's first explanation—the role of habit. A theory, says Kuhn, consists of a complex set of concepts, assumptions, and methods that reinforce one another. Adherents of any such system have internalized this complex over a long period of time. They cannot shed it like a coat, but it is part of them in a way that facial expressions are part of a personality. To drop the theory would be to lose an important part of oneself. One can't always do that, even

though one tries. Thus Kuhn finds it understandable that arguments against old theories are seldom accepted by established practitioners. They can always find some way to save at least a semblance of the old theory. The new argument, if successful, can only take hold among new practitioners who are deciding which of two or more systems to make their own. See *The Structure of Scientific Revolutions* (Chicago: University of Chicago Press, 1962).

30. Galbraith, *Economics and the Public Purpose,* p. 43.
31. The thesis that ownership and control are progressively separated was first advanced in Adolf A. Berle and Gardiner C. Means, *The Modern Corporation and Private Property* (New York: Macmillan, 1932). An updated version of that thesis discussed within the confines of a pluralist theory of power is offered in Berle, *Power Without Property* (New York: Harcourt, Brace and World, 1964).
32. Galbraith, *The New Industrial State,* p. 111.
33. Ibid., p. 161.
34. Ibid., p. 202.
35. Gorz, *A Strategy for Labor* (Boston: Beacon Press, 1967), p. 11.
36. Ibid., p. 67.
37. A thoughtful critique of the assumed connection between indispensability and power is developed in Anthony Giddens, *The Class Structure of Advanced Societies* (New York: Harper and Row, 1973), pp. 177 and 262–263.
38. Gorz, *A Strategy for Labor,* p. 106.
39. Ibid., p. 104.
40. Ibid., p. 127.
41. Ibid., p. 122.
42. Ibid., p. 65.
43. Ibid., p. 65.
44. Gorz, *Socialism and Revolution* (New York: Doubleday, 1973), p. 168.

2
INEQUALITY, THE AMERICAN WAY

■ Dimensions of Inequality

Income refers to the money returns from wages, gifts, and so on, that enable one to purchase goods. Wealth refers, in its broadest sense, to the market value of the property one owns; in a more restricted sense, it means the ownership of income-producing assets such as bonds and corporate stock. To understand a system of inequality, one must understand inequalities in both wealth and income. But inequalities in wealth are particularly important. For those with wealth can use it to create income directly, and they can also employ it as a power resource to protect or extend their high status and privileges.

In the United States the top 10 percent of income earners control 56 percent of the nation's wealth; the bottom 10 percent have negative wealth—debts that outstrip their ownership of property.[1] When we restrict our terms to the ownership of corporate stock, a singularly important source of control over productive resources, the concentration of wealth becomes even more apparent. One half of 1 percent of the adult population controls 33 percent or more of such private wealth, and the wealthiest 2 percent holds over two thirds of the nation's corporate stock. State and local bonds, mortgages, and notes are distributed a bit more broadly. But even when these interest-producing assets are included, 20 percent of the population controls 77 percent of the nation's private wealth.[2] Eighty percent of the population divides the remaining 23 percent of productive wealth among itself, and most of the available wealth represented in that figure consists of those interest-producing bonds and notes that enhance individual income but do not compare to corporate stock as a source of power. If the idea of class is to refer primarily to ownership of the means of production, then in America today the capitalist class, that is, the class with the capital, consists basically of 2 percent of the population. Perhaps another 15 to 20 percent can be viewed as junior partners in that class.

Significant, if less extreme, inequality in the distribution of income has persisted in the United States throughout the twentieth century. In 1910, for example, the top fifth of the population received about 46 percent of the nation's income and the bottom fifth received 8 percent; by 1978 those figures had become 44 percent and 5 percent, respectively. As Table 2-1 shows, the proportion of income received by each fifth of the population has remained remarkably stable since 1947. And as Figure 2-1 indi-

TABLE 2-1   *Percentage Share of Aggregate Income, Received by Each Fifth of Families, 1947–1978*

	1947	1957	1967	1972	1978
Poorest fifth	5.1	5.0	5.5	5.4	4.3
Second fifth	11.8	12.6	12.4	11.9	10.3
Middle fifth	16.7	18.1	17.9	17.5	16.9
Fourth fifth	23.2	23.7	23.9	23.9	24.7
Richest fifth	43.3	40.5	40.4	41.4	43.9
(Richest 5 percent)	17.5	15.8	15.2	15.9	16.6

Source: U.S. Bureau of the Census, *Current Population Reports,* Series P-60, No. 90 (December 1973) and No. 121 (February 1980).

cates, in 1978 the bottom 80 percent of all households received slightly more than half of the aggregate income, and the top 20 percent slightly less than half.

These income statistics certainly underrepresent the income of the top fifth of the population, because they do not include capital-gains receipts and because respondents regularly underreport income from interest, dividends, and rentals.[3] Robert Pechman and Benjamin Okner, for example, estimate that in 1966 the actual money income of the top fifth was as high as 47.9 percent and that of the bottom fifth as low as 3.7 percent.[4] These estimates, if correct for 1966, would remain relatively constant today. Finally, while the figures summarized so far cover pretax income, the posttax percentage of income of each income fifth is not substantially changed. Pechman and Okner conclude "Because there is

Figure 2-1 Cumulative Index Shares by Household, 1978

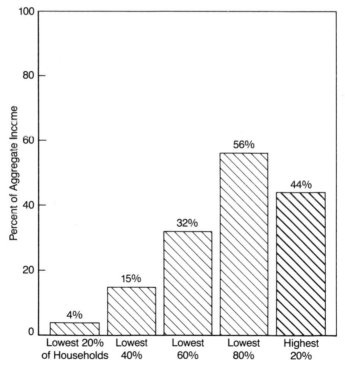

Source: Adapted from U.S. Bureau of the Census, *Current Population Reports,* Series P-60, No. 121, February 1980.

so little difference in effective rates over most of the income distribution the tax system has very little effect on the relative distribution of income." [5]

Income-distribution figures merely summarize the relative purchasing power of each fifth of the population. But there is a substantial connection between occupational affiliation and income level, and unequal purchasing power is therefore merely one dimension of the entire system of inequality. In the United States occupational categories form a hierarchy in which professional and managerial positions typically receive the highest incomes, followed by semiprofessional, skilled or manual, routine white-collar, and unskilled manual occupations in roughly that order. Table 2-2 illustrates this ranking.

The figures for Table 2-2 are for 1972, but by 1978 these differentials had, if anything, increased slightly. Thus 78 percent of professional and technical employees earned over $15,000, while 61 percent of laborers, farm workers, and service workers earned less than $15,000. [6]

Table 2-2 indicates the connection between income level and

TABLE 2-2   *Occupational and Employment Status, by Head of Household, by Total Income, 1972*

	Under $4,000	$4,000– 6,999	$7,000– 9,999	$10,000– 14,999	$15,000– 24,999	$25,000 & above
Professional and technical	4%	7%	12%	26%	35%	17%
Managers and administrators	4	6	10	25	33	20
Sales workers	7	11	14	26	29	13
Craftsmen and kindred workers	4	10	18	35	29	4
Operatives	7	17	23	33	18	2
Clerical	8	20	23	29	18	3
Farmers and farm managers	22	22	19	18	15	4
Laborers, except farm	12	21	25	27	13	3
Service workers	22	23	19	20	14	2
Farm workers	34	32	19	15	8	1

Source: Adapted from *Current Population Reports,* Series P-60, No. 89 (July 1973), p. 22.

occupational affiliation but probably understates it. First, it underreports nonsalary incomes by those in upper occupations. Second, since opportunities for advancement within the upper categories surpass those in the lower categories, and since the risk of periodic unemployment is significantly greater in the lower categories, the *lifetime earnings* (the only time span worthy of close attention) of the typical manager or professional and the typical laborer will be much more unequal than revealed here. Third, these categories fail to distinguish those working in the corporate system from those working in the market system; but in fact blue-collar workers in the former tend to earn more than their counterparts in the market system. (The Department of Commerce defines its categories as if we lived in a market system, making interpretation of its data difficult for those who know better.)

When the connection between income distribution and the occupational hierarchy is established, several other dimensions of our stratified system become visible. Thus managers, professionals, and other technicians in the corporate system not only receive comparatively high incomes but their sick-pay benefits, health insurance, pension plans, long-term economic security, expense accounts, clean and healthy working environments, degree of control over work schedules, roles in decision making, and status outstrip by far the benefits received by blue-collar workers in these areas. Similarly, blue collar workers in the corporate system tend to fare better on most of these dimensions than their counterparts in the market system. The system of income inequality, then, is simply *one manifestation* of a complex of cumulative inequalities anchored in the occupational system. To think only of income distribution when appraising inequality is to divert attention away from the cumulative nature and institutional basis of the distribution system.

The importance of keeping the entire system of inequality in view can hardly be overemphasized. At the time the Ford Motor Company, for instance, announced a new program of preventive health care for its 4,000 salaried headquarters employees to cut down the incidence of heart attacks, alcoholism, and other "stress-related ills," another study revealed that of 1,266 poor households in Nashville, Tennessee, only 13 percent of those with health problems were receiving proper medical attention, 95 percent lacked proper dental care, 94 percent lacked a nutritious diet, and 50 percent lacked health insurance of any sort.[7] If the United States balanced its system of unequal income with equal access to health-care facilities for all citizens, the system of inequality would be somewhat less onerous than it is. But, in fact, our system of income inequality is merely an index of a cumulative system that bestows a vast range of privileges and benefits upon some segments of the population while it imposes the most painful burdens and risks on others. Our distribution system creates its own nobles, peasants, and paupers, and only failure to acknowledge that the occupational system is the backbone of the distribution system can hide that fact from those who study inequality.[8]

■ The Burdens of Inequality

Since the money income (in constant dollars) of those in each income fifth in 1978 was higher than that of those equivalently placed in the income hierarchy in, say, 1952, many observers have concluded that the absolute standard of living of each income group has significantly improved between 1952 and 1978; only its position relative to other groups has remained constant. Those at the lower levels of the income system may be worse off than today's rich, but they are better off than yesterday's poor. In the jargon of social science, they are not absolutely deprived, only relatively deprived.

There is some initial plausibility to such an interpretation. Thus 27 percent of the population had incomes of $4,000 or less in 1952, while only 14 percent did in 1978. But we doubt that those in the bottom two fifths are actually much better off today than in 1952 (or some earlier date) despite definite increases in real money income. In fact, the proponents of the theory of relative deprivation fail to take into account the changing costs of partaking of the services and institutions that prevail at different times in the development of a technological society. If a family's dollar income grows (that is, constant dollars controlled for inflation) while *luxuries* of one era literally become *necessities* in the next, the actual change in welfare over the intervening years cannot be captured by reading off increases in real money income.

In 1924 one could store food in an icebox because the iceman delivered ice regularly and because the corner store made it convenient to buy groceries on a daily basis. But today the iceman no longer delivers ice and the corner store has disappeared. The electric refrigerator has replaced the icebox as the available means of food storage, and the supermarket now makes weekly shopping the most convenient and least expensive way to acquire food. The refrigerator has become a household necessity not merely because everybody habitually uses it but because the food-distribution system requires its use.

The shift from the icebox to the refrigerator merely symbolizes, of course, the changed social and economic context in which today's consumers must make choices. If cheap cuts of meat are no longer available in the supermarket (perhaps they are not profitable enough), I must buy the more expensive cuts. If the "consumer durables" of today, such as television sets, washing machines, hot water heaters, refrigerators, automobiles, and even houses, wear out faster than in a previous period, I must simply replace them more often at the going prices. If public transportation is unavailable, I must purchase a car to drive to work and to shop. If the risks and costs of automobile accidents are growing, I must purchase expensive automobile insurance. If cars are more complicated than in the past, I must pay to have them repaired rather than fixing them myself. If building codes, plumbing regulations, and electrical specifications required by law are too complicated for the handyman of yesterday to understand, I must hire specialists to install and repair these household systems. If the breakdown of extended kinship ties threatens to leave my offspring unprotected in the event of death or injury, I must buy life and disability insurance to provide for their security. If home heating costs are going up, I must buy home insulation. If crime is increasing, I must buy locks and police dogs and alarm systems to protect my family. If my children today must go to college in order to attain positions equivalent to the one I took as a high school graduate, I must try to pay their way through college.

These are just some of the ways in which systems of health care, transportation, schooling, security, food distribution, and household repair, which were introduced initially to meet the desires and budgets of middle- and high-income groups, can become necessities for lower-income groups living in the same society. What is for the affluent a new and better social service is often for the poor a new and costly regulation or necessity of life.

It is difficult to ascertain the exact effect of such changes in the prevailing system of social services on the welfare of lower- and moderate-income groups, but recent studies by the Bureau of Labor Statistics can give us some indication.[9] The bureau calculates three hypothetical budgets, *lower level, intermediate level,* and *higher level,* for a family of four living in an urban area.

In 1972, for instance, the lower budget was $7,386, the intermediate $11,446, and the higher $16,558. By 1978, these three budgets were inflated to $11,546, $18,622, and $27,420, respectively! According to the bureau, the intermediate budget provides a "modest but adequate" standard of living. It enables the father to buy a new suit every two to four years, the mother to purchase one new coat every five years; the family to purchase a new refrigerator or stove every seventeen years, a used car every four years; the parents to attend a movie once every six weeks. It is not exactly a model budget in the affluent society. And it makes no provision for extended illness, unemployment, vacations, a college education for the children. These problems, plans, and obligations are assumed away, for the children are young and the father is healthy in this hypothetical family. The minimum budget is still more austere, merely providing minimal food, clothing, and housing for the family under optimistic assumptions about its health and the availability of the proper items. These two budgets are so high in dollar figures and so low in purchasing power, we think, at least partly because of the social services any family must acquire if it is to live in an urban or suburban area.

But even by these austere standards the American economy does not live up to its image of near-universal affluence punctuated by occasional poverty. In 1978 about 26 percent of American families had incomes of less than $11,500, placing them below the minimum budget for a family of four. Fifty-eight percent of the families had incomes below the intermediate budget level, and 75 percent were placed below the higher budget.[10] These figures cover families living in a variety of circumstances, so they must be interpreted with caution. Thus families living in rural areas or with fewer than two children face lesser financial burdens than assumed in the budgets. And families with more than two children, children in college, serious illnesses, or two adult breadwinners—over half now have two breadwinners—face higher expenses for medical care, education, transportation, day care, and meals than the budget assumes.

Certainly, then, these figures indicate that a majority of American families find it difficult today to make ends meet, even though their dollar incomes would generate a comfortable life in many other societies. They are deprived not merely of luxuries they would like to have but also of the opportunity to participate in the established universe of consumption. The expenses imposed by the social infrastructure of consumption in America generate the most powerful set of pressures to resist significant reductions in the system of inequality. In an order where the disciplines of schooling and work are justified largely by the promise of affluence, those with a tight budget and power resources will use those resources to maintain the differentials already established. This feature of the economy indicates, as we shall later argue, that any attempt to reduce inequality significantly cannot succeed until it is joined by an effort to reconstitute the social infrastructure of consumption.

But the burdens of a stratified system are not sufficiently catalogued even after we have identified the unequal chances for security, health care, recreation, education, fulfilling work life, and consumer goods that flow out of the system. The myth of equality of opportunity within a system of unequal rewards—the idea that individuals have a fair chance to move to significantly higher positions in society if they are especially energetic, intelligent, skilled, and lucky—contributes other injuries as well. Following the lead of Sennett and Cobb in their sensitive study, *The Hidden Injuries of Class*,[11] we can identify a series of traps faced by the low-income breadwinner seeking to serve the best interests of a family under adverse conditions.

People need to believe that they can play some role of importance in shaping their own lives, in living up to ideals and principles they accept in providing for the current welfare and future chances of their children. In a class system where people are classified and rewarded according to prevailing standards of worthiness, those at the lower end of the scale may deny in the abstract the validity of a system that first gives them lowly jobs and then blames them for being so lowly but, when one thinks about his own life, one tends to blame oneself, at least in part, for failure to climb further up the occupational ladder. Perhaps, the worker thinks, I did not apply myself enough in school or I am too stupid (and therefore deserving of low pay and status) or I have given in to the desire for a new car or a vacation rather than planning ahead. Perhaps I have done—or failed to do—any number of things that together explain why I remain near the bottom. The system of classification and differential reward, combined with the myth of equality of opportunity, generates self-doubt and self-reproach among those who stand at the lower levels of the stratification system. "If I hadn't quit school to make a fast buck, I wouldn't be where I am today," is the typical remark of a blue-collar worker in the Sennett and Cobb interviews.[12]

Partly to make up for that lingering sense of unworthiness,

partly to ensure that the next generation can escape this plight, blue-collar employees often work long hours to give their children a chance to move up the occupational ladder. These workers are not primarily motivated by the goals that energize the "economic man" of mainstream economic theory; they are willing to sacrifice now so that their children will not have to experience the same hardships and low self-esteem in the future. But this motive, while effective from the point of view of the employer as an incentive to work, further complicates the life of the worker.

If the breadwinner is unsuccessful in helping the children escape, then the sacrifice has been all for nothing. If, on the other hand, success is attained, it will probably be at the expense of losing too much time away from the family in whose name the sacrifice was made. And if, as is very common, both parents work to promote their objective, that consequence is doubled. Moreover, if the progeny do move on to higher positions, their new geographic and class location will separate them from the parents. The very network of extended kinship ties that can provide solace and support to people suffering hardships is undermined by the mobility of the children. In our system working-class parents can hardly help feeling ambivalent about the future of their children because, win or lose in the struggle to lift the next generation up, something of importance is lost.

To compete for the few promotion opportunities available, the worker must meet the expectations and attitudes of superiors more than fellow workers. Once again, whereas losing the promotion can mean failure, in winning it, the worker loses too. For now the task is to enforce rules and policies previously experienced as a burden, against workers once identified with.

Sennett and Cobb help us to understand such hidden injuries of class inequality and to comprehend as well the intense resentment and hostility people in such positions often feel against both intellectuals and welfare recipients: they help us, that is, to see the forces at work that divide constituencies that would have to be united if the system of inequality were to be changed significantly. If the welfare recipient can get income and food even when unemployed, a central source of meaning in the worker's life has been nullified: a willingness to *sacrifice* for one's family no longer seems so necessary. Why then make the sacrifice? If intellectuals call for expanded welfare programs; if they "coddle" criminals; if they criticize consumerism, they in effect ridicule the sacrifices and goals that give meaning (are available as a source of meaning) for the workers. The system of inequality, supplemented by the myth of equality of opportunity, thus deepens the hardship of those at the lower levels while dividing them from others who are potential allies in opposing the system itself.

■ Apologies for Inequality: The Functionalist Theory

Each person, most of us believe, has the capacity to feel pain and experience satisfaction, to formulate and act upon personal projects, to enter into complex relationships of love, trust, resentment, friendship with others, to suffer grievously from the loss of a loved one, and to feel indignation if the dignity of another is improperly denied. Since each of us has these capacities, we expect arrangements that undermine the satisfaction, projects, and dignity of some while magnifying those of others to receive some special justification. Why, we reasonably ask, are some placed so low while others are placed so high? Are those at the bottom lacking some of the characteristics we generally attribute to human beings? If so, that would constitute a justification; for we do not complain if someone fails to treat a worm like a person, only if someone treats a person like a worm. Or if it is not the lack of these human capacities that justifies inequality, is it perhaps to the benefit of the entire society to distribute rewards unequally?

It is useful to regard theories explaining inequality as efforts to answer these moral questions. Some theories explain inequality so as to justify the system sustaining it; others do so in ways that open the system to moral condemnation. It is appropriate to view the functionalist theory of inequality in this light. If the functionalist theory is basically sound, no sensible person would condemn the system that sustains inequality. The burdens it generates would be seen as necessary costs required to maintain a good society, just as we think of long practice as an essential prerequisite to becoming a concert pianist. To put it another way, to criticize the American system of inequality, one must first show flaws in the functionalist theory, which is so often advanced to explain and justify those arrangements.[13]

A functionalist in social science is one who seeks to understand the operation of an institution like the family, government, religion, the market, or a class system by showing how each contributes to the maintenance of the larger social system within which it operates. Each institution is understood in terms of the *functions* it performs within the entire system. And some institutions, according to theorists of functionalism, are functionally imperative in all complex societies; no stable system can survive without them. Inequality is thought to be one such functional imperative of any complex society.

A succinct statement of the functionalist theory of inequality was presented some years ago by two sociologists, Kingsley Davis and Wilbert Moore.[14] Every society, they assert, must first distribute its members into the various jobs or roles defined by the society and then motivate them to perform their tasks efficiently. Some roles or positions are more important than others in the sense that the successful performance of them is crucial to the welfare of the whole society. In addition, some tasks require skills that are either difficult or scarce because they require a good deal of special training. In order to ensure that the most important and difficult tasks are performed competently, every society rewards the performance of these tasks highly. The system of unequal rewards thereby functions as a set of incentives to channel the most competent people into the most important and difficult roles and then ensures that they will perform these tasks efficiently. The greater the division of labor in society, the greater the range must be between the positions with the lowest rewards and those with the highest. "Social inequality," in the words of the authors, "is thus an unconsciously evolved device by which societies insure that the most important positions are conscientiously filled by the most qualified persons." [15]

The general theory, as stated, is incomplete. If you explain why my heart pumps blood by showing me that its function is to keep sufficient blood flowing through my body to maintain life, you have displayed the heart's role in maintaining my life but have not yet explained why it performs that function. We don't yet know why the heart works, only what work it does. Similarly, to claim that inequality places the most qualified people in the most important positions (its function) is not to explain how the system of inequality is created and maintained.

When they turn to this question, Davis and Moore explicitly deny that the power of some over others is the principal means by which inequality is maintained: "It should be stressed that a position does not bring power and prestige because it draws a high income. Rather it draws a high income because it is functionally important and the available personnel is for one reason or another scarce." [16] But then they shy away from stating explicitly why these functional requirements are met.

We can correct this omission by specifying an assumption often acknowledged by functionalists and surely implicit in the theory of Davis and Moore. (If this is not the correct assumption, we must be informed which one *is* and how it squares with the other dimensions of functionalist theory.) Stability, in a system where each position receives approximately the level of reward required to get the most qualified people into it and to motivate them to work conscientiously, is based on the *consent of the population,* or in the jargon of social science, on the consensus of beliefs and values accepted by the majority of the population. Acceptance of the established system of inequality is part of the consensus. The population comes to understand that inequality is functional; it comes to see that a system of unequal rewards works to the advantage of the whole system by ensuring that roles central to society's welfare are well carried out. The population thus voluntarily accepts, or consents to, the system of inequality.

Put another way, a central tenet of the functionalist theory of inequality is that the population more or less tacitly comes to adopt that theory as part of its own understanding of established inequalities and to consent to established inequality because of that understanding. Thus only if the participants were to accept another theory of inequality, one that finds the established inequalities unnecessary and exploitative, would it be necessary to employ large doses of coercive power to maintain the system. As long as the dominant ideology is functionalism, we will have a consensus behind the system of inequality; if that ideology is challenged, the inequality must be maintained in some other way.

The functionalist explanation of inequality is deeply rooted in the traditions of American intellectual life. Thus James Madison, while laying out fundamental principles of the American Constitution in *Federalist No. 10,* expressed such views very clearly. The separation of powers, checks and balances, and division of powers between the states and the national government were designed to disperse and obstruct the power of those who might develop a "rage for paper money, for an abolition of debts, for an equal division of property, or any other improper or wicked project." [17] And Madison justified the unequal division of property in terms quite congenial to contemporary functionalists:

> From the protection of different and unequal faculties of acquiring property, the possession of different degrees and kinds of property immediately results; and from the influence of these on the sentiments and views of the respective proprietors ensues a division of society into different interests and parties. [18]

Madison was not as optimistic as modern functionalists that a consensus could be built around the established inequalities. He thought therefore that the "first object of government" was to protect the division of property because the division itself was essential to the welfare of the system.

Today Milton Friedman holds that the market is the most efficient way of filling the most important posts with the most competent people and that equality of opportunity is the principle that allows the market to select the most competent individuals. Inequality of position, in a market system, reflects functional imperatives, and both the market and the inequality it sustains are supported by a broad social consensus: "No society can be stable unless there is a basic core of value judgments that are unthinkingly accepted by the great bulk of its members. I believe that payment in accordance with product has been, and in large measure still is, one of these accepted value judgments or institutions." [19]

Others who believe that the market is increasingly displaced by a rather benevolent corporate elite limited by labor, government, a broad consensus, and the conscience of its own managers, also conclude that the established system of inequality is basically sound. As one exponent of this view puts it, "The system is not equalitarian . . . nor probably should it be. Superior character, high ability, greater capacity to render those services which society needs not only can but should be rewarded more highly." [20]

Many writers in a variety of fields accept the functionalist theory of inequality, and they are ready to draw the appropriate moral conclusion: if inequality works to the advantage of the whole system, it should be maintained. What other view could one reasonably hold *if* the functionalist theory is correct?

The theory, however, is open to telling criticisms, criticisms that do not destroy it completely but radically narrow the range of inequalities that can be justified as functional imperatives.

1. While it is usually easy enough to tell which skills are in scarce supply, it is not so easy to tell which tasks are the most important to the welfare of a particular society. Garbage collection is terribly important today, probably more important than, say, advertising detergents, writing comic strips, or selling used cars. But is it as important as managing a corporation, teaching young children, psychoanalyzing public officials? How would one decide? In practice, functionalists shift from assessing the relative

importance of any particular position to assessing its relative *skill* level and the *scarcity* of that skill in the population. Fortunately for them, the skills required to psychoanalyze public officials are more scarce today than those required to collect garbage.

2. Scarcity of needed skills becomes the primary test, then, but if a profession is strategically located in a restricted market economy, it can do much to make sure that the supply of skilled personnel in its profession is limited. It thereby ensures its practitioners a high income. This is surely why doctors are paid so highly. The profession limits the supply of physicians through control over entry to medical schools and then, through the American Medical Association, lobbies government effectively to make sure that physicians do not lose the right to set fees privately. The *market power* of the medical profession is surely a better explanation of its very high income level than is the functionalist interpretation of its position offered by Davis and Moore: "Modern medicine, for example, is within the mental capacity of most individuals, but a medical education is so burdensome and expensive that virtually none would undertake it if the position of the M.D. did not carry a reward commensurate with the sacrifice." [21]

It is plausible to explain much of the expense of medical education, the small number and size of medical schools, even the length of medical education as artifacts of unionized control over access to the profession rather than as necessary features of medical practice. Similar points apply to lawyers, accountants, skilled crafts, and so on. *Once the first criterion of the functionalists—functional importance—recedes to the background, the functionalist interpretation of the second—scarcity of needed skills—becomes very problematic.*

3. Functionalists emphasize the affirmative side of their theory —the need to identify scarce talent and to motivate those who possess it to work efficiently. But if their assumptions about human motivation are correct, there is another side to functionalist theory as well. Since those at the lower end of the income stream cannot be motivated by high rewards, they must be motivated by such "incentives" as the belief, whether true or false, that a good performance will be rewarded with promotion, the fear of unemployment, the need to provide for a family even under the most adverse circumstances. And as workers at the bottom get older, the first incentive must give way to the others. Only then will it be possible, on functionalist assumptions, to ensure that the most dangerous, demeaning, dirty, and routinized

jobs are "conscientiously filled by the most qualified persons." High income cannot be the incentive, for according to the theory, low income at this level must provide the differential needed to fill the higher positions with qualified and conscientious workers. It should be no coincidence, then, from the vantage point of functionalist theory, that not only low income but poverty, unemployment, and the continual threat of unemployment are concentrated among those jobs where the skill level is the lowest and the supply of skills the greatest. These threats are the functional requirements of a stratified society. They ensure a supply of menial workers at low cost to the society. And these agents often supply service at low cost to high-income personnel, rewarding the latter even more for performance of their skilled tasks. It is a beautiful theory (and system) when all its assumptions are spelled out: the carrot at higher levels *requires* the stick at lower levels.

4. The functionalists assume that the incentives to work that prevail in our society must prevail in every society. In that respect the theory is quite close to classical and neoclassical economic theory. But it could be that inequality in our society is so great in part because work in our society is organized basically around *external* and *individual* incentives. An external incentive is one, like money, that stands outside the work process itself. It is in contrast to an internal incentive, such as the fulfilling or challenging nature of the task. An individual incentive is in contrast to a shared incentive, as when the work itself involves fulfilling social relationships (an internal, social incentive) or when the object of work will be a contribution to some collectivity with which one identifies. It seems likely that a broader mix of external, individual, internal, and social incentives is *possible* in the organization of a society's division of labor. If so, it could be that our system of inequality is functional relative to the division of labor and incentive forms we have developed. But then our system of inequality would not reflect universal functional imperatives, but the imperatives of our particular system of production and work. And that would really amount to a refutation of functionalist theory: it would point toward reform of our system of production and work so as to relieve (among other things) the burdens of inequality. Why should we tolerate those burdens if they are remediable? The answer to that question also reveals why functionalist theory must view the incentive system prevailing in our society as the incentive system of society per se.

5. For the system of inequality to operate smoothly, a majority

of the population must see it as the functionalist theorists see it— as working to benefit the entire society. And most of the members of the system must also believe that their assigned roles and reward levels reflect their abilities and the relative value of their services to the society. When these conditions are met, the stratified system will rest upon a consensus; even those at the lower levels will understand that the threat of unemployment is needed to keep them working. But if these conditions are met, only those at the higher levels can *both* believe in the system and have a sense of self-esteem. (Those who accept functionalist theory wholeheartedly tend to be clustered near the upper end of the income stream). The others must see themselves as at least partly responsible for their own lowly fate. My incompetence, laziness, or lack of discipline is responsible for my low position and for the restricted life chances of my children. In this way, acceptance of (popularized versions of) functionalist theory becomes one of the burdens of class. It generates exactly the shame and self-doubt Sennett and Cobb identified as the hidden injuries of class.

■ An Alternative Theory of Inequality

The factors that explain the historical development of an institution do not necessarily explain how it is maintained today. Thus if members of a village select and follow a leader during a siege, his position emerges through community consent. But if, after the siege is over, he uses the resources at his disposal to retain his position even against opposition, his position of preeminence is now based on his exercise of power over his followers.

We will argue that an expanding and powerful industrial elite played a crucial role in creating the structure of inequality that prevails today. One of the effects of this process was to allow an accumulation of capital for further industrial expansion; another was to push the industrial working class into a subordinate and precarious economic position. Now that the system of inequality is solidified, the corporate elite continues to play some continuing role in its maintenance. But the stability of the system itself is further enhanced because the system of inequality itself divides groups that would have to be united if the system were to be altered. Each subordinate group, to put it starkly, is both exploited and a willing or unwilling participant in the exploitation of others. The result, in broadest outline, is a stable hierarchy, graded by power, in which every "new pressure or imposition moves along the line of least resistance which, though not in its first stage, usually and eventually runs in a descending direction." And, as Georg Simmel, the author of this imagery, reminds us, the pressure in such a structure of inequality flows inexorably downward until it reaches those at the bottom:

> This is the tragedy of whoever is the lowest.... He not only has to suffer from the deprivations, efforts, and discriminations which, taken together, characterize his position; in addition every new pressure on any point whatever in the superordinate layers is, if technically possible at all, transmitted downward and stops only at him.[22]

We begin by considering briefly the development of the modern wage-labor system in one industry—the steel industry—around the turn of the century. The pressures at work in that industry existed in other basic industries too, and the outlines of our modern corporate system and the system of inequality attached to it were created.

Before 1892 the production of steel required a group of highly skilled craftsmen who held a strategic position in the production system. "At every point rollers, roughers, and heaters had manually handled the metal. They were men of long experience and at a premium in America." [23] These craftsmen would negotiate a fixed rate of pay per unit of production with management and then "contract out" wages to semiskilled and unskilled workers who worked for them.[24] If the skilled workers were dissatisfied with working conditions or with their pay scales, they could strike until management was ready to negotiate. For when the members of the Amalgamated Association, the union of steel craftsmen, went on strike, there were no skilled craftsmen to replace them.

But as the market for steel expanded and as new technologies allowed pig iron (the crude iron from which steel is made) to be produced faster than finished steel, the steel owners saw possibilities for new profits in the mechanization of the entire process. Moreover, if they could create a process in which every required skill could be easily acquired and therefore every skilled worker could be replaced easily, they could gain more control over the work force. They could then set wage rates that seemed appropriate to them, regulate the conditions of work, and discipline or fire stubborn workers. They could do all this by developing a production system in which no group of workers possessed scarce and indispensable skills.

The Carnegie Company, with Andrew Carnegie at the helm, had

both these objectives in mind when it set the stage for the classic steel strike of 1892 in Homestead, Illinois. As a partner in the Carnegie Corporation said, "The Amalgamated placed a tax on improvements, therefore the Amalgamated had to go." [25]

Henry Clay Frick, the chief executive of Carnegie's operation, prepared carefully for the 1892 strike. He converted the factory into an armed fortress, hired three hundred Pinkerton detectives, and then announced that the company would no longer recognize the union but would negotiate with each worker individually. The Amalgamated then called a strike. After dozens of deaths, the intervention of the state militia, Pinkerton detectives, scabs, and the courts on the side of the company, the union was finally broken. Several consequences followed.

1. Blacks from the South, driven north by repression and increasing unemployment in their home states, were employed as strikebreakers.[26] This created deep animosity between white and black workers, neither group comprehending (or able to consider) the plight faced by the other. Similar incidents in future labor-management conflicts plus the fact that the blacks when eventually given regular employment in the steel factories held the most debilitating and low-paying jobs helped to divide these two segments of the labor force from one another. This historical development, rather than some hypothetical racism indigenous to blue-collar workers, fostered the persistence of racial conflict within the working class.

2. With the Amalgamated Association broken, the owners were able to mechanize the production of steel. Output was soon increased, the number of working hours was expanded to ten or twelve hours per day (often seven days a week), and work skills were defined so that no group of workers became indispensable to the enterprise. The system was structured so that managers did almost all of the *thinking, organizing,* and *commanding* while the workers *monitored* specific pieces of machinery or did other *physical* work. Craftsmanship was thus replaced by labor in the steel industry. And while production increased rapidly during the next ten years, wage rates increased only modestly. "The accomplishment was possible," according to historian David Brody, "only with a labor force powerless to oppose the decisions of the steel men." [27]

3. Despite a significant reduction in the range of skills required for steel production, management soon found that a hierarchical system of wages, a set of "job ladders," was needed to motivate

men to work efficiently and to weaken their ability to unite in organized opposition to management policies. As one manufacturer
himself explained it in the early 1920s:

> When all are paid one rate, it is the simplest and most inevitable
> thing for all to unite in the support of a common demand. When
> each worker is paid according to his record there is not the same
> community of interest.... There are not likely to be union strikes
> when there is no union of interest.[28]

By *record,* the manufacturer meant less the levels of skill of the
workers than their attendance, their cooperation with management, the pace at which they worked, their opposition to unionism, and their willingness to accept overtime. The "job ladders"
became a device for controlling workers while increasing their
efficiency. Some of those who played the game by the new rules
were pushed up the ladder while the others stayed behind. The
result was to further divide workers from one another and thereby
to make them and the wage rates they received easier to control.
As the new system matured, one steelworker described the difficulties it presented to those who sought to organize a new union:
"Naw they won't join the union; they're all after every other
feller's job."[29] The "equality of opportunity," operating within
the job ladders, focused each worker's attention on his chances
for individual promotion and away from the risky possibilities for
collective improvement of the position of the working class.

4. The migration of Slovaks, Poles, Croats, Serbs, Magyars, and
Italians, encouraged by United States immigration policies and
depressed economic conditions in Eastern Europe, swelled the
labor force, weakened the possibilities for collective organization
because of an available supply of labor to replace strikers, and
created division and resentment among the various ethnic groups
as each new wave found jobs below the groups that had migrated
ahead of it. Since many of the immigrants came without wives
and planned to return to the homeland as soon as possible, they
were often willing to work hard for low pay. They usually avoided
the established workers, who viewed them as a threat to their
job security. The immigrants themselves often had few illusions
about America. Letters to the homeland often concurred with
the judgment of a Hungarian churchman: "Wherever the heat is
the most insupportable, the flames the most scorching, the smoke
and soot the most choking, there we are certain to find compa-
triots bent and wasted with toil."[30] The immigrants suffered, and
the pay rates of the workers who had arrived before them were

depressed by the new supply of labor. All this increased conflict within the working class, intersecting with the racial conflicts already present. When labor conflicts emerged again in the 1920s, corporate owners exploited these conflicts by playing one ethnic group against others.

Our thesis is this: once management, through its destruction of the old craft union and craft system of work, had introduced the new factory system, the system itself developed self-perpetuating tendencies. The job ladders, the principle of advancement through individual effort, the ethnic divisions, the replaceability of unskilled and semiskilled workers, the technology adapted to the needs of management control, the continuing flow of new labor into the region—all these forces divided workers and allowed corporate owners, always with the willing assistance of the state, to break efforts at collective organization with a minimum of difficulty. What emerged was not a functional system of inequality (the workers did not consent to it voluntarily; it was not the only possible way to organize production, to accumulate capital rationally, or to motivate workers to work; and it benefited some groups unnecessarily at severe cost to others). It was (and is) a hierarchical system of exploitation in which each occupational level is exploited, though to different degrees; each participates, often unwittingly, in the exploitation of the groups below it. Employers gained the loyalty of top managers, professionals, middle-level technicians, and foremen first by paying them highly and providing job security, later by recruiting most of them not from inside the factory but from universities where they are socialized to congenial values and expectations. The "loyalty" of the others was retained through job ladders with uniformly low wage ceilings, corporate welfare, and job insecurity.

This pattern was duplicated, with important variations of course, in each of the basic industries (roughly in what Galbraith calls the corporate or planning system). It is important to see that the successful organization of industrial trade unions in the 1930s occurred well after the basic consolidation of the industrial system of private corporations. The trade-union leadership did not challenge the established pattern of private ownership, the structure of work, the distribution of income between workers and managers, even (much) the established balance between privately incorporated production for private consumption (depending on private income level) and the social provision of public goods (energy, health care, transportation systems, public life insurance). The trade unions did introduce a measure of job security through seniority rules, press for social security and other retirement benefits, establish a system of due process for workers treated arbitrarily by management, and most important for the purposes of our inquiry, redistribute income within the working class.

Galbraith's thesis that our economy is marked by a subordinate market system (service industries, farming) and a dominant corporate system is pertinent to the question of how unions help to redistribute income within the working class and how they often unwittingly contribute to inequality and divisions within the working class. Established industrial unions in the United States have never challenged the right of corporate owners to make investment decisions, relocate, set prices, or determine the basic form of the assembly line. So when these unions demand higher wages for workers, corporate owners can comply and then raise prices to more than cover the increased wage costs. The cost of living then goes up, taking some of the wage gains away. But workers in the market system, who are seldom organized into unions and for whom unions cannot have much leverage even when they are organized, then find their cost of living has gone up also. Their employers are restricted by market competition and, most important, by the necessity of conforming to the terms of trade set by the large corporations who buy many of their products. Workers in the market system, then, cannot match the cost-of-living increase with an equivalent wage increase. In effect, the wage increase of the organized workers in the corporate system contributes to the higher cost of living faced by workers in the market system.

Functionalist theory is not completely wrong; it is just radically overstated by its proponents. And this overstatement unjustifiably legitimates an extreme inequality in the distribution of wealth, income, working conditions, job satisfaction, job security, health care, pension plans, and other fringe benefits that has persisted for decades and that stratifies the population in roughly the following order: corporate owners, market entrepreneurs, managers and professionals in both systems, white-collar workers in the corporate system, skilled manual workers in the corporate system and selected market areas, clerical workers in the market system, unskilled workers in the corporate system, unskilled workers in the market system. Our alternative interpretation, we suggest, accounts for the stability of this stratification system in terms of a complex set of political controls and divisive pressures within the production system. It also undermines the legitimacy of established inequalities, lending legitimacy to those who would reduce their scope.[31]

■ The Poverty of Liberal Reforms

In 1875 Karl Marx criticized those "vulgar socialists" who sought to reform the system of *distribution* while leaving the system of *production* basically intact:

> Vulgar socialism (and from it in turn a section of democracy) has taken over from the bourgeois economists the consideration and treatment of distribution as independent of the mode of production and hence the presentation of socialism as turning principally on distribution.... The distribution of the means of consumption at any time is only a consequence of the distribution of the conditions of production themselves.[32]

That criticism applies today to liberals who seek to redistribute income through government programs and yet are eager to leave the system of work and ownership intact. Their programs can at most result in very modest success; at worst they will fail miserably (remember the "war on poverty") and play into the hands of corporate conservatives, who have insisted all along that these programs cannot succeed.

Liberal proposals have included job training for the unemployed, expansion of welfare programs, a negative income tax to provide income floors for those at the bottom of the system, and most ambitiously, a graduated income tax that would significantly close the gap between high- and low-income earners. All these proposals, it must be emphasized, leave the system of ownership and production untouched and introduce only marginal effects in the infrastructure of consumption, a situation that helps generate political pressures for inequality. They seek to reform the system of distribution without altering the political economy in which it is anchored.

The first problem with these proposals (though they are not unique in this respect) is that they are unlikely to receive the support of a majority of the electorate in the existing political economy. It goes almost without saying that the most powerful interest groups in the system will oppose the most ambitious of these reform proposals. But more is involved.

It is easier in our system of political economy to build an electoral majority of 51 percent from the top down than from the bottom up because the top has more benefits to dispense to the middle than the bottom does. Not only is the blue-collar work force divided from within by the forces we have described, but corporate elites have impressive resources available in the prevailing system to maintain the loyalty of managerial and professional employees by providing them with high salaries and special benefits. These groups together can also align themselves politically with entrepreneurs, white-collar workers, and sometimes skilled blue-collar workers over a broad range of issues. Thus they can coalesce to protect or extend tax breaks for each group; to promote those military expenditures that provide investment and employment opportunities for each group; to provide public support for technical education so that corporate employment needs are financed through public funds and so that all taxpayers contribute to a system that primarily benefits children of middle- and upper-middle-class taxpayers; and so on.

During normal times, then, an electoral majority is easier to create from the top down than from the bottom up. This is largely because of the power of corporate elites to dispense benefits directly to potential allies and to play an important indirect role in securing benefits from government favorable to the same constituencies. Divisions, struggles, hard feelings certainly do emerge within these loosely forged coalitions, especially between its fringe members at lower occupational levels and its core members. But as George McGovern demonstrated in his 1972 campaign effort to redistribute income modestly through the tax system, these squabbles are ignored when class interests in the existing system of income distribution are at issue. This difficulty applies, of course, to other strategies for redistribution too, but it is a decisive obstacle to those liberals who seek to achieve significant tax reforms through government while leaving the basic system of ownership and production intact.

Suppose, however, that the situation were to change (perhaps an economic crisis opened up new coalition possibilities) and liberals were able to push through a highly progressive income tax combined with an income floor while leaving everything else in the system intact. The reforms simply would not take. We would have to expect American investors to divert a larger portion of their investments abroad. American corporations with a multinational capability already established would also move part of their production abroad, where higher profits are possible. Workers at the bottom of the occupational hierarchy would loaf on the job (there is no reform of work life, remember; many of those who had to choose between deadening, demeaning work and a somewhat lower income without work would choose the latter— and rationally so). The demand for a range of private consumption goods previously reserved for the middle class would increase (remember that there is no shift from private goods to collective goods) just at the time production was lagging; and thus inflation would accelerate. The reforms, in short, would fail, and very soon a militant top-down coalition would organize to restore the old system of inequality. Egalitarian policies, having failed, would once again get a bad name, and the ideal of equality would lose a place on the liberal agenda for another generation.

The failure must be expected because the established system of inequality is largely *functional,* not in the universal sense claimed by functionalists, but as it operates in a historically specific system of private ownership, instrumental organization of work, and production oriented primarily to private consumption. Reform in these latter areas is an essential part of any meaningful effort to reduce inequality.

More specifically, two major structural changes are required to open the way for a reduction in inequality:

1. The system of production for private profit and private consumption (think of cars, individual houses, fashionable clothes) must be modified extensively to allow the expansion of public ownership and a greater emphasis on the production of collective goods. Mass-transit systems, health centers, recreation centers, and schools are goods that can be made available to any citizen. To the extent that these collective goods become established in various spheres of life, the effective scope of inequality will be reduced.

2. The system of work must be reformed so that, first, more jobs become fulfilling in their own right, and second, those necessary jobs that are not open to such reform become increasingly the part-time responsibility of all able-bodied members of the society, whatever their major occupations. These reforms will lessen the need for extreme pay differentials as an incentive to work, and they will have the important direct effect of reducing the extreme inequality of working conditions. Of course, these reforms will also require public ownership of more firms; private owners will not accept meaningful reform voluntarily because, as the earlier example of the old craft unions in the steel industry made clear, meaningful work reform erodes the ability of private owners to control the productive system in their private interests.[33]

These reforms are not in principle unachievable. There is no technological imperative that makes their implementation impossible. They are, of course, unacceptable to major interests in the system and unfamiliar to many citizens who would benefit from them. But the political obstacles to such reduction in inequality are not in themselves an argument against our theory of inequality or our proposals for change; rather they reflect the inadequacy of the system that obstructs such programs. The first move toward revising that system is to deny its beneficiaries the ideological cover, that is, the ideology of functionalism within a market system, that has previously justified an oppressive, exploitative system of inequality.

There are some signs that the pressures to reduce inequality will emerge with renewed force during the next decade. First, an increasing number of workers are aware that not all countries organize work and income incentives the way we do; they are less easily convinced today that the established ways are the only ways. Finally, as the economic system faces increasing pressures from resource depletion, environmental decay, growing international constraints, internal inflation, unemployment, and a population overeducated for the jobs available, we can expect an increase in labor unrest. *Since many of these constraints set limits to the old ideal of an indefinitely expanding economy, with its promise of growth in money income for most workers, the pressures to divide the existing pie more equitably are likely to grow more intense.*

It is not clear how successful renewed pressure for a reduction in inequality can be. But even if immediate success were marginal, a social movement organized around these objectives would still be worthwhile. As we have seen, one of the hidden injuries of class is the low self-esteem that often accompanies a low-class position. Those who even partly accept the functionalist ideology internalize an ethic that places blame on themselves for the burdens they and their children bear. Acceptance of an alternative ideology, which locates the structural sources of inequality within the established political economy, would externalize that responsibility; it would thus help to lift a burden of shame that has unjustifiably been projected onto the victims of the established system. This process of externalization is important in itself; it is also essential to the development of a political movement for equality.

Finally, since acceptance of a radical theory of inequality places liberal schemes for redistribution in critical perspective, it also enables the left to dissociate itself from those redistributive programs doomed to fail in the present system. It thereby helps to maintain a good name for equality even while the misconceived egalitarian schemes of liberals falter.

NOTES

1. *Business Week,* August 5, 1972.
2. See Ferdinand Lundberg, *The Rich and the Super Rich* (New York: Bantam Books, 1969), Ch. 1.
3. See *Current Population Reports,* Series P-60, No. 89 (July 1973), p. 3. The income of the bottom fifth might be underrepresented too, since respondents often underreport income from public assistance and social security.
4. *Who Bears the Tax Burden?* (Washington, D.C.: Brookings Institution, 1974), p. 46.
5. Ibid., p. 6.
6. See *Current Population Reports,* Series P-60, No. 121 (February 1980), p. 42.
7. The Ford plan was announced in *Business Week,* June 8, 1974, p. 24. The Nashville study is summarized in the *New York Times,* October 23, 1974, p. 88.
8. For further discussion of the connection between income inequality and the occupational system, see Frank Parkin, *Class Inequality and Political Order* (New York: Praeger, 1971).
9. See *Three Standards of Living for an Urban Family of Four Persons,* Bulletin 1570-51, Bureau of Labor Statistics (Spring 1967), and *Urban Family Budget Updated to Autumn 1972,* Bureau of Labor Statistics, Vol. 96, No. 8, updated to Autumn 1978 in Vol. 102, No. 8.
10. *Current Population Reports,* Series P-60, No. 121 (February 1980); data are taken from pp. 3, 4, and 27. These figures do not correspond perfectly with the budget levels set by the Bureau of Labor Statistics. The figures cover both rural and urban families, and the family sizes vary (two-person, 37 percent; three-person, 21 percent; four-person, 20 percent; five-person or more, 23 percent). But these discrepancies are surely compensated for by the fact that the bureau budget assumes an established couple married fifteen years, a nonworking wife, children not yet of college age, and the absence of serious health problems or accidents.
11. (New York: Random House, 1973).
12. *The Hidden Injuries of Class,* p. 187.
13. More developed discussions of the connections between explanatory theory and normative judgment can be found in Charles

Taylor, "Neutrality in Political Science," and William Connolly, "Theoretical Self-Consciousness," in *Social Structure and Political Theory,* edited by William Connolly and Glen Gordon (Lexington, Mass.: D. C. Heath, 1974), pp. 16–39 and pp. 40–68.

14. "Some Principles of Stratification," *American Sociological Review* (April 1945), pp. 242–249. Reprinted in Connolly and Gordon, *Social Structure and Political Theory.* Quotations are taken from this book of readings.
15. Ibid., p. 114.
16. Ibid., p. 119.
17. *Federalist No. 10* (Indianapolis: Bobbs-Merrill, 1954), p. 19.
18. Ibid., p. 12.
19. Milton Friedman, *Capitalism and Freedom* (Chicago: University of Chicago Press, 1962), pp. 166–167.
20. Adolf Berle, *Power without Property* (New York: Harcourt, Brace and World, 1959), p. 145.
21. Davis and Moore, "Some Principles of Stratification," p. 115.
22. Quoted in Kurt H. Wolff, ed., *The Sociology of Georg Simmel* (New York: Free Press, 1950), pp. 236–237.
23. David Brody, *Steelworkers in America: The Non-Union Era* (New York: Harper and Row, 1960), pp. 31–32.
24. Actually, the contracting system was more complex and variable than presented here, but the complexities do not affect our thesis. For further information, see Katherine Stone, "The Origin of Job Structures in the Steel Industry," *Review of Radical Economics* (Summer 1974), pp. 113–174. Our presentation of developments in this industry is indebted to her essay, to the above study by Brody, and to Jeremy Brecher, *Strike!* (Greenwich, Conn.: Fawcett, 1974).
25. Brody, p. 54.
26. The bind of the black workers, driven from the South and despised in the North by whites whose jobs they threatened, is explored sensitively by Stanley Aronowitz, *False Promises: The Shaping of American Working Class Consciousness* (New York: McGraw-Hill, 1973), esp. Ch. 3.
27. Brody, pp. 48–49.
28. Stone, p. 131 (our emphasis).
29. Ibid., p. 134.
30. Brody, p. 99.
31. A complete account would include a more detailed discussion of women, the elderly, the chronically unemployed, the infirm. We simply want to suggest here that these categories, important in their own right to a thorough picture of the stratification system, can be comprehended to a great extent through the occupational categories that set the crucial terms within which inequality operates. The occupational system is the fundamental dimension of the system of stratification, though it alone is not sufficient to full understanding of it.

32. Marx, *Critique of the Gotha Programme* (1875) (New York: International Publishers, 1970), pp. 10, 11.
33. The reduction of inequality, it should be noted, does not necessarily require the elimination of all job ladders in specific occupations, although the difference between the top and bottom levels *between* occupations must be reduced greatly. If younger workers earn less than middle-aged workers within an occupation, this is not an inegalitarian practice unless the younger workers cannot expect eventually to move to those higher levels. It is not equality in any particular year that counts, but equality over a lifetime.

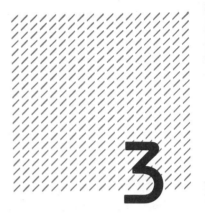

NATURE AND ITS LARGEST PARASITE

Ecology deals with the balance between organisms and their environment—between human beings and nature. The issues posed by such a relationship touch the very survival of humanity on the planet Earth. We depend on nature for air to breathe, soil to grow food, water to drink and to sustain vegetation, fossil fuels to provide heat and to power the production system, metals to provide material for commodities. But if nature is our host, we are its parasites. We abuse it unmercifully, robbing it of nonrenewable materials, straining its self-restorative capacities.

Parts of this chapter are drawn from "Market Images and Corporate Power: Beyond the 'Economics of Environmental Management,'" by Michael H. Best and William E. Connolly, pp. 41–74 of *Public Policy Evaluation,* Kenneth M. Dolbeare (ed.), © 1975 Sage Publications, Beverly Hills, with permission of the publisher.

If some economic systems are more parasitical than others, the structure of that relationship, and the problems it spawns, must be confronted before the host collapses from the strain. This is particularly pertinent today. For as corporate capitalism, the ultimate ecoparasite by any measure of resource use or waste disposal, faces a new round of internal crises, ecology is apt to lose its popularity as a political issue. Such a lapse must be challenged, because the current maladies of the system are partly rooted in a long-term debt to nature that is coming due.

Any reasonable assessment of the policy sciences in America must account for the lag between the escalation of ecological assault and its recognition by social scientists. Respected textbooks in political science and economics written before 1965 paid little heed to the issue. The social costs of environmental misuse became a national disgrace before they became the serious object of policy analysis by mainstream social scientists.[1]

Perhaps, though, the omission looks like a deficiency of theory only by hindsight. Perhaps the adverse environmental effects of the political economy of corporate capitalism were until recently too unobstrusive to be captured within the conceptual net of any intellectual system. Unfortunately, the earlier work of two maverick social scientists—K. William Kapp, an economist, and Grant McConnell, a political scientist—suggests that this is not true.[2] Their intellectual frameworks allowed them to detect abuses of nature resulting from prevailing forms of production and consumption even while these connections remained obscure to those trapped within the categories of pluralist political and neoclassical economic theory. In *The Social Costs of Private Enterprise* (1950), Kapp documents the

> destructive effects of air and water pollution . . . [and] occupational diseases . . . , the competitive exploitation of both self-renewable and exhaustible natural wealth such as wildlife, petroleum and coal reserves, soil fertility and forest resources . . . ; the diseconomies of the present transport system.[3]

These social costs had gone unnoted and untended, according to Kapp, because they "do not enter into the cost calculations of private firms." And economists failed to detect them too, not because they indulged in "wilful apologetics" for the private-enterprise system but because "the phenomena of social costs" seem to "have no room in the conceptual system of traditional value and price analysis."[4] Particularly important, he thought, was the faulty attempt by his professional colleagues to separate economic from political analysis, as if each could be treated as a distinct system. The ironic outcome of such an effort was a set of assumptions and concepts that maintained an unacknowledged and thus undefended "union between economic analysis and political liberalism." [5]

McConnell's early analysis of the political obstacles facing any conservation movement was built on ideas quite similar to Kapp's. He castigated pluralist political scientists for their refusal to see that compromises among organized private interests often produced results harmful to the public interest (his corollary to Kapp's idea of the social costs of private transactions). He criticized them for their failure to identify the corporation as "the most important form of private government in America today" and particularly for their continued acceptance of the "historic liberal" image of "an autonomous economy and its corollary, an autonomous politics." [6]

The prescience of Kapp and McConnell would be merely of historical interest (and academic embarrassment) amid the universal attention given to environmental issues today except for one further development. Adopting ideas very much like those Kapp and McConnell thought had blinded their predecessors to the environmental impact of the American political economy, contemporary policy scientists today purport to have a program to restore environmental integrity while retaining the autonomy of the market economy.

In contemporary America, policy scientists who perceive the economy as a competitive market system invariably see pluralism as its mirror image in politics. Indeed, since pluralist theory is basically market theory transposed to politics, we can say that each image is a mirror to the other: if one is blurred, the other will shift out of focus also. We will argue that the assumptions and policy priorities of social scientists who favor market images of the economy and polity are still disconnected today from the very environmental problems their predecessors failed to detect yesterday. Only an analysis linking private consumerism and industrial waste to our system of power, product designs, work-life incentives, and economic inequality can account adequately for the dangerous imbalance between human beings and nature that results from the political economy of corporate capitalism.

■ The Market Model of Environmental Management

The market, according to neoclassical theorists, is still a sound mechanism for coordinating economic transactions. But there are more and more *unpriced* effects of market transactions that must be incorporated into the market's pricing system. Air, water, and soil pollution are not automatically translated into market costs because the environmental effects of particular economic transactions are diffused over a wide population and to some extent projected onto future populations. Under such circumstances, it is irrational for any individual producer or consumer to accept voluntarily the higher costs involved in curtailing pollution of the environment. Thus a company that purifies the water used in production before disposing it into streams adds to its own costs, fails to benefit from the purified water flowing downstream, and weakens its competitive market position with respect to those companies unwilling to institute purification procedures. Since it is reasonable to assume that other companies in a market system will not voluntarily weaken their position in this way, it is irrational for any single company to choose to do so.

The same logic applies to the purely self-interested consumer who assesses the economic rationality of, say, placing an emission-control device on an automobile exhaust system. As shown in Figure 3-1, if the individual desired pollution abatement, a good situation would exist if everyone purchased the control device. But it would be better if everyone else purchased the device and the individual did not, since the individual then would get the benefit of the product without paying for it. Similarly, it might be a bad situation if no one at all purchased the device, but it would be worse if the individual purchased it and no one else did. For then the individual would have paid for the device but would not have received the desired benefit. Thus, regardless of what others might do, the individual would always be in a better position in not purchasing the emission-control device, even though pollution abatement would be worth much more than the price of the device.

Figure 3-1 Individual versus Collective Rationality in the Purchase of Pollution-Abatement Devices

		Everyone Else	
		Purchases	Doesn't purchase
Individual	Purchases	Good	Worst
	Doesn't purchase	Best	Bad

Thus practices that are desirable from the viewpoint of the public are irrational from the viewpoint of any particular consumer or producer. And policies that are rational for individual consumers and producers go against the collective interest in preserving nonrenewable productive resources and maintaining the environment's capacity to assimilate wastes. This is the "tragedy of the commons." [7]

To cope with this problem most economists think the government should establish by law a system of charges and subsidies; the adverse side effects of market transactions are then priced high enough to make it economical for producers and consumers to conserve nonrenewable energy resources and to establish waste-disposal systems that preserve the purity of air, water, and soil. As a secondary bonus, the new system of prices stimulates private business to produce improved disposal and recycling facilities since there is now profit in such enterprises. Much recent environmental legislation is based on this theory.

We do not say that such a program is inherently irrational; for any viable environmentalist program must somehow find a way to incorporate environmental costs into economic transactions. But if such a scheme were really to work, it would require basic alterations in the system of political economy. We will first identify some problems internal to the market theory and then turn to an alternative interpretation that places such a pricing system in a quite different context.

First, it is not at all clear that the intrusion of politics into the marketplace on the massive scale required to "internalize the externalities" would not create severe dislocations in the delicate, self-adjustive market mechanisms. Certainly a huge bureaucracy is required to identify the environmental costs of so many production processes and waste-disposal systems and to administer a tax and subsidy program reflecting these assessments.

Moreover, the problems of measuring and assessing environmental costs become magnified when considering costs to future generations. What will motivate today's voters, many of whom are treated unjustly within the prevailing economic system, to incorporate by law the needs and claims of future generations into current market transactions? Why should proponents of this model, who assume that individuals are inherently self-interested, think that current generations will be willing to build the interests of future generations into the pricing system? [8]

Finally, a market system that retains private control of the investment and pricing functions requires continued economic growth as a spur to investment. But a point may well be reached when growth itself is incompatible with environmental imperatives. Some experts believe, for instance, that a steady rate of growth will eventually (within several generations) generate atmospheric heat levels incompatible with human life.[9] Many suspect that other factors such as the depletion of key resources before adequate substitutes are found will force an end to, or a profound slow-down of, economic growth. The ecological effects of economic processes are often delayed, but when they emerge, they can be overwhelming. If it is true that capitalism flourishes on growth and dies on stagnation, then the market response to the environmental crisis so long ignored by its theorists may be woefully inadequate to the magnitude of the problem.

A number of revisionist market economists, reacting in part to problems internal to neoclassical theory and in part to a growing perception that the theory does not correspond to the actual economic system at crucial points, have introduced some adjustments into this framework. A recent study by A. Myrick Freeman, Robert H. Haveman, and Allen V. Kneese, *The Economics of Environmental Policy*,[10] applies such a revisionist view to an understanding of environmental issues. They seek to show how the "economics of environmental management" can enable us to curb the worst effects of pollution within the parameters of the market economy. Their basic acceptance of the market model is expressed when they assert that "unlike most other kinds of resources, choices involving the allocation of environmental resources cannot be left to individuals acting separately in unregulated and decentralized markets." [11]

But then some adjustments are made in the theory they employ. They concede that manipulative advertising affects consumer choices in important ways. They acknowledge that a highly unequal distribution of income allows privileged minorities to impose the heaviest burdens of pollution and the largest costs of pollution control on low-income groups. They agree that their proposals to incorporate ecological costs into the pricing system are inadequate to cope with costs to future generations. They agree that biases in the pluralist political system make it an exceedingly intractable vehicle for incorporating environmental costs into the market system. Indeed, they conclude, "the most formidable barrier to controlling pollution is probably not technology, population or public attitudes, but the politics of power." [12]

These adjustments could provide the catalyst for a quite different analysis of environmental issues. But these leads are not pursued by the authors. Inequality is noted as a problem, but neither its causes nor environmental effects are explored.[13] The costs for future generations are mentioned, but *institutional reforms* that might enable citizens to forgo immediate consumption benefits to preserve the future environment are never considered. Biases in the pluralist political system are described as the most "formidable barrier" to ecological integrity, but only a brief (and rather quaint) reference is made to "institutional arrangements such as the congressional seniority system and loose campaign financial regulations that encourage economic power to be readily transformed into political power."[14] In effect, these modifications function to protect specific parts of the theory while its basic form remains untouched: the newly identified factors, though admitted to be important, are neither explained within the model nor reflected in policy proposals drawn from it.

Such an analysis moves too hesitantly beyond those very assumptions that led social scientists to ignore the environmental effects of prevailing arrangements until they reached near crisis proportions. The analysis is abstracted from the basic structure of corporate capitalism. The technical proposals for reform do not show a grasp of the political constituencies and structural reforms required to implement them. In fact, proposals to incorporate environmental costs into the market system while retaining the structural arrangements that have generated these effects promise to divide the very constituencies that must be united if environmental deterioration is to be forestalled.

These are the charges we seek to sustain. To do so, we must move beyond the artificial division between the economic and political systems postulated in the market model to a perspective that probes connections between the dangerous deterioration of the natural environment and the political economy of corporate capitalism.

■ Product Alternatives and Corporate Priorities

To specify the cause of a problem is to establish as well its appropriate remedy. If otherwise healthy markets fail to price the social costs of resource depletion and pollution, the solution is to build those costs artificially into market transactions. But if the power of corporations to impose their priorities on governments and markets is part of the problem, and if some of those priorities in turn flow from structural tendencies in the politicized economy, then the remedy will involve major reforms in the political economy. It is the latter hypothesis that we wish to defend. We will start by exploring three related areas of production and consumption: transportation, energy, and petrochemical products.

TRANSPORTATION

A national transportation system built around automobiles, trucks, and airplanes uses fuel and metal resources extravagantly, imposes an enormous load on the self-purification capacities of the ecosystem, undercuts the cultural and recreational attractions of downtowns, and eventually drives up the cost of alternative modes of transportation.

The rising cost is linked to the self-destructive appetite of the American car, which uses about half of all oil consumed in the country, as compared to about a sixth of the oil consumed in Europe and Japan. On average each of the over 100 million U.S. cars consumes 2 tons of fuel annually; to reduce that consumption to the 1-ton-per-car level of Western Europe would save more than the total oil consumption of Canada or South America.[15] Yet as Table 3-1 shows, an average-occupancy car gets approximately a fifteenth the passenger miles per gallon used by a fully loaded bus and rail vehicle. A fully loaded car averaging 30 miles a gallon can reduce the proportion to about a fifth of a fully loaded mass transit vehicle.[16]

TABLE 3-1   *Fuel Consumption by Transport Mode*

	Miles per Gallon	Average Occupancy	Passenger Miles per Gallon	Maximum Occupancy	Passenger Miles per Gallon
Car	30	1.3	39	4	120
Rear-engined double-decker bus	7	16	112	75	525
Two-car diesel railcar	4	35	140	150	600
London transport seven-car tube train	0.75	105	79	840	630
Light-transit two-car set	2	50	100	240	480

Source: R. G. Harmon, "Fuel in Transport," *Traffic Engineering & Control* 15 (1974).

Cars use a range of other limited resources, such as iron, steel, aluminum, lead, zinc, and copper, the prices of which will also rise as the rate of depletion rises. While public transportation uses these same materials, it does not use them so inordinately.[17]

The advantages of public urban and interurban transportation are not restricted to resource savings. A French study estimates that mass transit there has the potential capacity to move 50,000 passengers during rush hour as compared to 3,000 by car, for no matter how many freeways are constructed, the small Paris streets will only absorb cars at 5–10 miles per hour.[18] Similar though less dramatic comparisons could be made in the United States, and they suggest a close link between our dependence on the automobile and the rise of congestion and urban breakdown.

Why does the United States depend on such an irrational transportation system, and what stops it from shifting to one more economical? Part of the answer lies in the structural characteristics of alternative modes of transportation, and part in the rising influence of the automobile corporations in the first part of the twentieth century in shaping both the transportation market and government policy. We will examine both factors.

Transportation choices provide a paradigm of how the split between individual and collective rationality operates.[19] As individuals shift from the rail to the road, they simultaneously drive up the cost of road *and* rail transportation. Figure 3-2 illustrates the relationship between increasing motorists and rising costs of transportation. An accurate positioning of the curve would require inclusion of the costs of congestion, resource scarcity, pollution, the thousands killed and millions injured annually by car accidents, insurance and legal fees, policing, and the public space lost to roads and car parks. Whereas C_1C_2 indicates the social cost to any one individual of purchasing a car, C_1C_3 indicates these costs plus the external costs—that is, uncompensated costs imposed on all *other* car owners by the new car buyer. Rail transportation, on the other hand, generates collective *benefits*. A new train rider reduces the costs to all other train riders. This is illustrated in Figure 3-2 by the downward movement of curve R_1R_2 from right to left.[20]

Given these characteristics, the market will lead to higher prices for both road and rail transport as long as the rail system serves only a small proportion of the populace. At any single transportation mix—for example, point P or P' in Figure 3-2—the self-interested individual will choose the road over the rail, and

Figure 3-2 Interdependency of Road and Rail Transportation Costs

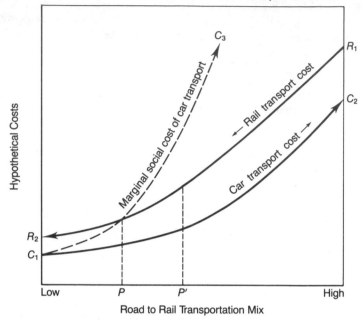

Source: Adapted from C. A. Nash, *Public versus Private Transport* (London: Macmillan, 1976), p. 46, by permission of Macmillan, London and Basingstoke.

the collective effect of these choices will increase the congestion and pollution costs to all road users, whether traveling by bicycle, rail, or foot.

In an area such as transportation, the reduction of individual and social costs (toward point P from P') requires public coordination of individual product choices. The market will not lead consumers, acting alone, toward the socially rational mix at point P; instead, private consumers responding to market signals individually will push the actual mix toward increased reliance on the road and ever higher transportation costs (to the right in Figure 3-2).

A decreasing-cost industry such as a rail or a mass transit system provides a basis for public subsidy. While public transportation is often opposed as a welfare program or subsidy to the poor, it is in fact rational from the point of view of social cost and the efficient use of scarce resources. A comparison of London Transport (LT) and Paris's public transport service (RATP) is instructive. Responding twenty years ago to the vicious cycle of deteriorating service, higher prices, and fewer passengers, RATP lowered fares and increased subsidies. Consequently, the fare per kilometer today (see Table 3-2) is less than one-third that of London Transport, having dropped from a previous cost of 10 minutes of average working time to 4 minutes. The LT rate, however, remains at the equivalent of 10 minutes of average working time. Since 1970, RATP's business has expanded by 20 percent and LT's has dropped by 16 percent, so that the former now carries 1 million more passengers daily. While LT's service is deteriorating, RATP has been reaping the benefits of better, cheaper service through the replacement of old trains with modern, comfortable, quiet vehicles; the refitting of old stations to make them safer and more attractive; and the elimination of queues by the widespread use of unlimited travel passes purchased periodically.

Clearly the potential for developing a rational railroad transportation system exists, but public coordination is required to close the gap between the result of the market and collective rationality. This potential has not been realized in the United States. Instead of subsidizing rail transportation in the twentieth century, the government intervened to subsidize its automobile competitor with a massive highway program, price controls on fuel, and tax advantages to suburban home owners. To understand better the transportation crisis gripping America in the 1980s, we must examine the corporate pressures that have shaped

TABLE 3-2 *Fares and Subsidies in London and Paris*

| | | Fare (pence) | | Operating Subsidy | |
		Per Kilometer	Per Journey	Amount (£ million)	Percentage of Operating Costs
London	Rail	5.9	44	135	26
	Bus	5.6	19		
Paris	Rail	1.8	16	417	59
	Bus	1.5	N.A.		

Source: Anatole Kaletsky, "Why Fares Are So High in London Transport," *London Financial Times,* June 23, 1980. Reprinted by permission of the *London Financial Times.*

government policy and the transportation choices available to the populace.

During the 1920s the United States had rather extensive trolley transit and rail systems, and there was ample potential to expand these services to meet the needs of a growing industrial population. As Bradford Snell has documented in a report to the Senate Judiciary Subcommittee on Antitrust and Monopoly, the competitive situation of the 1920s was short-lived.[21] During the middle of the decade, General Motors, often in conjunction with Standard Oil of California and Firestone Tire, launched an investment program enabling it first to control and then to dismantle the electric trolley and transit systems of forty-four urban areas in sixteen states. Often operating through a holding company, National City Line, the three corporations acquired electric rail systems, uprooted the tracks, and substituted diesel-powered bus systems. After acquisition and conversion, the systems were sold back to local groups, but only with a contractual clause precluding the purchase of new equipment "using any fuel or means of propulsion other than gas." [22]

The life of a diesel bus is 28 percent shorter than that of its electric counterpart; its operating costs are 40 percent higher. Thus the typical result of substituting one system for the other was "higher operating costs, loss of patronage, and eventual bankruptcy." [23] General Motors pursued a similar program of acquisition and conversion with rail lines.

General Motors and its satellite companies benefited in two ways from this acquisition policy. First, its profits from the sale of buses and diesel-powered locomotives have been higher than from trolleys and electric trains. Second, the financial difficulties faced by these converted transportation systems encouraged consumers to buy more cars. General Motors' incentive to make cars and trucks the basic vehicles of American ground transportation is clear enough: its gross revenues are ten times greater from cars than from buses, and twenty-five to thirty-five times greater from trucks than from locomotives.[24] Its expansion into mass-transportation systems enhanced its ability to attract consumers to cars and trucks.

The General Motors policy of acquiring, converting, selling, and ultimately strangling mass-transportation systems, in combination with escalating pressure from the American Road Builders Association, the American Trucking Association, and the American Petroleum Association to launch massive state and federal highway-construction programs, helped to make trucks and automobiles dominant vehicles for shipping and transportation in the country.[25] For example, the government, responding to these pressures, spent $156 billion for highway construction between 1945 and 1970. Sandwiched between a private corporation with impressive market power over ground transportation and government bias toward those organized corporate interests, mass-transportation systems inevitably lost out.

But as profitable as the operation has been for the corporations involved, it has been disastrous for the country. Besides the strain it has imposed on our fuel resources, it has created cities crisscrossed with highways, straddled by distorted housing patterns, and smothered in toxic emissions of carbon monoxide, lead, and other deadly chemical combinations from gasoline-powered vehicles.

Consumer desires and fantasies, of course, played a prominent role in implementing this conversion process. It is absurd to argue that consumers chose cars and trucks over transit and rail systems after consideration of each option in light of its comparative costs and benefits, including the costs of highway construction and the effects on the environment. Rather, a few corporations with effective market power, including control over information about alternative transportation, helped to eliminate some modes of transportation as viable consumer options. The demand of consumers uninformed as to the collective costs of these individual transactions then validated the transportation option favored by corporations. Thereafter, the hegemony of the automobile was solidified as national patterns of employment (in automobile manufacture, oil production, and highway construction) and satellite entrepreneurial activities (motels, tourist businesses) developed around this system and established a vast constituency whose immediate interests were tied to the maintenance and expansion of an ecologically irrational transportation system.

The cost today of extending the highway system and paying the price of the resultant pollution or of rebuilding the railroad system would be many times the cost earlier of a gradual upgrading of a train-based system. Today several obstacles converge in the same direction: increased road congestion has driven down the quality of car transportation; the rise in pollution has led to expensive antipollution regulation; the depletion of oil has driven up the cost of car transportation; and train services have become too emasculated to provide an option for most people. Given the spatial layout of most American cities, people are now dependent on the car as a way of life: it is essential for getting to and from

work, stores, recreation spots, and relatives' and friends' homes—
in short, for living as we know it.

ENERGY

Between October 17, 1973, and January 1, 1974, Americans became painfully aware of the nation's dependence on foreign energy supplies. At that time Arab nations imposed a boycott on
oil to industrial nations, restricting energy use by American consumers and nearly quadrupling the price of crude oil from $3.01
to $11.65 per barrel. While some economists, most notably Milton
Friedman, were predicting that competitive forces would break
the new Organization of Petroleum Exporting Countries cartel
(OPEC) and send prices tumbling downward, the price of crude
oil again shot up in 1979–1980 to over $30 per barrel. It is pos-
sible that, in a depressed world economy, these high prices will
produce a short-term supply glut and price discounts, but the
slack will be soon absorbed by cutbacks in OPEC production and
renewed economic growth.

The energy crunch, it is often asserted, converted the recession
of the mid-1970s into a near depression, one that took the form
of high inflation and high unemployment.[26] But this explanation
stops where it should begin. Why has the United States become
so dependent on Arab oil and thereby so vulnerable to boycotts
and price increases? What do our expanding energy needs imply for the future?

As shown in Table 3-3 and Figure 3-3, in historical terms oil
is a recent source of energy. Oil production did not begin until
late in the nineteenth century, but it grew rapidly, with the United
States producing and consuming well over half the world's sup-

TABLE 3-3 *World Oil Production, 1890–1974**

Year	North America	Middle East	World
1890	6.4	—	9.9
1910	29.2	—	44.5
1930	128.6	6.4	192.9
1950	284.3	87.8	519.3
1970	563.3	706.0	2286.5
1974	563.9	1077.5	2791.0

Source: E. N. Tiratsoo, *Oilfields of the World*, 2nd ed. (Houston: Gulf Publishing,
1976).

* In million tons. One ton equals 7.3 barrels of oil.

Figure 3-3 World Oil Production, 1890–1974

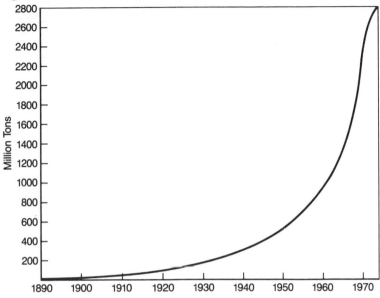

Source: Table 3–3.

ply until the 1950s The $2–3 per-barrel price of oil in the 1950s and 1960s certainly did not signal an impending shortage. Prices were raised only after the transportation, industrial, agricultural, commercial, and housing stock of the nation were built and in place. Today the society is a prisoner of these past investments and hostage to the decisions and priorities of domestic and foreign owners of oil resources.

The magnitude of the world oil-depletion problem is shown in Table 3-4 and illustrated in Figure 3-4. The date of depletion of finite reserves is highly sensitive to the rate of consumption, even with substantial differences in reserve estimates.[27] If the world consumption of oil were to continue to increase by 7.5 percent a year as it did from 1940 to 1973, the remaining *known* recoverable reserves would be depleted in eighteen years or by the year 1991. At the 7.5 percent rate, the discovery of an additional 965 billion barrels of recoverable reserves (an amount widely predicted by geologists) would delay the depletion a mere eight years, to 1999. If the post-1973 growth rate tapers off to 2.5 percent per year, as predicted by Exxon's *World Energy Outlook* (and in fact the actual rate for the 1974 to 1980 period), then

TABLE 3-4 *Estimates of Ultimate Recovery of Crude Oil (Billions of Barrels)*

	Cumulative Production to 1973	Proved and Prospective		Undiscovered Potential
		1974	1978	1974
North America	110	58		147
United States	103	51	76	76
Canada	7	7		71
Latin America	44	39		91
Western Europe (including North Sea)	3	21	24	45
Middle East	69	430	370	131
Africa	16	61	58	86
Far East	9	27	20	93
Communist countries	46	104	94	350
Other				20
Total	297	740	642	963

Sources: Columns 1, 2, and 4 from J. D. Moody, *The Petroleum Economist* (June 1975), p. 204.

Column 3 from *Oil & Gas Journal* 76, no. 52 (December 25, 1978), pp. 102–103. Reprinted with permission of *Oil & Gas Journal,* December 25, 1978.

known reserves would last twenty-six years or until 1999. Known reserves plus the 965 billion barrels of estimated reserves not yet discovered would last forty-five years or until the year 2018. If the growth rate had slackened to zero in 1973, then dates of exhaustion would be delayed to 2010 for known reserves and 2056 for known plus undiscovered reserves.

This consequence of geometric progression in depletion dates is not limited to oil; it holds for all finite resources. For example, Jimmy Carter's National Energy Plan called for a 13 percent growth rate in coal production. Estimates for the remaining coal deposits at present levels of consumption vary between 600 and 3,000 years. If the rate of growth is increased to 13 percent annually, the depletion of coal will occur in thirty-three years if the lower figure is correct and forty-six years if the higher figure is right.

The preceding figures are used primarily for illustrative purposes. Predicting the availability of undiscovered reserves is clearly problematic. A variety of economic and political factors could increase or decrease the estimates enormously. Certainly, as de-

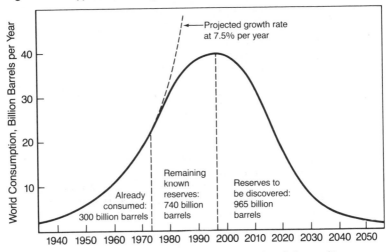

Figure 3-4 Hypothetical Depletion Curve for World Oil Reserves

Projected growth rate
at 7.5% per year

World Consumption, Billion Barrels per Year

Already
consumed:
300 billion barrels

Remaining
known
reserves:
740 billion
barrels

Reserves to
be discovered:
965 billion
barrels

1940 1950 1960 1970 1980 1990 2000 2010 2020 2030 2040 2050

Source: Adapted from M. King Hubbert, Statement before Subcommittee on
the Environment of the House Committee on Interior and Insular Affairs,
June 4, 1974.

pletion approaches, price rises and political intervention will
shrink consumption rates.

We can say that the estimated 30-35 billion barrels of oil remaining in the United States will be gone early in the 1990s if the
present annual production rate of 3.5 billion barrels per year continues and no major new domestic reserves are discovered.[28] The
United States consumption rate of oil is seven times the world
average and three to four times the European average. It is reasonable to assume that these levels will be impossible to sustain
in the future, and the necessary reductions will require massive
changes in the organization of the American economy.

Consider some of the implications.

1. The waste in our energy system is truly massive. We have
already noted the energy inefficiency of the car transport system,
which accounts for one-half of U.S. oil consumption. Half of the
fuel used in car transportation is for trips of less than five miles.
Short car trips could be substantially reduced with increased
mass transit, bicycle paths, and pedestrian walkways. Energy
wastefulness in housing is also commonplace. An analysis of
New York City concluded that perhaps three-fourths of the heat-

ing energy now used could be saved by a conservation and solar-energy program. The program would involve insulation, weatherization, and the use of solar hot water and solar walls to provide heat in winter and cooling in summer. The program is labor-intensive and would generate jobs in the local economy.[29] A Council on Economic Priorities study estimates that insulating homes properly could reduce energy consumption by approximately 40 percent, while the American Institute of Architects claims that the United States could save one-third of its entire energy consumption by installing energy-effective systems.[30]

Our system of energy production is also woefully inefficient. Centralized power stations far removed from the point of energy use dissipate energy into the atmosphere. In the case of fossil fuels, two-thirds of the available energy is wasted in this way, and over 95 percent is lost by nuclear reactors.[31] Europeans have reduced this form of waste somewhat by the cogeneration of both electricity and heat in a single power plant located in the community or building complex. Through cogeneration the heat used in producing electricity is captured and utilized for space and water heating; conversely, steam used for heat is also employed to create mechanical motion for electricity.

Some industrial firms have experimented with energy conservation with enormous success. Dow Chemical, for example, has boasted that by rearranging its heating processes, it has cut energy consumption by 20 percent and has saved enough energy for "New York City (to) operate its subway for two years."[32] The post-World War II shift from labor-intensive to energy-intensive production techniques also contributes greatly to energy waste.[33]

2. The rising price of oil has led to immense income transfers at the international and national levels. The same physical amount of exports in 1980 brings ten times the oil revenues that it did in 1973. Oil and gas monies received by the major exporting countries went from $37 billion in 1973 to $116 billion in 1974. The figure shot up to $213 billion in 1979. One authority estimates that even on the most favorable assumptions, the OPEC countries will receive between $350 and $450 billion over the 1980–1985 period.

Each dollar in purchasing power gained by the oil exporters is lost by consumers in the oil-importing nations. The U.S. fuel bill has climbed from $5 billion or 0.4 percent of gross national product in 1972 to $81 billion or 3.1 percent in 1980. It is predicted that it will reach $167 billion by 1985. But the underdeveloped countries have been hardest hit. Their foreign debt rose from $150 billion in 1975 to $385 billion in 1980 and will climb to an estimated $440 billion by 1981.[34]

The distributional shifts within the United States have also been dramatic. Since direct and indirect energy consumption represents nearly 10 percent of national income, a 100 percent rise in energy costs (which is the order of magnitude of the 1973–1980 increase) reduces real income of consumers by 10 percent. But the drop is shared very unequally: the richest 10 percent of the population spends only 5.2 percent of its income on energy, while the bottom 10 percent spends 34.1 percent.[35] Thus the poorest lose between six and seven times as much of their income as the richest. This loss, however, is a drop in the bucket when the beneficiaries of higher oil prices are brought into consideration. The value of U.S. oil and gas reserves has increased from $200 billion at 1973 prices to more than $2 trillion at 1980 prices.[36] Since less than 1 percent of the population holds over 75 percent of corporate stock, this increase will amount to a massive income transfer from oil and gas consumers to some of the very richest Americans.

In general, the oil companies defend their hefty profit hikes at a time of declining incomes with the claim that oil exploration and drilling have become more costly (which is no doubt true) and that the conversion to a new energy system will require immense investment funds. We could better trust their foresight and judgment on long-term energy policy if they had warned the American public in the 1950s of the potential hazards of building an oil-energy-intensive economy. Furthermore, oil companies are now using high energy profits to diversify into nonenergy areas including real estate, retailing, printing, synthetic fibers, shipping, hardware, computers, publishing, shipbuilding, trucking, food stores, electronics, and data processing.[37] One company even attempted to buy the Barnum and Bailey Circus. The profits held by oil companies have placed them in a commanding position to make the critical decisions determining the country's energy future.

3. The alternatives to oil now considered by the state and the corporate system are potentially ruinous. Long before the magnitude of the oil crisis had become public knowledge, the oil companies were preparing for the future by buying up alternative energy sources. Primarily, they went after coal and uranium reserves. By the mid-1970s at least seventeen of the twenty-five

largest oil companies had entered the coal business, and five domestic oil producers along with three other companies controlled 80 percent of the uranium reserves.[38]

Coal was the energy source that ushered in the Industrial Revolution; but it was superseded by oil. The 1980s will witness a return to coal in the United States and elsewhere, since recoverable coal resources are estimated to surpass oil resources many times over.

Unfortunately, the ecological implications for coal are not sanguine. The sulfur dioxide emission of coal burning combines with water vapor in the atmosphere to form acid rain. Existing levels of acidity are already blamed for destroying over one hundred lakes in the Adirondacks, and, according to one report, acid buildup in the rainfall is fifty times the level of twenty-five years ago. A scientist who examined 2 million death certificates in the country estimated that 9 percent of all deaths are associated with pollution; and sulfates were identified as one of the major culprits.[39]

Solid coal has thermodynamic efficiencies in cogeneration and ground transportation that would provide it with a promising future if techniques for dealing with pollution were developed. But the $88 billion synthetic-fuels program recently considered by Congress has severe environmental drawbacks. Shale oil production in the West would require more water than is available in the region at the same time that water is becoming a scarce national resource. It is likely that the massive upheavals of terrain required by strip mining would permanently scar the land. The harsh carcinogenic effects of shale oil on workers were established over one hundred years ago.[40]

4. The resurgence of coal is not based on a carefully conceived public strategy. It represents a rebound from the failure of the heavily subsidized nuclear-energy program. Nuclear proponents initially argued that nuclear energy would be so inexpensive that metering would be unnecessary, and so safe that the risk of personal harm was comparable to the chance of an individual's being bitten by a poisonous snake while crossing a street in Washington, D.C.[41]

It took the Three Mile Island crisis to alert the American population to the safety hazards of the new technology. But the public has also been seriously misled by corporate and government agencies on the costs of nuclear energy. Nuclear power is strictly an electricity producer, but electricity constitutes only a small portion of the total energy used in the United States. To use nuclear-generated electricity to heat homes and water is comparable to buying a Mercedes-Benz to make a weekly trip to the supermarket. It would be much cheaper to insulate, to invest in cogeneration, to shift to solar and wind energy, and to reduce inefficiencies in appliances.

Nuclear costs have skyrocketed. The Long Island Lighting Company (LILCO) started a nuclear plant in 1973 at the projected cost of $300 million. It may be completed a decade later for an actual cost of $2.2 billion. Unless the company gets further consumer rate increases, plant completion will be delayed at least until 1984, and the cost will go up to $2.7 billion.[42] And the costs do not stop there. Nuclear plants generate wastes that remain hazardous to human health for 250,000 years. The risks and expenses of storing and guarding this material are not factored into the recognized cost of nuclear energy.

While substantial supplies of natural gas can be relied upon for a medium-term strategy,[43] the long-term solution to the energy crisis is the development of renewable energy sources. A number of forms of solar energy show the greatest promise from an environmental point of view. The possible varieties include biomass production of alcohol and methane, gas, wind, geothermal, photovoltaic cells, and tidal waves. The selection of an energy program for the future is far too important to be left to corporate decision makers. If it is, we can expect a continued shift toward synthetic fuels, nuclear breeders, and nuclear fusion. And if it is to be taken out of their hands, it will have to be done in conjunction with a significant restructuring of the American political economy.

PETROCHEMICALS

The chemical revolution of the post-World War II period allowed many commodities to be made of synthetic rather than organic substances. Detergents replaced soap; synthetic fibers replaced cotton and wool; plastics substituted for leather, rubber, and wood; and large infusions of synthetic fertilizers for intensive land cultivation replaced the organic fertilizers tied to more extensive land use. Barry Commoner has demonstrated that this conversion to synthetic materials is almost always incompatible with ecological imperatives: the "chemical substances . . . which are absent from biological systems are, for that reason, frequently toxic and/or non-biodegradable." [44] Typically, too, each synthetic material requires more energy for its production than does its organic counterpart.

The American beef industry stands alone in energy waste even in a food industry that is energy-intensive. Since cattle consume ten protein units for every one they yield in meat, the energy that now goes into cattle feed could be reduced significantly with no loss in protein available for human consumption. However, the change would involve a shift toward a more vegetarian diet. In recent years cattle have been removed from the land and placed in feeding lots, a practice that has broken the nitrogen cycle and created widespread and costly market side effects. Today, unlike leaves that drop from the tree, beef cattle no longer return to the soil what they have removed. Rather than being deposited in the soil where it rebuilds humus, the nitrogen in manure is flushed into the water system, where it leads to algae buildup, depletes oxygen, and adds to the pollution of rivers and lakes. Meanwhile the farmer compensates for the loss of nitrogen with nitrates that have a deadly side effect: they kill nitrogen-fixing bacteria in the soil, a situation that leads to yet greater application of nitrates. The farmer is set onto a chemical treadmill in fertilizer use, which drives up the demand for oil and increases production costs. [45]

Again, neither sovereign voters nor sovereign consumers can be said to have chosen these materials over their organic counterparts in the light of an informed assessment of the comparative utility of each option. In agriculture, once a few farmers began to use more synthetic fertilizers, market competition led to widespread emulation by other farmers. Oligopolistic soap companies found that detergents were more profitable than soap— even though wastes from soap are far less destructive of soil and waterways. And petrochemical companies generally found the sale of synthetics to be more profitable in the short run than the sale of organic materials.

In the areas of transportation, energy production, and petro-chemicals, then, product decisions with adverse environmental effects reflect the private priorities of corporations with market power. This market power in turn generates a work force and a set of satellite companies that depend on these corporations for employment and market outlets. Thus if environmentalists press to convert to energy resources and product forms that are better for the environment, a set of dependent workers and businesses will emerge as a powerful political constituency in support of prevailing corporate policies. Truckers will oppose a shift to rail-freight systems; auto and steel workers will oppose mass-transit systems; tire-manufacturing, oil-production; and highway-construction firms will make political payoffs to protect the status quo.

Moreover, since the multinational corporation retains autonomous investment and pricing prerogatives, it can arouse these dependent constituencies when government regulatory policies threaten to become effective. For example, if domestic regulations prove too stringent, the corporation can divert a portion of its capital to other countries where environmental controls are weaker. The resulting threat of domestic unemployment will mobilize affected workers and businesses to support the corporation's domestic economic policies.

The multinational corporation's domestic and foreign market power helps create powerful political leverage in support of its economic autonomy. The resulting combination of power over markets and power over government policies makes market theories of the economy and pluralist theories of politics increasingly anachronistic.

Corporate product priorities are incompatible with and ignore the imperatives of ecology: long-term husbanding of natural resources and pollution-absorption capacity, maintenance of ecological balances to sustain the delicate biosphere essential to life, maximum durability of products, and styles of social life that provide meaning without depending on the proliferation of new private-consumption goods. A rational ecology policy requires, therefore, that the large corporation, presently unaccountable to the public, be brought under full public control. The political coalition needed to advance that policy, we will argue, can emerge only if white-collar environmentalists revise their priorities to reflect more closely the pressing needs of blue-collar workers.

■ The Environment and the Worker

In the political economy of corporate capitalism, the work environment of the blue-collar worker is too often filled with deadly fumes, carcinogenic dust, high noise levels, and intense heat. Periodically a major mine disaster or a particularly harsh outbreak of cancer among workers handling deadly chemicals arouses public awareness and mobilizes support for reform of the work environment. But typically conditions return to normal as public attention shifts elsewhere. One earlier incident, exceptional in the death and injury produced, exposes strikingly this cycle of brief uproar followed by long periods of benign neglect.

In 1930, as the Depression was worsening, workers were too weak to insist on health standards, and the public was kept ignorant about the most oppressive conditions of work. A subsidiary of Union Carbide began a hydroelectric project in the southern part of West Virginia, diverting water from two rivers through a tunnel to be constructed near the town of Gauley Bridge. The Gauley Bridge disaster, as it came to be known when it finally became a public issue five years after the fact, involved a group of unskilled workers, mostly black, who dug the tunnel through silica rock.

Working for extremely low pay, breathing carbon monoxide fumes as they rode into the tunnel every day, the workers also inhaled the heavy clouds of silica dust created by rock blasting in the tunnel. Engineers wore masks inside the tunnel, for the adverse effects of silica dust inhalation were known even then to health officials. But no masks were assigned to the workers. As increasing numbers of workers died from exposure to the dust, Rinehart-Dennis, the subcontractor on the project, hired a local undertaker to bury the bodies at $55 per corpse.

When the U.S. Public Health Service probed the disaster in 1935, it concluded that 476 men had died and 1,500 had been disabled. The case was eventually tried in the courts and congressional hearings were held, but the effective legal and legislative response was negligible. The settlements for survivors were extremely small; some defense lawyers were even caught accepting bribes from the company. The congressional hearings did not result in effective health regulations. And none of the companies involved, New Kanawha Power, Rinehart-Dennis, and Union Carbide, ever faced official punitive action.[46]

Despite recent legislation designed to protect the health and safety of workers, the classic cycle persists. Consider some of the facts about work and health in America today:

The Public Health Service estimates that each year prolonged exposure to toxic chemicals, dusts, noise, heat, cold, and radiation kills 100,000 workers and disables 390,000 more.

A federally sponsored, and more intensive, study of workers in a variety of factories and farms disclosed that three out of every ten workers suffered occupationally related illnesses. Ninety percent of these illnesses were not reported through regular channels, suggesting that the Public Health estimates are seriously deflated.

While Congress was moving in 1974 to reduce Occupational Safety and Health Administration (OSHA) funds for inspection of safety and health protection of employees in small businesses, another study showed that one out of every four workers in a sample of small businesses incurred an occupationally related disease. Eighty-nine percent of these were not reported to the Labor Department. The diseases included chronic respiratory disorders, loss of hearing, eye cataracts, and increased lead absorption in the blood.[47]

Within these general statistics are particular areas of extreme suffering and neglect:

Three million workers in fabricated metals, stone, clay, and glass products suffer a very high incidence of irreversible respiratory diseases such as silicosis, bysinosis, and emphysema.

The death rate among coal miners from respiratory diseases is five times higher than that of the general population.

Asbestos workers are disproportionately afflicted with asbestiosis, which is in turn linked to cancer of the lung, stomach, colon, and rectum.

Coke workers in steel factories assigned to the ovens for five years or more incur a risk of cancer ten times greater than that of the general population.

One out of every six uranium miners will die of cancer within ten years.

Employees in petroleum-based mineral oils suffer a very high incidence of cancer.[48]

Passage of the Occupational Safety and Health Act of 1970 seemed to promise rectification of this miserable record of worker illness and death, but the effectiveness of its administrative and research arm, OSHA, has been severely limited. Of the half million synthetic substances introduced into the work environment, threshold limits had been established for only 250 by 1974.

By 1974 OSHA was hamstrung in a variety of ways: with less than 800 inspectors in the field, the average employer will see an inspector once every sixty-six years; after three years of operation only two firms had been convicted of criminal violations; and the average fine for OSHA violations is $25.[49]

Clearly the workplace is a major site of ecological assault, but just as clearly corporate and business elites use the impressive resources at their disposal to hide the facts about worker disease, to deflect pressures for reform of the work environment into other channels, and to malign those who would convert the oppressive conditions of work into a public issue. The U.S. Chamber of Commerce reflected this orientation when it told health officials, "The health of American industry is eroded every time a new standard is issued." [50]

Blue-collar workers have traditionally been wary of environmentalism, partly because the issues as defined by leading environmentalists have bypassed the workplace. It has appeared to many workers, and often correctly so, that environmental reforms would undermine the standard of living of the working class without bringing tangible benefits in return. But if the ecology movement, currently facing hard times, were to identify the workplace itself as the crucial place to promote environmentalism, the prospects for a political alliance between workers and environmentalists would be enhanced.

■ Work Life and Incentive Systems

Workers are victimized not only by the workplace as a collection point for pollution and safety and health hazards. The structure of work itself is deadening for vast numbers of blue- and white-collar workers: the incentive system that structure sustains and the motivational system it accentuates produce exactly the set of consumer pressures that must be displaced if environmental degradation is to be forestalled.

Routinized, repetitive, mindless work that only imperfectly produces goods and services for the general welfare cannot be intrinsically satisfying to workers. In such circumstances, work must be organized almost completely around external incentives. Since continuous interclass and intergeneration movement in a highly stratified society officially committed to class mobility ("equality of opportunity") erodes extended kinship ties and breaks up stable neighborhood communities, the external incentives to work must be restricted to a narrow range. Incentives tied to the general welfare of internally unified collectivities (for instance, community recreation centers, health programs, transit systems) tend to be displaced by incentives tied to private consumer goods (like stylish clothes, exotic foods) or to goods that can be enjoyed by the individual primarily within the nuclear family (for instance, cars, television sets, private houses).

We do not say, of course, that all consumer satisfactions geared to private individuals and to nuclear families are evil; nor do we think that a work-incentive system tied strictly to collective goals would be feasible or desirable. But it is clear that private incentives are unnecessarily accentuated by the structure of work and social life that prevails in our society, while the connection between fulfilling work and the attainment of more durable, collective interests is ignored. Deprived of the opportunity for communal satisfaction in and out of work, workers seek their satisfactions privately. This limited range of private satisfactions must then become the main incentive to work and the main form of consumption.

The organization of work, the restriction of opportunities for improvement to *individual* mobility, and the resulting erosion of stable communal ties combine to sustain (or to require) a private mode of life that is intrinsically unfulfilling and opposed to the imperatives of ecology. Public policies that seek to convert patterns of *consumption* to ecologically rational forms while leaving this historically specific set of *productive* and *social* arrangements untouched are doomed to magnify the discontent of those caught in the bind. Until these structural sources of consumerism are confronted, either consumerism itself will prevail or its magnitude will be reduced by forcing "sacrifices" from those who are already the most exploited.

For instance, should I voluntarily support a transit system in this area when I can improve my own life chances best by moving elsewhere in a few years? Are the costs of recycling and of modernizing waste-disposal systems worth it to us when there is no internalized we that any of us naturally identifies with? Is the future condition of this stream, this park, this local atmosphere, this soil of deep concern to me when my relatives live elsewhere and my children are also likely to move? When I am likely to be a transitory resident myself? Will I tolerate high tax levels and the curtailment of consumer purchases to protect the environment for others when the promise of consumer pleasures and the dangers of personal insecurity provide my basic incentives to work?

Economists and other social scientists gripped by the theory of abstract individualism, by the view of individuals as private utility maximizers, are unable to explore the ecological import of these structural arrangements. They simply assume that the incentives to work must always and everywhere match those dominant in our society. They suppose the private consumer satisfactions predominant here to be the paradigm satisfaction available to the human species. In effect, they take as given what needs to be explained. When confronting the basic dimensions of work, social life, and patterns of motivation in our society, we must not lose sight of the simple insight enunciated in another context by E. E. Schattschneider:

> Anyone watching the crowds move about Grand Central Station might learn something. . . . The crowds seem to be completely unorganized. What the spectator observes is not chaos, however, because the multitude is controlled by the timetables and the gates. *Each member of the crowd finds his place in the* system *(is organized by the system) because his alternatives are limited.*[51]

Those who, analogously, comprehend that the prevailing patterns of work and opportunity in our stratified social order provide a set of timetables and gates to shape and limit the modes of life open to citizens will understand as well that efforts to channel consumption habits into ecologically sound forms will be resisted bitterly by those confined within these structures. In the absence of new possibilities for fulfillment in work itself, in the absence of new possibilities for stable community relationships that extend beyond the nuclear family, apprehensive blue- and white-collar workers will militantly oppose environmental management programs that threaten the private forms of satisfaction currently available. The organizations to which they belong can be expected to coalesce with corporate interests to oppose environmental controls.

There is nothing about the environmental crisis itself that ensures the political will and muscle to correct it. The pressures against environmentalism are indeed very strong. But an environmental movement that connects prevailing structures of work and opportunity with persisting patterns of environmental destruction has the best potential to build a progressive coalition that could correct the one form of exploitation while coping with the other.

■ Inequality and Social Services

We have already considered arguments for, and barriers to, a reduction of economic inequality. It remains to add that ecology and equality are closely connected; progress in one area can contribute to success in the other.

The basic relation, enunciated in a different context by Jean Jacques Rousseau, is quite simple and powerful. In a highly stratified, individualistic society, those with the most wealth and income seek private solutions to collective problems, often deepening the collective problems as they escape them individually.

Those in the lowest positions, however, lack both the means to secure private remedies to these troubles and the power to impose public solutions. In an egalitarian society, by contrast, it is rational for each citizen to support public solutions to those collective problems that none is in a position to escape privately. And for such a disposition in favor of the public interest to prevail, it is not necessary that absolute equality be established: "As for equality, this word must not be understood to mean that all individuals must have exactly the same amount of power and wealth, but rather that power must be exercised . . . so that no one shall have so much of it as to be able to do violence upon another and that no citizen shall have so much wealth that he can buy another, and none so little that he is forced to sell himself." [52]

In the American class system the affluent evade urban pollution, congestion, noise, and heat by private expenditures that at once accelerate environmentally destructive practices and undermine the political will of privileged minorities to cope with these public consequences. The affluent can secure work that is environmentally safe, move to suburbs where the air and water are cleaner, live in large, private homes, escape summer heat through air conditioning, take vacations by jet to undefiled areas, locate residences away from nuclear plants, replace shoddy products that break or perish. Indeed, in the absence of *public* policies to attack the pertinent environmental problems, it is rational for the affluent to use private resources to fund such *private* escapes. But since they must then commute to work in the inner city by automobile, their private escape worsens the pollution problem in the city they left behind. Their dependence on air conditioning, wasteful heating systems, air travel, and shoddy products similarly increases the load imposed on the environment. Most important, since they have invested heavily in private escape and since their own affluence often flows from ecologically unsound business enterprises, they tend then to oppose public policies that would make energy production ecologically safe, establish mass-transit systems, improve building-construction codes to reduce the energy wasted in heating and air conditioning, restore urban parks and waterways, improve urban garbage and disposal systems, ensure the production of more durable goods, encourage the shift from synthetic to organic materials in consumer goods, and so on. The very availability of expensive private escape routes makes the affluent unwilling to accept the tax assessments, changes in production processes, and alterations in privileged life styles necessary to apply collective solutions to these public problems.

In these interconnected ways, inequality combines with the system of corporate priorities, the structure of work, and the weakness of communal ties to encourage the growth of ecologically devastating forms of consumption. It imposes the most direct and oppressive effects of these unsound systems on a politically weak underclass. Inequality encourages the affluent to seek private escape routes that deepen the system's debt to nature. And it dampens political support for effective public programs. These are the reasons that redistribution, a worthy objective in its own right, will also form an essential part of any political movement that seriously hopes to cope with the environmental crisis. These considerations also reinforce the case for bringing the private corporation under effective public control, for inequality cannot be materially reduced until corporate pricing, investment, salary, and location decisions are subjected to public debate and accountability.

A more egalitarian society would not *necessarily* maintain rational ecological policies, but it would be *more likely* to do so. To paraphrase Rousseau, when life chances are distributed so that all can feel the effects of collective achievements and collective failures, so that all are in a position to benefit from a public resolution of common problems, and so that none can afford to escape the problems through the use of private resources unavailable to others, then the political system is very likely to generate collective responses to the common risks and burdens imposed by the depletion of non-renewable energy resources and the deterioration of air, water, and soil supports essential to human life.

■ Environmental Imperatives and Political Realism

With all the public attention given environmental problems in the last two decades, it might seem that we have come a long way from the Gauley Bridge disaster of the early 1930s. But public perception is barely keeping pace with the rash of assaults on the environment. Love Canal shocks the public today as the Gauley Bridge disaster did in the 1930s.

Love Canal has become a symbol of the country's toxic-waste problem. Unbeknownst to the residents of this district of Niagara Falls, their homes were constructed over an abandoned dump site. The consequences were described vividly by *Time* magazine in June 1980:

For the past two years, one report after another has told harrowing tales of noxious odors leaking into homes, of sinister-colored sludge seeping into basements, of children playing in potholes of pollutants and, worst of all, of abnormally high rates of miscarriages and birth defects, of nerve, respiratory, liver and kidney disorders and of assorted cancers among the people of Love Canal.[53]

Finally in 1980, after outside researchers discovered a high incidence of genetic damage to residents of Love Canal, President Carter declared a state of emergency in the area. He empowered environmental agencies to relocate over seven hundred families.

How did it happen? Between 1943 and 1953 Hooker Chemicals and Plastics Corporation buried 21,800 tons of chemical wastes on this property. It then sold the land to the local board of education in 1953. The company claims that the dumping was legal under existing laws and that in any case it was absolved of all responsibility once it sold the property to the board of education.

Love Canal is probably the tip of an iceberg. According to the Environmental Protection Agency (EPA), some 30,000 to 50,000 sites around the country are contaminated by hazardous wastes generated over the last few decades by three-quarters of a million industrial concerns. The tonnage in these burial grounds is estimated at 100 billion pounds, equivalent to the combined weight of every car now on the road. No more than one-tenth of these wastes are disposed of properly and safely, according to the EPA.

Are there other Love Canals to be discovered? "There are at least 1000 Love Canals around the country," asserts an EPA official. "We know of 4000 to 5000 potential ones right now." This prognostication is reinforced by an administrator of the EPA:

Let me predict now that the process we are starting will turn up information and situations which will shock our nation. We will find waste sites which are now unknown. We will document leaching of chemicals into aquifers which we have assumed were safe. We will gather hard data on a problem whose dimensions we now can only guess. But we will have begun the difficult transition from a time when wastes, once out of sight, were out of mind.[54]

Can this difficult transition be successfully accomplished under the guidance of the market model of environmental management whose theoretical props have been stripped away? We doubt it, but to solidify those doubts, we must consider the fall-back position advanced by advocates of the market model today.

In our society, market theorists say, it is unrealistic politically (that is, it is naive, utopian, impractical) to try to reform existing modes of work, consumption, exchange, and community in order to reduce the gap between our economic practices and the requirements of ecology. At least the mainstream program of "internalizing the externalities" within existing market mechanisms has a chance, they say, of gaining political acceptance. We agree. But a few additional points are required to fill this picture out.

1. If the market program is now to be justified not because it copes effectively with imperfections in an otherwise healthy system but because theoretically viable alternatives are unacceptable to corporate and government elites, the argument for political realism becomes an indictment of the American political economy rather than a justification of the market system.

2. Neoclassical economists and pluralist political scientists who have helped to legitimize the market images of the economy and the polity bear a measure of responsibility for the political unrealism of efforts to institute structural reforms today. Scholars who now see defects in assumptions underlying these models and who define themselves as defenders of the truth are today obligated to explore the theoretical viability of alternative responses to environmental control, even if those alternatives presently face intractable political barriers.

3. The policies of the environmental managers may gain limited short-run support, especially from constituencies who can easily assimilate the costs involved or displace them to subordinate classes. But initial successes, as the "war on poverty" demonstrated, can contribute to defeat over the longer run. The program of the environmental managers, as we have argued, promises to drive that segment of labor employed in the corporate sector into an alliance with corporate elites against environmental reform. The immediate difficulties in our strategy are outstripped only by the long-run political unrealism of the economics of environmental management. Moreover, labor-corporate backlash threatens to heighten the repressive tendencies in American politics.

4. When the problem is construed as political rather than technical, it is clear that the most important strategic objective is to mobilize a progressive labor-environmentalist coalition around issues immediately compelling to each and thus to generate momentum for more basic reforms at a later date. Such a strategy is not easy to develop. But the most promising focal point is the workplace itself. Workers and environmentalists can find common ground in an effort to eliminate the hazards of pollution with-

in the workplace. And as environmentalists come to see that the reform of work life is an essential precondition to sound environmental control, that alliance could develop into a movement for broader structural reform.

Clearly, the direction the environmental movement takes in the next decade will help to determine whether a labor-environmental or labor-corporate coalition gains ascendancy. If economic growth no longer matches the pace of the 1960s (as we expect) and if the organized labor movement does coalesce with corporate elites, we can expect a suppression of environmental issues while labor in the corporate sector solidifies its advantages over labor in the market sector of the economy. If, alternatively, an emerging alliance between environmentalists and organized labor forestalls these developments, there is a chance that the "economics of environmental management" can be replaced by the politics of work-life reform, income redistribution, and environmental integrity.

No one group can alone shape forces as large as those discussed here, but a strategically alert environmental movement can encourage the labor-environmentalist coalition necessary to attack the institutional sources of environmental decay.

NOTES

1. In Paul Samuelson's classic text *Economics* (New York: McGraw-Hill, 1948, 1951, 1955, 1958, 1961, 1964, 1967, 1970, 1973), there is no discussion of pollution until the 1961 edition, in which a very brief mention of smoke is made. By 1964 there were a couple of paragraphs on "external diseconomies" in general; by 1967 a brief justification of government intervention to compensate for market externalities such as air and water pollution. There is no comparable classic text in political science. But Frederic Ogg and R. Orman Ray, *Essentials of American Government* (New York: Appleton-Century-Crofts, 1932, 1936, 1940, 1943, 1947, 1950, 1952, 1961, 1963, 1969), covers a long span and has been widely used. The 1950 edition contains a brief, optimistic discussion of recent government protection of land, soil, water, forest, and mineral resources. By 1969, William and Sara Young, who revised that edition, warned that "our forests are still being slashed and depleted; soil is being washed and blown away. . . . Bays and estuaries, rivers and lakes are brown with silt and rank with wastes. Our cities are choked with traffic, smog and blight" (p. 400). A more contemporary, behavioral text, Marian D. Irish and James W. Prothro, *The Politics*

of American Democracy (Englewood Cliffs, N.J.: Prentice-Hall, 1959, 1962, 1965, 1968), has four chapters dealing with the "outputs of the political system," but none touches the politics of ecology.

2. K. W. Kapp, The Social Costs of Private Enterprise (Cambridge, Mass.: Harvard University Press, 1950); Grant McConnell, "The Conservation Movement: Past and Present," Western Political Quarterly (December 1954), pp. 463–478, and Private Power and American Democracy (New York: Alfred A. Knopf, 1966).

3. Kapp, p. 229.

4. Ibid., pp. 229, 230.

5. Ibid., p. 236.

6. McConnell, Private Power and American Democracy, pp. 129, 247.

7. This analysis is developed in Garrett Hardin, "The Tragedy of the Commons," Science (December 13, 1968), pp. 1243–1248, and Kenneth Arrow, "The Organization of Economic Activity: Issues Pertinent to the Choice of Market Versus Non-Market Allocation," in Public Expenditures and Public Analysis, edited by Robert Haveman and Jerrold Margolis (Chicago: Markham, 1970).

8. There are other difficulties more or less internal to this theory that we cannot discuss here: the assumption of a smooth exchange function between any two items (how many ice cream cones will you exchange for your left arm?); the assumption that the environment and animal life are merely to be viewed and valued as human resources; and (a view we will oppose in our alternative model) the tendency to reduce complex social relationships to exchange relationships between private utility maximizers. For impressive elaboration and criticism of these tendencies among utilitarians in general and market economists in particular, see Stuart Hampshire, Morality and Pessimism (London: Cambridge University Press, 1973); Robert Paul Wolff, The Poverty of Liberalism (Boston: Beacon Press, 1968), Ch. 5; and Lawrence Tribe, "The Policy Sciences: Science or Ideology?" Philosophy and Public Affairs (Fall 1972); pp. 66–110.

9. See Robert Heilbroner, "The Human Prospect," New York Review of Books, January 4, 1974, pp. 21–34.

10. (New York: John Wiley, 1973).

11. Ibid., p. 33.

12. Ibid., p. 170.

13. As the authors put it, "We must assume that there is some political mechanism through which collective choices are made and that through this political mechanism the society has determined the rules that govern the distribution of income and wealth in the society." Ibid., p. 70.

14. Ibid., p. 168.

15. For data on energy consumption by country, see Gerald Foley, The Energy Question (New York: Penguin, 1976), p. 62.

16. While Amtrak's mileage was recently being reduced, a Congressional Budget Office report demonstrated the potential energy savings from U.S. rail and bus transportation by comparing the 450 passenger miles per gallon (pmg) of a loaded 18-passenger train pulled by two locomotives and the 250 pmg for intercity buses with the 36 to 62 pmg for passenger jets and the 20 to 40 pmg for average commuter cars. Cited in *In These Times* (March 12–25, 1980), p. 11.

17. C. A. Nash, *Public Versus Private Transport* (London: Macmillan, 1976), p. 29.

18. Cited in Michel Bosquet, *Capitalism in Crises and Everyday Life* (Sussex, England: Harvester Press, 1977), p. 33.

19. Externalities are discussed more fully in Chapter 5.

20. Curve $C_1 C_2$ is the conventional average, and curve $C_1 C_3$ the conventional marginal cost curve of microeconomic theory with the inclusion of external costs.

21. Bradford Snell, *American Ground Transport: A Proposal for Restructuring the Automobile, Truck, Bus, and Rail Industries,* presented to the Subcommittee on Antitrust and Monopoly of the Committee of the Judiciary, U.S. Senate (Washington, D.C.: Government Printing Office, 1974).

22. Ibid., p. 37.

23. Ibid.

24. Ibid., p. 38. General Motors did, according to findings by the Interstate Commerce Commission, make cost claims for its diesel locomotives to potential buyers that were "erroneous," "inflated," and "manifestly absurd" (ibid., p. 41), and corporate elites knew about the dangerous levels of pollution from cars and trucks as early as 1953. Nevertheless, our argument leans less on an assessment of corporate intent formed in the 1920s to dismantle trolley and train systems than on the identification of policy tendencies that emerge when a small group of corporations dominates all forms of ground transportation, some of which are more profitable than others. Moreover, as this brief review indicates, the acknowledgment by Freeman, Haveman, and Kneese that consumer "tastes and preferences are not strictly given, but are subject to the influences of advertising" barely scratches the surface of the forces at work in corporate capitalism that shape consumer demand by controlling product options (*The Economics of Environmental Policy,* p. 71).

25. A good summary of this development is found in Lawrence Kohlmeier, *The Regulators* (New York: Harper and Row, 1969). Notable in the history of this development was the presidential commission in 1944 that proposed the Highway Trust Fund, in which gasoline taxes are used only for highway construction. The commission "failed to give any consideration to the relative efficiency or need of rail, water and air, as well as highway transportation" (p. 154).

26. See, for example, the *New York Times* editorial, September 22, 1974.
27. Our estimate of depletion dates is based on the formula

$$T_d = \frac{1}{k} \ln (kT_o + 1)$$

where T_d is the time to depletion of a finite resource, k is the yearly growth rate of extraction, and T_o is the time the resource would last at current levels of consumption. Kurt H. Hohenemser, in "Energy Consumption and Gross National Product," *Environment* 20 no. 3 (April 1978): 2–4, brought the usefulness of this formula to our attention. For more on resource-depletion curves, see John M. Blair, *The Control of Oil* (New York: Random House, 1977) and Gerald Foley, *The Energy Question.*
28. In 1979, *Newsweek* predicted that the United States had 8.7 years of oil supplies remaining at prevailing rates of consumption. See "Why We Must Act Now," *Newsweek,* July 16, 1979.
29. Leonard Rodberg, "Employment Impact of the Solar Transition," Joint Economic Committee, U.S. Congress, April 1979, and Leonard Rodberg and Geoffrey Stokes, *The Village Voice,* February 18, 1980.
30. For references to these and other studies, see Maarten de Kadt, "Energy for Profits or Power for People," *Union for Radical Political Economics Newsletter,* May/June 1980; Lawrence Solomon, *The Conserver Solution* (New York: Doubleday, 1978); Rodberg and Stokes, cited in note 29; and Richard Barnet, *The Lean Years* (New York: Simon and Schuster, 1980).
31. A complete analysis of waste involves the second law of thermodynamics. The first law, that energy can be neither created nor destroyed, is familiar. The second law is more complex and holds that the work capacity of terrestrial energy is constantly decreasing. The fixed amount of useful terrestrial energy is irreversibly deteriorating with the passage of time and misuse by society. (Solar is the only nonterrestrial energy.) Once energy is converted to heat and work, that portion of the earth's endowment has been used once and for all. Future generations will no more be able to reverse the process and thus produce energy from heat or motion than they can construct a perpetual-motion machine. Barry Commoner estimates that 85 percent of U.S. energy supplies are wasted by second law mismatches between high-quality energy resources and low-quality energy uses. See *The Poverty of Power* (New York: Alfred A. Knopf, 1976), p. 203. One of the few economists to study the implications of the second law for economic efficiency is Nicholas Georgescu-Roegen, *Energy and Economic Myths* (New York: Pergamon Press, 1976).
32. This and other examples are described in Emma Rothschild, "Illusions about Energy," *New York Review of Books,* August 9, 1973.
33. Postwar agriculture led the shift to energy-intensive methods with mechanization; the petrochemical revolution in fertilizers, insecticides, and preservatives; and long-haul trucking. For the culmin-

ation of this process, see William Serrin, "Factory Methods Are Bringing Revolution in Hog Production," *New York Times,* August 11, 1980.

34. Data in the preceding two paragraphs are from Walter J. Levy, "Oil and the Decline of the West," *Foreign Affairs* 58, no. 5 (1980): 1001.
35. Lester C. Thurow, *The Zero-Sum Society* (New York: Basic Books, 1980), p. 30.
36. Robert Stobaugh and Daniel Yergin, "Energy: An Emergency Telescoped," *Foreign Affairs* 58, no. 3 (1979): 587.
37. For details, see "Oil Profits Running Wild?" *U.S. News and World Report,* November 5, 1979, pp. 24–28.
38. Robert Stobaugh and Daniel Yergin, eds., *Energy Future: Report of the Energy Project at the Harvard Business School* (New York: Random House, 1979), p. 98, and Barnet, *The Lean Years,* p. 93.
39. Hearings before the Senate Energy and Natural Resources Committee, U. S. Senate, June 1980.
40. Barry Commoner, *The Poverty of Power* (New York: Alfred A. Knopf, 1976), p. 70.
41. Commoner summarizes such arguments in *The Poverty of Power,* p. 88.
42. Alyssa A. Lappen, "Pay Now or Pay Later," *Forbes,* August 4, 1980, pp. 67–68.
43. For an analysis of natural gas as a "bridge" fuel between oil-based energy systems of today and solar-based systems of tomorrow, see Barry Commoner, *The Politics of Energy* (New York: Alfred A. Knopf, 1979).
44. Barry Commoner, *The Closing Circle* (New York: Alfred A. Knopf, 1071), p. 41.
45. Bosquet, p. 179.
46. A more thorough discussion of this incident and of many others as well can be found in Joseph A. Page and Mary Win O'Brien, *Bitter Wages* (New York: Grossman, 1973), Ch. 3.
47. Information for the preceding items is taken from the *New York Times,* March 4, 1974, May 12, 1975, and April 28, 1975.
48. These estimates and others are found in Frederick Wallick, *The American Worker: An Endangered Species* (New York: Ballantine, 1972); Jean Stellman and Susan Daum, *Work Is Dangerous to Your Health* (New York: Vintage, 1973); *Work in America,* Special Task Force Report to the Department of Health, Education, and Welfare (Cambridge, Mass.: MIT Press, 1973).
49. *Wall Street Journal,* August 9, 1974.
50. Ibid.
51. *The Semi-Sovereign People* (New York: Holt, Rinehart and Winston, 1960), p. 57.
52. *The Social Contract* (Chicago: Regnery, 1954), p. 76.
53. *Time,* June 2, 1980, p. 61.
54. Reported by Ralph Blumenthal, "Fight to Curb 'Love Canals,'" *New York Times,* June 30, 1980, p. B11.

THE POLITICS OF WORK

■ The Myth of the Happy Worker Explodes

Employers in the United States have traditionally taken an instrumental view of the work their employees do: the employer seeks to make a profit from production, and the employee's incentive to work efficiently is the promise of pay or the threat of unemployment [1] With notable exceptions, most American social scientists have taken this instrumental work ethic for granted in their studies of economic processes, social relationships, and political issues.

For a long time it seemed that workers themselves shared this view. If wages, job security, and fringe benefits could be improved, it appeared that workers would remain contented with their lot. Thus for years, between 80 and 90 percent of all polled workers responded affirmatively to the Gallup Poll question, "Is your work satisfying?" [2] And sociologist John Goldthorpe, in a detailed study of auto workers at a Vauxhall auto plant in England, found that most workers want their unions to "limit themselves to their specifically economic functions: only among the craftsmen was the idea of greater worker's control still largely upheld as a union objective." [3]

Robert Lane, a political scientist, thought he was able to explain why, despite evidence to the contrary, a small group of dissident social scientists, led by Erich Fromm and C. Wright Mills, continued to speak in the 1950s of the "increasing alienation of men from work, society, and government." [4] These social scientists, Lane concluded, must be projecting their own discontents onto a contented society:

> I have long suspected that they reflect their own discontent with society rather than any mass discontent. . . . Partly, too, I think their views reflect their own alienation from the field of endeavour where there is true *élan,* the field of science.[5]

But then some interesting things began to happen, which cast grave doubt upon prevailing methods of survey analysis, the findings it had produced with respect to workers, and the judgments Lane and others had made about the contrary findings (and skills) of dissident social scientists.

At the Vauxhall factory, for instance, where Goldthorpe had interviewed a number of contented workers, the workers themselves began to discuss the interviews and to reconsider the statements they had made to Goldthorpe. Many agreed that they had been *individually resigned* to their jobs, but few were really *contented* with their work. And when they began to discuss their *collective* situation comparatively—as members of a working class comparing their collective plight to that of employees in other occupations—their collective sense of discontent increased. Just as Goldthorpe's findings about the lack of class consciousness were going to press, the workers struck over a local grievance that might not have otherwise aroused them. The London *Times* report captures their response:

> Wild rioting has broken out at the Vauxhall car factories in Luton. Thousands of workers streamed out of the shops and gathered in the factory yard. They besieged the management offices, calling for the managers to come out, seizing the "Red Flag" and shouting "string them up." [6]

Indeed, this sequence has been repeated on several occasions. First social scientists interview workers individually, finding them to be relatively contented, and then the factory shortly thereafter erupts unexpectedly.[7] We will later have to ask why such interview techniques tend first to miss latent resentments among those interviewed and then to encourage the very eruptions the interviewers had thought so unlikely.

Evidence of worker discontent and resentment simmering beneath verbal expressions of contentment has flourished in recent history. In France, prior to 1968, many commentators had noted the quiescence of the working force; workers were, it was popularly thought, a relatively contented lot. But in May 1968 a demonstration of students was soon transformed into a general strike of workers against the state and the capitalist system. The country was brought to a standstill.

Two characteristics distinguished this strike from earlier ones. First, a new generation of young skilled workers, technicians, and white-collar workers assumed active leadership roles in this rebellion; many were recent university graduates who were supposed to be the future elite of French life. Second, the aims of the strike were nontraditional in many respects. The strikers demanded changes in the organization of work life and the system of managerial power over workers; they demanded employee participation in decisions, greater information on company activities, better training programs.[8] The general strike finally ended when President de Gaulle pledged to institute work reforms—a promise that has yet to be delivered

Undeniable evidence of deep worker discontent has also surfaced in the United States. The General Motors plant in Lordstown, Ohio, is its leading symbol. The Lordstown complex was designed to be a GM showpiece: new production technologies and quality controls were applied, costs were cut, worker efficiency was enhanced, high wage levels were introduced, and, most important, in the words of a GM spokesman in 1970, "The higher level of enthusiasm among employees at the Lordstown plant is producing craftsmanship to challenge any auto makers in the world." [9]

But by 1972 this enthusiasm had been replaced by increased worker absenteeism, slowdowns, sabotage, and car defects, and by management's introduction of speedups, harsh disciplinary tactics, and close job monitoring. The labor-management struggles erupted finally into a bitter twenty-two-day strike. Though the strikers were eventually defeated, by the time it was over these highly paid employees with highly regimented jobs had exploded the American myth of the happy worker.

If anyone continued to have doubts, further rumblings soon removed them. Discontent was expressed by secretaries herded together into secretarial pools, young lawyers tied to routine dead-end jobs, even young middle-level managers who, according to the American Management Association, often experience "a decreasing sense of personal reward and achievement" from the "highly bureaucratic, authoritarian structure" of today's corporation.[10]

When the HEW Report *Work in America* appeared in 1973, the available evidence overwhelmingly pointed in one direction. The report summarized studies connecting low status, little autonomy, isolation, and repetitiousness of the job to the low self-esteem, anxiety, tension, passivity, and social alienation of the worker. While inequalities in income and educational levels attached to various jobs play a role in these correlations, the design of work and the structure of power in the workplace are crucial factors as well.[11] And by the time it was widely publicized that only 24 percent of blue-collar and 43 percent of white-collar workers would choose the same job again if they had a chance, the problem of worker alienation had become a serious concern to those very managers and social scientists who had previously denied its existence, even though most of them translated the issue of alienation into a problem of worker "motivation." [12]

The myth of the happy worker had been dissipated by the early 1970s, but why had so many mainstream social scientists believed in that myth until *after* the worker unrest of the late 1960s and 1970s? One flimsy answer is that the workers were happy before, say, 1968, but not after. Such an answer, though, would cast doubt on the ability of survey analysts to predict future events and would hardly explain the persistence of the same working conditions and evidence of worker depression, and so on, before and after that date. A more promising course is to probe defects in the survey methods that produced the faulty findings. Such interviewing methods encourage answers that reflect the prevailing ideology of the day more than they test the actual congruence between that ideology and the life conditions of those interviewed. If the instrumental view of work is in ideological ascendancy, surveys of workers during periods of labor quiescence are likely to mesh with that ideology.[13]

When a worker is asked, "Are you satisfied with your work?", he tends to reply with the socially established model of work in mind. He says to himself, "I'm about as satisfied as one is supposed to be with work," and then answers, "yes." Moreover, when interviewed alone, he tends to *compare* himself with other workers in his job category. He is, generally, about as satisfied as they are; so again he is prone to answer yes. Finally, in the absence of available examples or theories of work that challenge the dominant work ethic and work system, the worker has no alternative conception against which to appraise his condition. Even a slave would say he is happy if his experience were so constricted that he believed slavery to be a natural and necessary condition for people like him. The worker's experience is not so thoroughly limited, but in modern capitalist society his experience with *alternative forms of work* has been severely restricted.

It is understandable, then, that workers who express satisfaction individually to interviewers have often changed their minds through collective discussion. For then *the terms of comparison* within which they are thinking and acting change. They begin to think more about their collective plight. The reaction to the interview itself encourages a shift in the terms of comparison. And, it must be remembered, statements about happiness, satisfaction, and contentment are always made within some framework of comparison, most often, given prevailing survey techniques, within the framework sustained by the society's dominant ideology.

But to insist, as we have, that the terms of comparison adopted are crucial in appraising a system of work is to raise a whole host of new issues: against what standards should the system of work that prevails in our society be appraised? What are the strengths and weaknesses of the instrumental model of work when compared to this standard? If its defects are grave, why has it retained for so long its dominant position in our society?

We will approach these questions by comparing two opposed models of work. The first one, we think, views work and workers primarily with the needs of owners and employers in mind; the second speaks more fully to the needs of workers themselves. The conflict between these two models plays a profound role in the politics of our society—in the class struggle between workers and owners—even though its influence is often hidden beneath a set of more acceptable, surrogate issues that dominate public attention.

■ Two Models of Work

TAYLORISM

Frederick W. Taylor, chief engineer for a steel company in the 1880s, founded the modern principles of scientific management. He was convinced that workers in a variety of occupations could be made more productive if management would follow rigorously a set of principles he had devised and tested in the field.

His experiment with an immigrant pig-iron handler earned him a good deal of acclaim and notoriety. Each "pig" weighed 92 pounds, and the handler had to pick it up and carry it a few yards to a pile. The average handler hauled 12½ tons per day. But Taylor, by carefully selecting a hauler of low intelligence and great strength, by rearranging meticulously the method and timing of the work, and by paying the handler a bonus for following his instructions to the letter and fulfilling his quota was able to increase that output fourfold. Taylor himself describes the monitoring process:

> Schmidt started to work, and all day long, and at regular intervals, was told by the man who stood over him with a watch, "Now pick up a pig and walk. Now sit down and rest. Now work—Now rest," etc. He worked when he was told to work and rested when he was told to rest, and half past five in the afternoon had his 47½ tons loaded on the car.... One man after another was picked out and trained to handle pig iron at the rate of 47½ tons per day until all the pig iron was handled at this rate and the men were receiving 60 percent more wages than the workmen around them.[14]

With the completion and publication of this experiment, the science of management was launched.

There are certain things taken for granted in Taylor's science. First, he takes as given the capitalist system of private ownership, production for profit, and wage labor. Second, his science is not a neutral science, or a science for just anyone, but a science for managers who seek to organize work so as to maximize profits and to exercise control over workers. Though Taylor insists that an effective system of work will promote "intimate, friendly cooperation between the management and the men," [15] he also insists that a precondition for such cooperation is that the workers accept the full authority of the managers over all aspects of the production process.

The science embodies several key components.

1. Management must master and monopolize all the knowledge needed to produce a given product efficiently. The size and responsibilities of the managerial core are thus magnified under Taylor's system:

> The managers assume new burdens, new duties and responsibilities never dreamed of in the past ... for instance, the burden of gather-

ing together all of the traditional knowledge which in the past has been possessed by the workmen and then of classifying, tabulating, and reducing this knowledge to rules, laws and formulae which are immensely helpful to the workers in doing their daily work.[16]

2. Management divides the production process into a series of simple components or tasks so that each task can be repeated by the same worker throughout the day. Each task is then studied intensively until the single most efficient way of doing it is discovered. This "one best method and best implement can only be discovered or developed through a scientific study and analysis of all methods and implements in use, together with accurate, minute time-and-motion study." [17]

3. Workers are selected who have the intelligence and skills needed for each particular task. Taylor thinks that most tasks should be very simple because most workers are quite simple and because the rapid repetition of simple tasks is more productive than the slower performance of complex tasks. Moreover, the "science which underlies each act of each worker is so great and amounts to so much that the workman who is best suited to actually doing the work is incapable of fully understanding the science . . . either through lack of education or through insufficient mental capacity." [18]

4. After studying the process, dividing it into a series of simple tasks, and preparing a time-and-motion study of each task, management gives each worker an assignment fitted to his abilities and then specifies precisely how he is to perform it.

> The work of every workman is fully planned out by the management at least one day in advance, and each man receives in most cases complete written instructions. . . . This task specifies not only what is to be done but how it is to be done and the exact time allowed for doing it.[19]

In short, the objective is to have management do all the *mind* work while the workers do the *physical, mindless* work.

5. Each worker who performs the assignment successfully is to be paid better than those who work under different systems or who do not perform well under this system. The worker's only incentive to work is for the promise of higher pay; "personal ambition always has been and will remain a more powerful incentive to exertion than a desire for the general welfare." [20] Taylor's system of instrumental work and graded pay scales requires the very hierarchy of incomes that the theory of functionalism (as we have seen) assumes to be necessary in every industrial society.

To maintain this system of work, we must have *gradations* of pay within the work force and a significant difference in the pay between those who manage and those who are managed. Taylorism and extreme inequality therefore encourage each other: an industrial system that emphasizes either will tend to support the other as well.

Taylor demonstrated how his system of management greatly improved the productivity of pig handlers, bricklayers, shovelers, inspectors of ball bearings, and steel cutters, but he claimed that the principles could and should be applied to any productive task whatsoever: this science of management is applicable to all systems of work. And he denied the charge, already made by his critics at the turn of the century, that his system would turn workers into "wooden men." Workers might complain, he conceded, when first encountering his system, but they would soon adjust to it; they would particularly come to appreciate the increase in income it allowed. It is better, he claimed, to be a trained specialist in one area than to try, as the old frontiersman had, to be "an architect, housebuilder, lumberman, farmer, soldier and doctor" all at once. One "would hardly say," Taylor argued while carefully picking his example, that the "life of the modern surgeon is any more narrowing, or that he is more of a wooden man than the frontiersman." [21] Besides, "all of us are grown up children," and each "will work to the greatest satisfaction of both himself and his employer, when he is given each day a definite task, which constitutes a proper day's work for a good workman." [22] When managers are willing to organize work properly and to pay workers fairly for a fair day's work, and when workers come to understand that their interests harmonize with those of an enlightened management, workers, managers and the general public will all benefit. Peaceful labor-management relations will flourish in a production system that improves the prosperity of all citizens. All this, according to Taylor.

While Taylorism has acquired a bad name among many students of management and administration, its basic principles are accepted even by many who criticize this or that detail. The separation between management and workers, the assignment of mind work like planning and managing to the former and of mindless work to the latter, the division of work assignments into simple and repetitive tasks, the dependence on monetary incentives and the threat of unemployment as primary instruments of worker discipline and motivation, the use of time-and-motion studies and programmed budgets to organize work efficiently—these are still the central ingredients of modern management theory and practice. The "human-relations" approach emphasized by some managerial theorists today does not undermine these basic principles in any essential way; rather it aims at surrounding the established system of work with a physical and human environment that makes it more bearable for the workers. Indeed, the human-relations theorists are not as far from Taylor even in that respect as they sometimes say they are, for he, too, emphasized the need for friendly relations between workers and managers. Taylor wanted managers to be friendly and considerate while maintaining their managerial prerogatives and while managing the work others did.

Nor have political scientists or economists, save for some dissenters, subjected Taylor's principles to searching criticism. Usually these principles are taken for granted as the *natural, undebatable background* against which economic activities are studied and political issues investigated. They are thought to be outside of economics and separate from politics. Political scientists have failed to ask, for instance, why the Taylorist system of work did not become a public issue earlier in American history. It became an issue for them only after it became an issue for the public. And economists have generally adopted the principle of comparative advantage in their research: they have assumed that of two agents, if A can do one task more efficiently and B can do another more efficiently, it is rational to divide work so that A does only the first task and B only the second. A professor, for example, who can both type and write scholarly essays should never do the former if there are secretaries who write essays less effectively and type more efficiently. The secretary should only and always type while the professor should always write. Such a principle, and the minute division of labor it implies when consistently pursued, is unproblematic only to those who never consider the possible adverse effects on the people whose working lives are dominated by one activity that they repeat over and over. The principle, that is, presents no problems only to those who tacitly accept Taylor's theory of managerial control, divided work, and worker incentives.

Some critics challenged the Taylorist model of work even before it was formalized into a complete theory. Alexis de Tocqueville, for instance, studying the emerging manufacturing enterprises in the United States during the first third of the nineteenth century, was appalled by the effects this new system of work had on workers:

> When a workman is increasingly and exclusively engaged in the fabrication of one thing, he ultimately does his work with singular dexterity; but at the same time, he loses the general faculty of applying his mind to the direction of his work. He everyday becomes more adroit and less industrious. In proportion as the principle of the division of labor is more extensively applied the workman becomes more weak, more narrow minded, and more dependent. The art advances, the artisan recedes.[23]

THE MARXIAN MODEL OF WORK

Karl Marx's early writings, especially the *Economic and Philosophical Manuscripts,* set forth an alternative model of work and workers.[24] The human being, says Marx, is a "species being": "Conscious life activity distinguishes man from the life activity of animals . . . ; he is only a self-conscious being, i.e., his life is an object for him, because he is a species being." [25] It is within the capacity of human beings to appraise critically their past conduct and to revise their future activity on the basis of that appraisal. We are also able to enter into fulfilling social relationships with others, relationships that involve mutual respect and promote shared ends. Since we can appraise our common history, since we can create new projects on the basis of those appraisals, we are beings capable of self-conscious action. The capacity for self-consciousness is in fact the species character of human beings; it is what distinguishes us essentially from other forms of life.

Work, organized properly, is the most important medium through which our species life, our potential as a species, unfolds. Work is the core of our "life activity." When it is "free, conscious activity" it fulfills us. When it exercises the mind and the body together, when it involves us in cooperative endeavors with others, when we can see the results of our work projects, and when the work serves a valuable social purpose, it becomes a medium for our development and gratification. Fulfilling work cannot "be made merely a joke or amusement. . . . Really free labor, the composing of music for example, is at the same time damned serious and demands the greatest effort." [26] It is the *structure* and *purpose* of work and the *social relations* within which it is embedded that are important for Marx, not simply the difficulty or ease with which it is done.

In modern capitalist society, labor increasingly alienates workers, separates them from their species life. First, the work is undertaken out of material necessity alone; workers do it "only as means for satisfaction of a need, the need to maintain physical existence." [27] Work becomes instrumental only rather than becoming also a source of fulfillment in itself. Second, since work assignments are so narrowly defined, the workers cannot see the individual results of the labor performed; their life activity is not ratified through viewing the product of their own craftsmanship. Third, the products a worker helps to produce are made more in the interest of making a profit for the owner than serving community welfare. The worker seldom takes pride in the social purpose served by the labor sold to another. Fourth, the fruits of labor go more to the owner and less to the worker; one works, under compulsion, not for oneself, but for another who reaps the greatest rewards from others' efforts. Fifth, and very important, the *productive process* itself is controlled not by workers but by owners; and the owners organize the process so that each worker's task is tedious and routinized. Labor neither exercises the mind nor involves cooperative relationships with other workers. It is mindless work controlled and organized by another for the other's profit.

The system of production alienates the worker, then, from the product, from creative activity, and from fellow workers—in short, from the species life:

> The more the worker produces the less he has to consume; the more value he creates the more worthless he becomes; the more refined his product the more crude and misshapen the worker; the more civilized the product the more barbarous the worker; the more powerful the work the more feeble the worker; the more the work manifests intelligence the more the worker declines in intelligence and becomes a slave of nature.[28]

Work in capitalist society is profoundly alienating, then, and the key to that alienation is the division of labor. It is important to see that Marx does not criticize specialization per se, although in one famous phrase (later retracted) he does celebrate the life in which one freely and frequently switches from one task to another. Rather, the "division of labor becomes truly such [is truly alienating] from the moment when a division of material and mental labor appears." [29] Such a division of labor forces some to work without thinking while it encourages others to think primarily about how to control workers. This division between mind work and mindless work is indeed a central ingredient in the class system of capitalist society.

We can see now that the models of work presented by Taylor and Marx are profoundly opposed. What seems to Taylor a rational system of ownership and division of mental and physical labor is seen by Marx as an alienating, exploitative system. The system of work that reflects human nature for Taylor treats human beings as wooden men and women, in the view of Marx. Indeed, Marx would contend that Taylor's ostensible science of management is actually a managerial ideology that falsely legitimates capital's control of worker for its own ends. Each new class in power, Marx says, "is compelled in order to carry through its aim, to represent its interest as the common interest of all members of society, put in ideal form; it will give its ideas the form of universality, and represent them as the only rational, universally valid ones." [30] Taylorism is the ideal form that owners and managers give to the alienating system of work they maintain in our society.

Marx would see Taylor as an ideologist whose doubtless honest beliefs serve the class interests of owners and legitimize an alienating system of work. But Taylor would think that Marxian theory is based on a faulty view of human nature and on a misunderstanding of the principles of modern production that create prosperity for all; to move away from the Taylor system would be to reduce worker productivity and to court disaster.

How is one to judge between these opposing models of work? We cannot here give that question the detailed treatment it deserves in its own right.[31] But one recent "historical experiment" does, in our view, help to shed some light on the problem.

When General Motors created the Lordstown complex, it applied Taylorist principles closely in order to maximize productivity. The management assumed complete control of the organization of work; jobs were defined very narrowly; time-and-motion studies were performed to make each worker's pace and motions more efficient; workers were paid at a higher rate than the average worker receives for similar jobs. Yet the experiment failed. Only the threat of unemployment kept workers on the job. The alienating conditions themselves both damaged the workers and contributed to the sabotage, absenteeism, and relaxation of quality controls management had sought to curtail. Workers were treated like wooden men and women, and so they treated the system and product with similar contempt. This occurred, we suggest, because Taylorism is at odds with basic human needs. Taylorism can never be a source of worker fulfillment. It requires wooden men and women, and if they are not already sufficiently pliable when hired, it tries to shape them into lumber.

We do not, of course, suggest that any industrial society can altogether dispense with monetary incentives or make every job equally challenging or eliminate all routine. But a mass of evidence does suggest that work can be organized more rationally, that the disjuncture between the managers and the managed, between the mind workers and the mindless workers, can be changed, that such production processes often even enhance productivity, and that workers in such arrangements are more fulfilled and more concerned about the quality of the product or service performed.[32] Under such conditions work is not merely instrumental, something done only for pay; but it is done partly for pay, partly because of the intrinsic interest of the work, partly because of a desire to create socially useful products, and partly because of a desire to gain the respect of others through the social contribution one makes. Such a mix of incentives shows that Taylor's false dichotomy between work for private gain and work for the general welfare loads the dice in the direction of his alienating model of work: the dichotomy itself unnecessarily undermines efforts to create modes of work geared to the needs of workers as human beings.

We will assume in what follows that the model of work and the theory of human nature developed by Marx is, if sometimes overstated, on the right track. To state our position schematically (and with the absence of qualification such schematism implies), Taylorism subordinates workers to the private interest of employers in the name of productivity and prosperity for all, while unalienating work subordinates the production process to the human needs of workers in the interests of productivity and the common welfare. If Taylorism was required at one stage of industrial development (we are not sure that it was), it is no longer a necessity today in most areas of the economy.

■ The Expansion of Taylorism

It is useful to see the politics of work as a struggle, often indirect and sublimated, sometimes more direct and open, between workers and owners in various occupations, each group trying to institute or maintain a different model of work.[33] The owners and managers seek to institute Taylorist principles of work and managerial control, and the workers seek to create space within which the worst forms of alienation can be avoided or eliminated.

The indirect, sublimated forms of the struggle are often subtle.

But in the workplace itself, the grievances of workers do form a pattern. Thus the Survey Research Center at the University of Michigan, studying a large number of workers in various occupations, found that workers themselves ranked the following dimensions of work in order of importance.

1. interesting work
2. enough help and equipment to get the job done
3. enough information to get the job done
4. enough authority to get the job done
5. good pay
6. opportunity to develop special abilities
7. job security
8. seeing the results of one's work[34]

Now certainly this ranking will shift as economic conditions change. In periods of high unemployment and high inflation, items 5 and 7 will move up the list. This would not indicate that they are the only things that matter to workers but that when job security and pay are missing, everything else crumbles too. Workers, then, prize working conditions that reflect their humanity and their capacities for craftsmanship. Owners and managers, on the other hand, would seldom provide this rank order when discussing what they hope to promote for the workers they employ. The priorities of each group are at odds with those of the other.

The politics of work is most often part of a daily struggle carried on in local settings. In the shop where the workers' movements are prescribed and the assembly line or the timer's watch sets the workers' pace, workers will typically collaborate to create space for themselves. Here is the advice of an experienced drill-press operator to a new worker about to face the rate setter:

> If you expect to get any kind of a price, you got to outwit that son-of-a-bitch! You got to use your noodle while you're working and think your work out ahead as you go along! You got to add in movements you know you ain't going to make when you're running the job! Remember, if you don't screw them, they're going to screw you! ... Every movement counts.[35]

Work in the factory embodies a recurring struggle between workers and managers. Management will define tasks, speed up jobs, impose new incentive systems in the interests of profit and control; workers will respond with shortcuts, group schemes, machinery breakdowns, and sometimes wildcat strikes to minimize the worst effects of the new system. Management will then introduce new measures to get around these responses, and workers will individually and collectively strive to create new ways to handle the new rules. A spiral of conflict emerges, with management seeing the workers as lazy and scheming and workers resisting those pressures and processes that treat them as wooden men and women. The struggle within the shop goes on continually, but it is a struggle in which the owners and managers hold most of the cards.

At the *public* level, when labor unions enter into negotiations with employers or press claims upon the government, the need for work reform is seldom a high-priority issue. But here, too, worker frustration with the conditions of work exerts its influence on those issues that are defined. The intensity with which unions press claims on those issues that can be legitimately defined within the system reflects in part the rage workers feel because of their inability to define the structure of work itself as a public issue of paramount importance. In our society, the politics of work is typically a sublimated politics.

The reasoning goes something like this: "Maybe we can't stop them from imposing inhumane work conditions on us, but they are going to have to pay for it with higher wages." Or: "Maybe we can't eliminate this mindless work, but we *can* struggle to make sure that the children of our race, our religion are given an opportunity to fill those few jobs that are satisfying." Or (think of medicine, law, professors, skilled crafts): "Everybody wants into our occupation because the others are so deadly, so we better organize to keep them out; if we don't we'll end up oversupplied with personnel and then *we'll* be ripe for the same routinization and authoritarian control they labor under." Or (think of truckers, assembly-line workers, janitors, low-level bureaucrats): "Why should those professors and public bureaucrats have it so easy? Why shouldn't they punch a clock like we do?" Or (think of the same constituencies): "Why should welfare mothers get paid for sitting around; let them work like everybody else." The grievances reflected in these demands for *higher wages, equal opportunity, protective unionism,* and *punitive legislation* against privileged professions and the unemployed are certainly important in themselves within the established system of stratification. But other pressures are involved as well.

First, these are in part surrogate issues. If significant reform of work life were established in a variety of occupations, some of these issues would dissolve and the others would diminish in intensity. In this way the politics of work operates in the background of many of the political issues with which we are most familiar. Since workers cannot, it seems, make effective inroads on that fundamental issue (and the issue of inequality to which it is connected), they are more intensely committed in those surrogate issue areas where they can make a difference.[36]

Second, these are exactly the issues that divide working-class constituencies along racial, sexual, ethnic, and status lines. If the issue of work-life reform which (to some extent) these constituencies share cannot be translated into a high-priority political issue, then the very factors that push the issue of work-life reform out of the public arena also help to divide the working class into warring factions. The working class pays dearly for its failure to translate the need for work reform into a viable political issue.

Why haven't unions simply defined work reform as a basic demand, pressing the government and corporations to respond affirmatively? A full answer must await our discussion in the next section of the structural constraints within which proposals for work reform are confined. For now we can say that American trade unions respond to these restraints in a fairly consistent way. They can deliver on the rank-and-file desire for higher wages because the cost to management of concession here can be transferred to consumers as higher prices. But management is more obstinate in dealing with demands for work reform; those reforms would threaten their control over the production process. A union that stakes everything on this issue would be likely to lose. It might also find itself losing the support of its own membership. Unions, then, often serve as a vehicle for converting work-reform needs into proposals for wage increases, protectionism, and other fringe benefits. Because workers are always struggling to make ends meet in an inflationary economy, the workers themselves accept success in the available area rather than risk defeat in the unavailable one.

This displacement of issues is profoundly important in American politics. And through such processes the politics of work emerges as an indirect, sublimated politics punctuated periodically by local wildcat strikes.

So far, though, we have concentrated on the blue-collar worker and have used work on the assembly line as our paradigm of Taylorized work. Since only 2 percent of all American laborers work on the assembly line today and since the white-collar worker is increasingly prevalent in the work force, some critics will undoubtedly say that the issue of work reform will soon disappear without recourse to a political struggle. As the proportion of blue-collar workers steadily declines, the pertinence of work reform will decline steadily too, until Taylorism slides gracefully into history. That contention, in our view, is thoroughly mistaken. To challenge it, we must look more closely at changes in the composition of the American work force.

Notice, first, the changing proportions of those who are self-employed and those who are dependent employees. In 1780, 20 percent of the labor force consisted of nonmanagerial employees, 80 percent were self-employed as farmers, merchants, lawyers, bankers, doctors, blacksmiths, and so on. By 1920 these figures were nearly reversed: 73 percent were nonmanagerial employees, 23.5 percent were self-employed, and 2.6 percent were classified as managerial employees. And by 1969, 83 percent were nonmanagerial wage and salary employees, only 9.2 percent were self-employed, and 7.2 percent were managerial officials. The first fact to note, then, is the massive shift in our work force from a middle-class society of the self-employed to a society in which the dependent employee is the prevailing type. Today well over 80 percent of all adults in the work force are dependent employees working in organizations that exert great influence over their pay, job security, and conditions of work.[37]

But those figures do not tell us how dependent employees are distributed among blue- and white-collar jobs. These internal changes are equally impressive. In 1870 white-collar workers made up 7 percent of the work force; by 1940 they made up 33 percent; by 1969, 47 percent. They outnumbered blue-collar workers by 50 percent in 1980. But accompanying this shift in the composition of the work force has been a corollary shift in the organization of work performed by white-collar workers. To speak of the first shift without attending closely to the second is to perpetuate a myth about white-collar work in America today.

We tend to think of white-collar work as work involving intellectual accomplishment, personal initiative, and some degree of managerial responsibility. But our image of the white-collar worker is drawn from the most prestigious, satisfying occupations within that category. In fact, most white-collar workers have more in common with blue-collar workers than they do with high-level administrators or technical experts. As C. Wright Mills put it in his classic study of the white-collar worker in the 1950s, "there are few, if any, features of wage work (except heavy toil, which is decreasingly a factor in wage work) that do not also characterize at least some white-collar work." [38]

Let us consider clerical and secretarial workers, by far the largest category in the white-collar force. If the old-fashioned bank clerk and private secretary were personally tied to their companies, if each had diverse and sometimes challenging responsibilities, that is decreasingly true today. In the modern office, secretarial pools often replace the personal secretary. In the largest operations each of the classical secretarial functions—filing, typing, recording, taking notes—is assigned to different personnel, sometimes to different pools. Time-and-motion studies are then performed on these separate tasks, and "secretaries" find themselves increasingly assigned to repeat one detailed operation while meeting performance quotas established by management.

The contemporary equivalent of the traditional clerk is also subject to Taylorist forms of work and evaluation in the large bureaucracies of today. One investigator summarizes the division of tasks among "clerks" in a typical modern firm:

> Characteristically, separate clerks open the mail, date and route orders, interpret customer information, clear credit, check the items ordered for clarity . . . , extend discounts, calculate shipping charges, etc.[39]

The work of secretarial and clerical employees is thus more and more subject to Taylorist principles in the large private and public bureaucracies. We are, in fact, witnessing today the emergence of white-collar factories, in which paper and data processing resemble the automobile assembly line in many ways.

As we proceed to the more prestigious sectors of white-collar work, we can see similar pressures emerging. Thus the computer, according to the testimony of its early enthusiasts, was to eliminate a great deal of repetitive white-collar work while generating new positions for highly skilled white-collar employees. Today we do see an impressive array of computer operatives graded by pay and status. The upper-level jobs, that of the systems analyst and the computer programmer, carry some degree of autonomy, and these employees do exercise some imagination and responsibility in their work. But these characteristics recede as we move down to the more numerous computer console operators, keypunch operators, tape librarians, and stockroom attendants. Workers in these areas experience a high degree of tension and boredom; their absenteeism and turnover rates are high; their promotion opportunities are slight.

Even programmers find their work less fulfilling than enthusiasts had anticipated. Listen to a 45-year-old programmer earning $18,000 a year (1974) describe not what he can buy with his income but what he gets out of his work:

> I like the people I work with. Good people.... It's just that I don't care about it. I spend eight hours a day, five days a week, doing something I don't care about.... I'd like some sort of social work, programming in alcoholism research or drug addiction control. But that's hard to find.... I think up questions so that I can talk with people. Legitimate questions. But it's a game of mine to get out of work. I'm like a boxer in the ring. I go to the ropes. Pace. Drink water. But sooner or later I have to start punching again.[40]

Here the problem is partly the work routine itself but partly too the lack of valuable social purpose served by the work. This concern is voiced at all levels of the occupational system, as by the woman on the Lordstown assembly line who told an interviewer, "I would never buy a Chevy." [41] It is accentuated as a problem in many higher-status occupations where work schedules are not so thoroughly routinized but where the product or service itself lacks those qualities of social utility and craftsmanship in which one can take pride.

There are satisfying jobs sprinkled throughout the occupational system. Even some lower-income jobs have their advantages: The mechanic in the small shop, the teacher in the small community, the clerk in the bookshop often control the pace of their own work and perform services of intrinsic social importance. And these examples increase as we climb the occupational ladder: technicians in highly automated and profitable industries such as oil refining and electrical equipment often have challenging work and a measure of control over their work environment. Indeed, because of their command of scarce skills and the favorable market position of their firms, such workers often press militantly and successfully for work reform. The professions of law, medicine, and college teaching also retain much of the autonomy and challenge that traditionally have made them favored professions for the sons and daughters of the middle class. Even here, though, the space within which these professionals work is increasingly subject to segmentation, performance quotas, and control by administrative personnel less thoroughly committed to the integrity of the profession.

The problem is this: the very jobs that challenge one's abilities, engage one's interest, and serve a social purpose worthy of personal commitment become, in a society where most work lacks these characteristics, the occupational targets toward which increasing numbers of young people understandably aim. The result is an oversupply of talent that threatens to drain the oases as everybody flees the desert. As individuals strive to locate fulfilling work in an occupational system dominated by Taylorism, Taylorism itself moves into new occupational outposts. And though important differences do exist, the grievances and aspirations of most dependent employees move increasingly in the same direction. Their common grievances reflect dependence within an occupational system oriented toward managerial prerogatives and private profit and away from worker prerogatives and community welfare. Listen to a medley of voices convey the frustrations and aspirations of the dependent employee:

> *The project coordinator:* Gradually your effectiveness wears down. Pretty soon, you no longer identify as the bright guy with the ideas. You become a fly in the ointment. You're criticized by your superiors and your subordinates not in a direct manner. Indirectly, by being ignored.
>
> *The stockbroker:* In this rip-off, we're treated with contempt by members of the stock exchange. They're really saying, "If you make too big a noise, we're gonna have a girl take the orders and the machine'll do the rest...."
>
> *The bureaucrat:* They get what they want out of people by threatening them economically. It makes people apple polishers and ass kissers. I used to hear people say "work needs to be redefined." I thought they were crazy. Now I know they're not.
>
> *The fireman:* I worked in a bank. You know it's just paper. It's not real. Nine to five and it's shit.... But the firemen, you actually see them produce. You see them put out a fire. You see them come out with babies in their hands.... I can look back and say "I helped put out that fire...." It shows something I did on this earth.
>
> *The union leader at Lordstown:* A unimate is a welding robot.... If the guys didn't stand up and fight, they'd become robots too.[42]

Blue- and white-collar workers sing the same song but with different voices and intonations. As dependent employees, they share thwarted aspirations for challenging, engaging, and purposeful work pursued in democratic settings. The politics of work will become a more public, militant politics when dependent employees in a variety of occupations begin to subordinate their differences in status, education, and pay levels to shared interests in reconstituting power relations and routines within the work-place itself.

■ The Prospects for Work Reform

The prevailing idea of work in our society is so deeply embedded in our production processes that it is easy to think of it as the only possible form, insusceptible to reformulation. We become resigned to necessity. Even our language reflects this sense of necessity and resignation. Thus we think of play and leisure as relatively trivial activities pursued for their own sakes; and we think of work, by comparison, as a more serious endeavor, inherently distasteful and pursued as a necessary means to feed our families, secure a better life for our children, and provide us with time for play and leisure. These categories fit much of our actual experience, but they also distort our perception of alternative styles emerging in certain occupations and potential alternatives inherent in others. If some find their work intrinsically satisfying, they tend to deny or understate it for fear that others will think they are being paid for playing. If others contemplate work reform in stultifying jobs, they are charged with wanting to play for money. Our *categories* themselves reflect Taylor's view that "it is a matter of ordinary common sense to plan working hours so that workers can really 'work while they work' and 'play while they play.'"[43] If the distinction between work and play could only be drawn in this way, common sense would also be good sense. But we must not allow our thought to be dominated by the Taylorist assumptions embedded in our language. Work *can* be nontrivial, demanding, instrumental, and intrinsically fulfilling all at the same time. To revise received distinctions in this way is to heighten our ability to bring a critical perspective to bear on alienating work routines. We expand our sense of the possible by reminding ourselves that Taylorist distinctions between work and leisure are not etched in stone.

Work as we know it is not work as it has always been practiced and known. For the early Greeks, work, *ponos,* was physical activity that was drudgery, a burden; the word itself was derived from the Greek word for sorrow. In feudal society the purpose of work was closely linked to God's will and purpose; a person worked out of Christian charity or as a remedy for temptation. And while many were ground down by heavy tasks, the prevailing model of work was provided by the idea of craftsmanship. Labor, as we define and measure it, was an alien idea; there was no unit of labor time as we know it today. Work and leisure, effort and pride, production and social life, were organically connected. The long hours of the craftsman were not strictly hours of labor time, because social relations were embedded in work relations. The "awareness of being part of a large social community permeated the work place, and the awareness of belonging to an occupational community dominated social relations of the job." [44] One does not have to understate the hard life faced by the peasant and the craftsman to perceive that work as they knew it was quite unlike work as we know it.

The ideas and forms of work prevailing at any time reflect and help to shape the entire society within which they exist. Put another way, significant changes in the structure of work must be accompanied by corollary changes in scientific knowledge, technological possibilities, educational institutions, moral codes, and patterns of political expectation. If work as we know it at this point in history is once again open to reconstitution, it can only be because a broad set of economic and social institutions are undergoing, or potentially open to, structural change.

To ask, What are the prospects for work reform? is to ask, What broader changes encourage or stifle a redefinition of the work ethic and a reconstitution of work processes? If the need for reform has persisted at least as long as Taylorism has flourished, what factors, if any, make it more possible to speak to that need today?

Consider, first, a set of tendencies that undermine the legitimacy of the old work ethic and provide potential openings for work reform.

1. Governments in Sweden and Yugoslavia, where work reform has gained a foothold, also have a commitment to the maintenance of full employment. Under these conditions managers cannot easily use the threat of unemployment to discipline the labor force; they must explore new incentives to enhance worker productivity. In Sweden the problems of absenteeism, turnover, and idleness did encourage management to experiment with modest work-reform schemes. Extensive unemployment, then, tends to suppress the issue of work reform, since the workers' first priority is to seek or retain jobs. But when organized labor secures a viable policy of full employment, it creates one of the preconditions for work reform. If employment levels vary significantly across occupational categories, as they do in the United States, we can expect those in highly skilled, undersupplied occupations

to have more leverage with respect to conditions of work than those in low-skilled, oversupplied areas. But even these differences in opportunities will be reduced if any large portion of the work force is insecure. As we have already noted, the sons and daughters of those in marginal jobs will strive to enter the more rewarding occupations, inflating the supply and increasing the hazards of unemployment at these levels. Thus a society with stable full employment is more open to pressure for work reform than one with high unemployment (or underemployment) in any areas.

2. In a similar way, a political economy that can and does control inflation is more likely to place work reform high on its agenda. If inflation eats away at incomes, workers must struggle to gain comparable pay increases, thereby pushing work reform to a lower position on their priority list. Moreover, if a political economy oscillates, as ours does, between periods of high unemployment and high inflation, the oscillation itself will limit workers' ability to translate the need for work reform into a viable political demand.

3. As the educational level of the working population improves, it is encouraged to expect work opportunities commensurate with its talents and its abilities to assume responsibility. The gap in the United States between the educational levels of the employee force and the intellectual demands of the jobs available in the occupational system creates space within which worker frustra tion expands and pressures for work reform grow. This uneven development between the educational and occupational systems helped to explode the myth of the happy worker in the late 1960s.

4. As the production system has matured, spewing out consumer goods in massive varieties and amounts, it has been necessary to accelerate consumer demand for goods through advertising. But such luxury advertising, to be effective, must appeal to the carefree life, the life of sexual liaisons, casual attitudes, self-indulgence. And luxury advertising, even though it is a requirement of the marketing system, almost certainly helps to undermine the instrumental work ethic central to the production system. This contradiction in modern capitalism is expressed as one imperative toward self-discipline and another toward self-indulgence; it surely encourages people to look upon the conditions of work with a critical eye. Burdens and grievances that were present all along now become more sharply defined and less acceptable.[45]

5. If the threats of unemployment and inflation have helped to

discipline a labor force subjected to Taylorism, the promise of future affluence has played its role too. Under Taylorism, the only function work has for the worker is to provide a means to subsistence and to affluence. But the promise of affluence seems to operate better as an incentive when its payoff is projected into the distant future: "We are working (struggling, sacrificing) today so that our children will have a better (more affluent) life tomorrow." By now, though, the sons and daughters of the upper-middle classes have tasted that promised affluence. And a crucial ingredient in the radicalism of the 1960s was the reaction of these young people against material opulence, environmental waste, and spiritual emptiness. Delivery on the promise of affluence has accentuated the lack of meaning and purpose in a materialist culture; the goal itself loses its ability to motivate and energize the young. Such a reaction must alter attitudes toward work. When people say they lack purpose and meaning in work, they mean in part that the old purpose and meaning—work as a means to affluence—has lost its significance. Affluence is shallow; it cannot serve as a viable incentive to mindless, repetitive work for those who have tasted its fruits. Thus delivery on the promise of affluence helps to undermine the very work ethic that contributed to its delivery.[46]

If, as many studies suggest, meaningful work reform often increases productivity, and if the factors mentioned before—full employment, low inflation, worker absenteeism, higher educational attainment of young workers, modern forms of advertising, and the shallowness of affluence—all seem to point toward work reform, why don't the pressures for reform become irresistible? What or who stands in the way of changes that would benefit the entire society?

There are, first of all, structural factors in the economy. If the inflation and unemployment spiral is endemic to contemporary American capitalism, then these forces will press against work reform. In that respect alone, the preconditions for work reform include the displacement of the economic system that repeatedly traps its workers in an inflation-unemployment spiral.

There are also technological limitations. Many industries have large investments in technologies organized around Taylorist principles. Marginal or declining industries (the auto industries are in the latter category) might have to limp along with the technologies they now have, making some work reform possible but significant change difficult. This obstacle, though, is not in itself insuperable throughout the economy.

More important is the fact that several of the factors noted before (educated workers, luxury advertising, and disillusion with affluence) have emerged relatively recently in the American political economy. And each of the elements is structurally related to the others. Thus a trend in the opposite direction is certainly possible. We could experience a long-term decline in employment, a decline in advertising aimed at self-indulgence, a reversal of educational opportunities for many Americans, and a decline in affluence. The need for a reconstitution of work would remain, but the political opportunities to promote it would be absent. The situation would not be exactly as we knew it, say in the 1920s and 1950s, for the population, having experienced and lost affluence, would be embittered by false promises. They would also be more alert to the limits posed by the environment to the endless pursuit of affluence. Threats and coercive pressure would then play a central role in disciplining those segments of the work force oppressed by Taylorism. But in the short run, at least, work reform probably would be subordinated to more pressing issues, even by socialists.

The pressures we have so far noted operate together to pose powerful obstacles to meaningful work reform within the present system. They are in fact so powerful because of internal instabilities within the capitalist system of political economy. But there are related pressures that demonstrate even more dramatically the contradiction between significant work reform and the maintenance of an economic system fueled by the private profits of private owners. These pressures show socialism to be a necessary, though not sufficient, condition of unalienating work for most working people.

Corporate owners and managers are alert to the studies in management journals connecting work reform to improved productivity. Why have most been extremely hesitant to act? Because the reforms that would decrease worker alienation and increase productivity pose a threat initially to managerial prerogatives and eventually to the system of private ownership itself. Corporate control over the work force would be jeopardized if jobs were redesigned and if channels of participation and information were opened. Recall, for instance, how the Carnegie Steel Company in 1892 reduced its dependence on skilled craftsmen in order to increase its control over the work process (see Chapter 3). A production process that engages skilled, knowledgeable workers creates a set of irreplaceable workers; if *they* lobby government or strike, owners and politicians must listen carefully. Meaningful work reform, in short, would make a larger number of workers in a variety of occupations less dispensable and more powerful. If they later challenged the prerogatives of managers and owners, they would have a more effective power base from which to launch the challenge.

But of course the connections we see between work reform and a threat to the private corporate system cannot serve as a motive for corporate opposition to work reform unless corporate elites themselves see it this way. They do. Though it would be impolitic for them to emphasize the point—it would feed the flames of worker discontent—enough signals have been given in publications read primarily by corporate and financial elites to get the message out.[47] We cite one example.

Thomas Fitzgerald, director of employee research and training activities at the Chevrolet Division, General Motors, published an essay in the *Harvard Business Review* in 1971, responding to those managerial theorists who have argued in favor of work reform. His essay is entitled "Why Motivation Theory Won't Work," and its contents are quite interesting.[48]

Fitzgerald acknowledges that American corporations face growing problems with worker absenteeism, turnover, idleness, featherbedding, and product defects. He agrees that these problems have provided impetus for a lively literature in business journals favorable to work reform. The authors don't always distinguish carefully enough, Fitzgerald notes, between those reforms that would increase worker *satisfaction* and those that would improve their *motivation* to work. The two may not always go together, and management, he implies, should be primarily interested in the latter.

He then contends that the problem of motivation is embedded in the structure of contemporary industrial society. The old work ethic is in trouble, and the classical sanction of unemployment is "partly neutralized by a full-employment welfare system and the protections possible for individuals through combinations (unions)."[49]

A number of traits once common to workers ("orderliness, punctuality . . . , success striving, deference to rank and authority, predictability . . . , reliance on rules and procedures")[50] are no longer to be taken for granted. But then Fitzgerald expresses skepticism about work reforms designed to cope with these changes in worker "traits." Over the long term the beneficial effects of "job enlargement" are likely to wear off just as the effects of increased pay schedules did (he says) in an earlier period. Also, managerial flexibility in "reallocating unskilled labor without loss of training investment would be reduced" if such reforms were introduced.[51] And since one job enlargement is likely to lead to another, managers should be hesitant in starting down this road.

He is even more wary of worker participation in decision making. First, he thinks, it won't succeed. He assumes, as early opponents to political democracy did, that workers will be too apathetic. More important, if it did work, it would lead to a challenge of traditional managerial prerogatives. Fitzgerald is eloquent on this point:

> Once competence is shown (or believed to be shown) in, say, rearranging the work area, and after participation has become a conscious, officially sponsored activity, participators may well want to go on to topics of job assignment, the allocation of rewards, or even the selection of leadership. In other words, management's present monopoly—on initiating participation, on the nomination of conferees, and on the limitation of legitimate areas for review—can itself easily become a source of contention.[52]

Meaningful work reform, Fitzgerald agrees, would involve job redesign, worker participation in the decision process, and worker access to the requisite information for intelligent participation. But inroads in these areas would increase the power and indispensability of workers while decreasing managerial monopoly over information and power. Once this process is started, it could easily get out of hand. So it is best not to allow it to start. "History," Fitzgerald warns, "does not offer many examples of oligarchies that have abdicated with grace and goodwill." [53]

For Fitzgerald these considerations constitute an argument for corporate opposition to work reform. Acknowledging difficulty in motivating the contemporary worker, but refusing to sanction work reform, he calls instead for a series of gimmicks within the present system of work, such as company recreation teams, contests, slogans, and managerial praise of workers with desirable traits.

The owning and managerial classes, entrenched in the most developed capitalist system in the world, will firmly oppose work reform that threatens their power base and prerogatives. They will oppose, that is, meaningful work reform. But if work reform is desirable in itself, and if it is connected to other important objectives like reducing inequality and establishing environmental integrity, then the issue of work reform must not be allowed to languish. Those pressures and elites within the capitalist political economy that obstruct work reform actually provide a case not for the retention of Taylorism, inequality, environmental degradation, and wage-price cycles, but for socialism. Although socialism does not guarantee that work reform and other objectives will be achieved, it is a crucial precondition for their promotion.

NOTES

1. The employer's purpose in designing work, we will argue, is to promote the highest efficiency of the worker compatible with the employer's ability to retain a high level of control over the work process. These two objectives are closely connected to the goal of private profit maximized over the long run. We return to this issue in our discussion of Taylorism.
2. Reported in *Work in America,* Special Task Force Report to the Department of Health, Education and Welfare (Cambridge: MIT Press, 1973), p. 14.
3. *The Affluent Worker* (London: Cambridge University Press, 1968), I: 108–109.
4. "The Politics of Consensus in an Age of Affluence," *American Political Science Review* (December 1965). During periods of affluence, "men feel more in control of their lives" (p. 879).
5. Ibid., pp. 879–880. The science from which Mills and Fromm were alienated, and to which Lane and Goldthorpe were committed, was the study of public attitudes through surveys.
6. The report of this incident is taken from André Gorz, "Workers Control Is More Than Just That," in *Workers Control,* edited by Gerry Hunnius, G. David Garson, and John Case (New York: Vintage Books, 1973), pp. 325–343.
7. These examples are also detailed in Gorz, pp. 334–335.
8. A summary of the strike can be found in David Jenkins, *Job Power* (Baltimore Penguin Books, 1974), Ch. 9.
9. Quoted in Emma Rothschild, *Paradise Lost: The Decline of the Auto-Industrial Age* (New York: Vintage Books, 1974), p. 100. Another excellent treatment of the Lordstown struggles is found in Stanley Aronowitz, *False Promises* (New York: McGraw-Hill, 1973), Ch. 1.
10. Quoted in Jenkins, p. 51.
11. The income, status, and educational level attached to a job are partly a function of the skill level and autonomy the job allows. It is not surprising that these factors cannot easily be unsorted, since a significant change in one requires significant changes in the others. These studies are summarized in *Work in America,* pp. 16, 76–93.

12. The distinction is important: the former asks how workers can achieve jobs and working conditions that engage their capacities and interests in fulfilling ways. The concern with worker motivation asks only how the worker can be made more efficient and reliable. If discipline and narrow job assignments prove more effective than fulfilling work, then they are judged to be the better motivators, regardless of the effects on the workers.

13. More careful, in-depth surveys can probe beneath this surface, but it is essential that survey analysts be exposed thoroughly to *alternative* theories, which they would seek to test during the interviews. It helps too, of course, if they are aware of how work is organized differently in other societies and ask workers to compare their actual experiences to likely experiences under those conditions. And, of course, individual interviews should be supplemented with group interviews. Then the interview technique can be of some limited value, still to be complemented by other modes of inquiry.

14. Taylor, *The Principles of Scientific Management* (1911) (New York: W. W. Norton, 1967), p. 47.

15. Ibid., p. 130.

16. Ibid., p. 36.

17. Ibid., p. 25.

18. Ibid., p. 26.

19. Ibid., p. 39.

20. Ibid., p. 95.

21. Ibid., p. 125.

22. Ibid., p. 120.

23. *Democracy in America,* edited by Richard D. Heffner (New York: Mentor Books, 1956), pp. 217–218.

24. We draw upon the translation in Erich Fromm, ed., *Marx's Concept of Man* (New York: Ungar, 1961). It is not our intent to ask whether the theory of alienation is still present in Marx's later work. The affirmative view has been defended by Shlomo Avineri, *The Social Thought of Karl Marx* (London: Cambridge University Press, 1970), and denied by Louis Althusser, *For Marx* (New York: Vintage Books, 1970). We suspect that Marx revised his earlier ideas about alienation but that in revised form they continued to play a role in his mature theory.

25. *Marx's Concept of Man,* p. 101.

26. Karl Marx, *The Grundrisse,* edited and translated by David McClellan (New York: Harper Torchbooks, 1972), p. 124.

27. *Marx's Concept of Man,* p. 101.

28. Ibid., p. 97.

29. Ibid., p. 204.

30. Ibid., p. 214.

31. Our thinking on the subject is summarized in two essays collected in William Connolly and Glen Gordon, eds., *Social Structure and Political Theory* (Lexington, Mass.: D. C. Heath, 1974): Steven Lukes,

"Alienation and Anomie," pp. 192–211; and Connolly, "Theoretical Self-Consciousness," pp. 40–67.

32. See the experiments summarized in *Work in America*, pp. 188–201, and in Jenkins, *Job Power*.

33. It is not always between workers and owners, but in the public sector between workers and controllers. We agree, of course, that alienating work can emerge in societies where private ownership is absent and centralized planning prevails. We will return to this question in the last chapter, where we consider the connections between planning and freedom. For now it is sufficient to say that our society is *objectively* in a better position than any in the world to promote unalienating work, since most socialist societies are at much earlier stages of accumulation than we are. Hence the key question is, what forces operate in our system to obstruct changes that are objectively possible? The dismal view that every evil manifest in our society also happens to be a requirement of industrial organization or human nature itself is one that has been popular with apologists throughout history (think of the defenses of slavery, the subordination of women, the early arguments against political democracy). In fact, the early arguments against political democracy had very much the same structure as contemporary arguments against industrial democracy.

34. Quoted in *Work in America*, p. 13.

35. Quoted in William F. Whyte et al., eds., *Money and Motivation* (New York: Harper and Row, 1955), p. 15.

36. The process by which more fundamental grievances that are illegitimate in the prevailing system are converted into less fundamental issues that are legitimate is crucial to the understanding of our system of issue formation and resolution. The best place to start in thinking about this process is E. E. Schattschneider, *The Semisovereign People* (New York: Holt, Rinehart and Winston, 1960), especially Ch. 4, "The Displacement of Conflicts."

37. These figures and the following ones are from Michael Reich, "The Evolution of the United States Working Force," in *The Capitalist System*, edited by Richard Edwards, Michael Reich, and Thomas Weisskopf (Englewood Cliffs, N.J.: Prentice-Hall, 1972), pp. 174–183.

38. *White Collar* (New York: Oxford University Press, 1951), p. 227.

39. Harry Braverman, "Labor and Monopoly Capital," *Monthly Review* (July-August 1974), p. 67. Our treatment of all workers in the white-collar category is indebted to this essay as well as to Braverman's book *Labor and Monopoly Capital* (New York: Monthly Review Press, 1974).

40. Interview in the *Boston Globe,* December 2, 1974.

41. The interviewer is Emma Rothschild in *Paradise Lost,* p. 96.

42. These quotations are excerpted from Studs Terkel's superb study *Working* (New York: Pantheon Books, 1972), pp. 341, 340, 347, 589, and 91, respectively.

43. Taylor, p. 87.
44. Edward Shorter, "The History of Work in the West," in *Work and Community in the West* (New York: Harper Torchbooks, 1973), p. 9. For a brief survey of changes in the idea of work over the ages, see Adriano Tilgher, *Homo Faber: Work Through the Ages* (Chicago: Regnery, 1930).
45. Of course, if the production system were more fully oriented to pressing social needs, it would not be so dependent on manipulative advertising. There would be a ready use and market for its goods. It is, then, the false priorities in production that require the expensive advertising, and the advertising then helps to generate criticisms against the production processes.
46. The argument that there is a "motivation crisis" emerging within advanced capitalism is developed by Jurgen Habermas in *Legitimation Crisis* (Boston: Beacon Press, 1974).
47. Public statements by corporate elites and sometimes managerial theorists are often part of the politics of work. While proponents of work reform seek to mobilize workers, proponents of the status quo must seek to immobilize them. They will thus temper public statements that might arouse the opposition. Their public statements must then be decoded with our understanding of such political considerations firmly in mind.
48. *Harvard Business Review* (July-August 1971), pp. 37–43.
49. Ibid., p. 39.
50. Ibid., p. 40.
51. Ibid., p. 41.
52. Ibid., p. 43.
53. Ibid,

THE STRUCTURAL ROOTS
OF STAGFLATION

■ Instability and Hard Times

A capitalist economy is inherently unstable, and the instability imposes heavy burdens on vast numbers of people. During the one hundred years between 1865 and 1965, the United States experienced twenty-five recessions, periods in which total production declined for at least six months (see Figure 5-1) The duration of these recessions varied greatly, from the relatively mild slowdown of the 1950s, running eight to thirteen months, to the sustained depressions of the 1870s and 1930s. Even in the relatively good times from 1945 to 1970, unemployment, according to official government counts, affected between 2.9 and 6.8 percent of the labor force.[1] Government statistics, however, underestimate joblessness. For instance, neither workers who have quit looking for work nor part-time workers are counted as unemployed in government statistics. One

Figure 5-1 Historic Fluctuations of the United States Economy

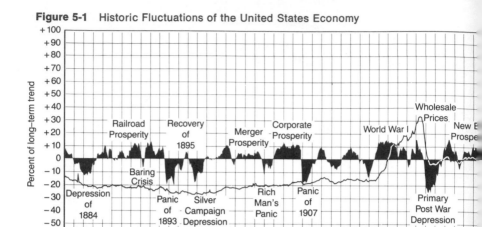

Source: "American Business Activity from 1790 to Today," by the AmeriTrust
Company, Cleveland, Ohio.

study has estimated conservatively that inclusion of the "dis-
couraged" worker would expand the rate of unemployment in
recent years by 40 percent, while further correction for those
who *involuntarily* work part-time would increase the rate to approximately 60 percent above the government figures.[2] If the
figures are adjusted to take these considerations into account,
the official unemployment rate for 1979 of 5.8 percent, or 6 million workers, corresponds to an actual unemployment level of
between 9 and 10 million people.[3] Furthermore, the number of
people unemployed at some point during any one year is equal
to about three times the number indicated by the average unemployment rate for the year. In other words, an average unemployment rate of 5.8 percent for 1979 indicates that approximately 18 million workers experienced periods of unemployment
some time during the year.[4] Finally, unemployment is spread
unevenly across race, sex, and age, as shown in Table 5-1. Black
female teenagers, for example, face an unemployment rate nearly
ten times that of white males over twenty years of age. Clearly,
the official unemployment figures understate the hard times confronting a large number of Americans when the economy operates
below its productive potential.

It is tough to be without a job in America. Table 5-2 itemizes
some of the quantifiable indicators of social stress that accom-

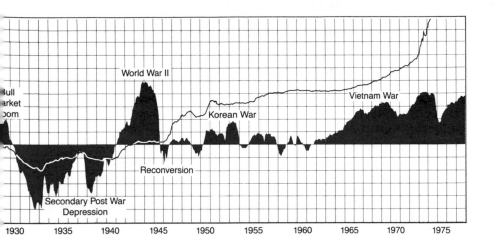

1930	1935	1940	1945	1950	1955	1960	1965	1970	1975

pany unemployment: a 1 percent increase in unemployment can be expected to increase rates of suicide, state prison admissions, and homicide by over 4 percent. To escape unemployment, Americans are expected to relocate geographically or to leave occupations of low demand for those of high demand. Thus, between 1870 and 1970 the percentage of Americans living on farms declined from over 50 percent to under 5 percent.[5] This migration from the farm to the factory or office was a painful, wrenching experience for millions of families. In any generation, many small entrepreneurs undergo trying times as their businesses fail. Sometimes, though, even geographical relocation or change in

TABLE 5-1   *Unemployment Rates by Race, Sex, and Age, 1979*

	White	Nonwhite
Males, total	4.4	10.3
Males, 16–19 years	13.9	31.5
Females, total	5.9	12.3
Females, 16–19 years	13.9	35.7
Both sexes, total	5.1	11.3

Source: Economic Report of the President, 1980 (Washington, D.C.: Government Printing Office, 1980), p. 238.

TABLE 5-2 *Cumulative Impact of a Sustained 1 Percent Change in Unemployment*

Social Stress Indicator	Change in Stress Indicator*
Suicide	4.1
State mental hospital admissions	3.4
State prison admissions	4.0
Homicide	5.7
Cirrhosis of the liver mortality	1.9
Cardiovascular-renal disease mortality	1.9
Total mortality	1.9

Source: M. Harvey Brenner, *Hearings on Social Costs of Unemployment.* Joint Economic Committee of U.S. Congress, October 31, 1979.

* Measured as a percentage of the total indicator incidence in the fifth year following a 1 percent change in the unemployment rate.

line of work does not result in a job. The Great Depression was such a time.

The voices of people who lived and suffered in the 1930s, captured by Studs Terkel in *Hard Times,* express the human dimensions of unemployment during other periods as well.[6] Time-honored means of livelihood were destroyed. On the farm:

> The struggles people had to go through are almost unbelievable. A man lived all his life on a given farm, it was taken away from him. One after the other. After the foreclosure, they got a deficiency judgment. Not only did he lose the farm, but it was impossible for him to get out of debt.

And in mining:

> 1929 was when it hit banking and big business. But we had suffering and starvation long before that. In the early twenties, mines shut down, nothin' for people to live on. Children fainted in school from hunger.

The loss of work affected the family in many ways. Sometimes the father left:

> The shame I was feeling. I walked out because I didn't have a job. I said, "I'm goin' out in the world and get me a job." And God help me, I couldn't get anything. I wouldn't let them see me dirty and ragged and I hadn't shaved. I wouldn't send 'em no picture.

Even when the father stayed, it sometimes wasn't much better:

I remember how, after dinner, he'd just lie on the couch in utter despair, night after night, for hours. A man who was interested in music, read all kinds of literature, novels, plays, history, economics and so on—there was this man so knocked out. We were afraid he was going to commit suicide. His close personal friend did take a header out of the fourteenth story.

Increased unemployment swelled the prisons. Times were bad there, too:

More people died during that depression phase than they ever did any other time. It wasn't starvation. They called it malnutrition. . . . They made you lose weight until the doctor got after them and said they have to get at least one meal a day.

Some gave up:

The majority of people were hit and hit hard. They were mentally disturbed, you're bound to know, 'cause they didn't know when the end of all this was comin'. There was a lot of suicides that I know of. From nothin' else but just they couldn't see any hope for a better tomorrow. I absolutely know some who did. Part of 'em were farmers and part of 'em were businessmen even. They went flat broke and they committed suicide on the strength of it, nothing else.

Feeding a baby in a family without a breadwinner wasn't easy:

I remember in Ainsloy that year, in the relief headquarters, a woman had been arguing and arguing to get some milk for her baby. You should have seen the things they were giving babies, instead of milk. I remember seeing them put salt-pork gravy in milk bottles and putting a nipple on, and the baby sucking this salt-pork gravy. A real blue baby, dying of starvation. In house after house, I saw that sort of thing.

Nor was the return home always pleasant for children of the Depression:

I got tired of hoboing and went down to see him and my daddy was all gray and didn't have no bank account and no Blue Cross. He didn't have nothin', and he worked himself to death. (Weeps). And the white man, he would drive a tractor in there. . . .

Housing conditions were often bad:

Here were all these people living in old, rusted out car bodies. I mean that was their home. There were people living in shacks made of orange crates. One family with a whole lot of kids were living in a piano box. This wasn't just a little section, this was maybe ten miles wide and ten miles long.

And for those who had a job it wasn't easy either. In agriculture:

In 1939, I went out as an itinerant farm worker. I got a job cutting asparagus, fifteen cents an hour, as fast as you could move. I remember standing up once to rub my aching back, 'cause you worked in a crouch almost at a running pace, and the straw boss yelling: "See those men standing by the road? They're just waiting to get you fired. If I catch you straightening up once more, one of them will be working and you won't."

Or in industry:

When I went to work in January, we were turning out 232 cars a day. When I was fired, four months later, we were turning out 535. Without any extra help and no increase in pay. It was the famous Ford speed-up.

And even some of the rich had it bad:

October 29, 1929, yeah. A frenzy. I must have gotten calls from a dozen and a half friends who were desperate. In each case, there was no sense in loaning them the money that they would give the broker. Suicides, left and right, made a terrific impression on me, of course. People I knew. It was heartbreaking.

Yet at the same time people were starving, too much was being produced:

He pointed out the great piles of oranges, the piles of lumber laying there idle.... They'd put up a rick of oranges and apples, put gasoline over it and set fire to them. Vegetables were being destroyed and everything. Everybody who cried so much later about federal programs destroying little pigs ... they should have seen what industry was doing at this time. To keep the price up.

This was perhaps the biggest paradox of the Great Depression: underconsumption side by side with excess production. A theoretical impossibility to the free market economists had become a fact of life to the nation. Certainly in human history it has often been true that even when everyone worked, there were not enough goods to go around. During the American Depression, however, so much needed to be done, but there were not enough jobs to go around. One question must have been asked a million times: Why were so many unemployed?

■ The Great Depression: A Revolution in Economic Doctrine

The free-market perspective, dominant among economists until the New Economics of the post-World War II period, holds that unemployment is the result of, first, workers' choosing leisure over work at prevailing wages (an unemployed person seeking work could always offer her or his services to an employer at a wage below the one already paid by the employer), and second, market interventions by protectionist labor unions and misguided government.[7] It fails to explain why suddenly in one period one of four workers should choose leisure over work. During the Great Depression there were long lines for every job available, labor unions represented less than 7 percent of the labor force, and the government had not yet introduced the New Deal legislation designed to promote full employment. Clearly, the classical doctrine hardly explained unemployment during this period. The Keynesian theory of unemployment provided an explanation of a policy responsive to the new problems created by this depression.

Heretical economists, notably the Physiocrats and, paradoxically, Thomas Malthus, had often argued that market economies suffer from periodic gluts marked by consumption below business production, unsold inventory buildups, and the resultant loss of jobs. But such "underconsumption" ideas lacked a theoretical base until the writings of John Maynard Keynes in 1936.[8] Keynes argued that employment is determined by *the level of aggregate demand* (composed of consumer purchases for the household, business investments on new plant and equipment, government spending and exports) *relative to productive capacity* (the output potential at full employment of labor and machines). Whenever the level of aggregate demand fell short of productive capacity, unemployment would be the result. The crucial element in Keynesian unemployment theory was the level of investment, which depended on *expectations* of business people regarding profitable opportunities. As Keynes put it, "The weakness of the inducement to invest has been at all times the key to the economic problem."[9]

The Keynesian model of unemployment is based on the notion that investment and savings have double roles. Investment, one of the two main components of private expenditure, is necessary to ensure high employment. But the very process of investing expands the productive capacity and thereby increases the level of demand required to achieve full employment in the future.

Savings, the release of productive capacity (both labor and machines or capital goods) from production of consumption goods, create the potential for the expansion of capital goods and thus for economic growth. But savings also establish a necessary condition for a business downturn: underspending. A downturn will occur if the capacity released from consumption is not employed in the production of new productive capacity. Put another way, a downturn will occur any time savings (a leakage from the expenditure stream) are greater than investment (an injection into the expenditure stream). And even a match between investment and savings can plant the seeds for future problems, for investment increases income, which in turn expands savings and therefore the level of investment required to sustain aggregate demand. In short, whenever investment fails to match savings (and is not offset by government or foreign spending), an economic downturn will follow.

The same tendency to instability of the market system can be perceived in yet a third way. In the owners' viewpoint, the workers play two incompatible roles: as *producers,* their low wages create high profits and potential for capital accumulation; as *consumers,* their high wages create larger markets for consumption products. To the extent that capitalists are successful in keeping wages down, their selling problem is intensified by a lack of demand; to the extent that workers are successful in driving wages up, the accumulation process is impeded by a lack of profits for investment.

In Keynesian theory full employment in a free-market economy without government intervention is a special case. According to the free-market perspective, unemployment is the special case. Aggregate demand would always tend to equal productive capacity. If households reduced their expenditures (increased savings), the level of investment would automatically expand to utilize the released productive capacity. The released labor and capital would simply be shifted from producing consumption goods to capital goods. Assuming flexible prices, the adjustment process would operate through the price of borrowing money, that is, the rate of interest: as savings increased, interest would drop. A drop in interest would increase the value of capital goods and induce an expansion in their production.[10] The process by which spending equals productive capacity and investment matches savings was referred to as Say's Law.

Keynes denied Say's Law, or any natural adjustment mechanisms ensuring full employment, and instead emphasized unemployment caused by the weakness in the inducement to invest compared with the propensity to save. He wrote: "The desire of the individual to augment his personal wealth by abstaining from consumption has usually been stronger than the inducement to the entrepreneur to augment the national wealth by employing labor on the construction of durable assets." As put by a follower of Keynes, the essence of the Keynesian revolution was in Keynes's ability "to shift economists from thinking normally in terms of a model of reality in which a dog called *savings* wagged his tail labeled *investment* to thinking in terms of a model in which a dog called *investment* wagged his tail labeled *savings*."[11]

The New Economics based on Keynes's writings undermined two central tenets of the free-market perspective and became the basis for the liberal government economic policies of the New Deal and later. It held, first, that inequality is not necessary to ensure a source of savings necessary for capital accumulation and economic growth, and second, that the government must intervene in the marketplace to ensure a level of demand sufficient to employ the nation's labor force fully. The classical defense for inequality—the view that capital accumulation, growth, and employment come from rich people's savings—was replaced by the Keynesian notion that high savings or low wages can easily result in underspending and are therefore often a barrier to growth and employment. The new view of savings and wages thus created a justification for government spending and progressive taxation. Taxing the rich and subsidizing the poor could stimulate demand, employment, and even profits.

But the implications of Keynesian theory for government intervention in the economy went beyond progressive taxation. Keynesian theory provided a rationale for interventionist government policies in pursuit of the four goals celebrated in every standard economics text: full employment, price stability, economic growth, and a favorable trade balance. These goals are to be pursued by an active government stabilization program composed of taxation, expenditure, and monetary policies. The New Economics promised an end to the business cycle and the birth of a new age of unprecedented prosperity based on ever-continuing economic growth. The riddle of unemployment had been solved, and the techniques for its elimination were now available. The only obstacle, or so it was thought, was the absence of a political will to implement the proper government policies at the right time.

■ The Rise and Fall of the New Economics

The Eisenhower years witnessed sluggish growth rates and unemployment levels that reached over 6.5 percent in two of the three recessions. With that background the New Economists found it relatively easy to convince President Kennedy that government policies of the 1950s had unnecessarily constrained the actual growth below the productive potential. What the economy needed, they claimed, was a boost in demand through tax cuts and increased expenditures. After a couple of years of political maneuvering, the president and (to a lesser degree) Congress were convinced; the 1964 tax cut was passed. The results matched the predictions of the New Economists. The lower-tax-induced spending increase propelled a 16.9 percent rise in gross national product and a 13.5 percent rise in government tax revenues over the ensuing two years.[12] Such success carried with it a smashing ideological victory for the New Economists. They were optimistic and exultant. Walter Heller, a chairman of the Council of Economic Advisors, wrote, "We have good reason to expect the U.S. economy to advance more steadily and, on average, more rapidly than either its long-run real growth rate of about 3 percent or its postwar rate of $3^1/_2$ to 4 percent." And, "The significance of the great expansion of the 1960s lies not in its striking statistics of employment, income, and growth but in its glowing promise of things to come." [13]

The high spirits were not confined to the economics profession. Successes of the New Economists gave the profession unprecedented popularity with the press, the business world, and the public. The acclaim was capped in 1968 by extending the Nobel Prize to include an annual award in the field of economics. As *Business Week* put it in 1966, the record of "remarkable growth— and remarkable stability—in the U.S. economy . . . has raised the prestige of economists—especially those who espouse the so-called new economics—to an all-time high." [14]

But by the late 1960s a new form of economic problem began to emerge. Keynesian policies seemed as helpless to cope with this new phenomenon as the free-market prescriptions had been during the Great Depression. Economists had been aware that full employment could not be achieved without some upward pressure on prices, but it was generally thought that a tradeoff existed between employment and inflation. The Phillips Curve predicted that unemployment rates above 5 percent would correlate with price deflation, while price inflation would surpass 4 percent only when rates of unemployment went below 2 percent. And, in fact, between 1952 and 1967 the facts conformed closely to these expectations: inflation stayed below 4 percent, and unemployment varied between 4 and 7 percent. But, as shown in Figure 5-2, a different picture emerged in the 1970s. Neither inflation nor unemployment has gone under 4 percent; and since 1974 inflation has been persistently in the double-digit range while unemployment has often surpassed 7 percent.

Lacking a coherent explanation, the New Economists generally blame a "confluence of random accidents." In the 1974 presiden-

Figure 5-2 Divergence of Actual Unemployment-Inflation Conditions from the Phillips Curve

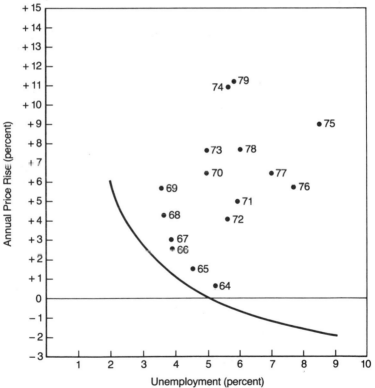

Source: Position of Phillips Curve from Paul Samuelson, *Economics*, 8th ed. (New York: McGraw-Hill, 1970), p. 810. Actual data from *Economic Report of the President, 1980*, Tables B-27 and B-49.

tial address to the American Economics Association, Heller defended the New Economics: "It is asking a lot of economists to expect them to have foreseen that the oil cartel would quadruple oil prices, that the world would suffer widespread and successive crop failures, that the Peruvian anchovies would go into hiding, and that the Soviet Union would 'solve our surplus grain problem' overnight." [15] James Tobin, another Kennedy advisor and author of *The New Economics: One Decade Older,* noted an unexpected steepness to the Phillips Curve at less than 4 percent unemployment rates, but he provided no explanation. He offered a series of minor modifications in fiscal and monetary policies that he believed, once the dislocations caused by the Vietnam War were over, would ensure a rebound in status for the New Economics.[16]

Milton Friedman, as expected, places the blame on the government: "The plain fact is that inflation is made in Washington, in ... the Federal Reserve System.... The government produces inflation, nobody but the government can produce inflation." Friedman asks, "Why does the Fed remain an engine of inflation? I confess that I am baffled." [17]

While the coexistence of inflation and unemployment creates a theoretical paradox for the mainstream economists, it creates a severe policy dilemma for the government. Successful stabilization policies had been based on the idea that unemployment and inflation are opposites, occurring not simultaneously but in a tradeoff relation. Unemployment was said to be caused by insufficient demand, and inflation, by excess demand; controlling the first therefore called for expansionary government policies, and controlling the second, for contractionary policies. But since inflation and unemployment now occur together, the technical solutions promised by the New Economics are no longer applicable.

The New Economics was an advance over the free-market perspective; it provided both an explanation of involuntary unemployment and policy measures for ending the Great Depression. But just as the Great Depression smashed the credibility of Say's Law, the *stagflation* (combined unemployment and inflation) of the 1970s demolished the notion of fine tuning the capitalist economy to sustain full employment, high growth, price stability, and a strong dollar in world markets. History applies a stern test to economic doctrines. The New Economists underestimated changes in the structure of the economy within which monetary and fiscal instruments were applied. Some of these changes were encouraged by government economic policies inspired by Keynesian theory. We turn now to an analysis that illuminates these structural changes.

■ Restricted Markets and Price Setting

The nature of the expansionary process today has been altered by two recent changes in the political economy of corporate capitalism: (1) the transition from the competitive, small-scale firm of the mid-nineteenth century to the corporate giant of the mid-twentieth century, and (2) the emergence of the state as a dominant force in shaping economic expansion. These structural changes have had far-reaching effects on pricing behavior and cost conditions and, we will argue, have qualitatively changed the nature of economic crisis.

In this section we will focus on an *immediate* cause of inflation: the pricing behavior of corporate giants. In the next sections we will examine the *root* causes of inflation: rising costs in a system of production for private profit.

The moderate price rises of the early 1960s were perceived by the New Economists as a necessary accompaniment to a booming economy. But the New Economists did not account for the fact that in the face of sluggish growth and slack demand, prices rose by over 125 percent in the 1967–1980 period. Every year of the 1970s meant unemployment for between 4 and 8 million workers by official count and excess productive capacity levels of between 15 and 27 percent (except briefly in 1973). The coexistence of rising prices and excess supply is impossible in a competitive-market setting, for, by definition, excess supply signifies falling prices. To explain this pairing, we must start (but not end) by examining pricing behavior in the light of the shift from competitive to monopolistic markets.

In the 1870s the American economy was composed mainly of small, one-product, geographically bounded, owner-managed firms operating in competitive markets. And, as shown in Figure 5-3, with the exception of two war periods, prices throughout the 1800s moved downward. But between the years of 1897 and 1905 the first of three great merger movements transformed business firms and market structures. The impact on the shape of American industry is described in a major study of merger activities:

> It transformed many industries, formerly characterized by many small and medium-sized firms, into those in which one or a few very large enterprises occupied leading positions. It laid the

Figure 5-3 Wars and the Consumer Price Index, 1800–1980 (1967 = 100)

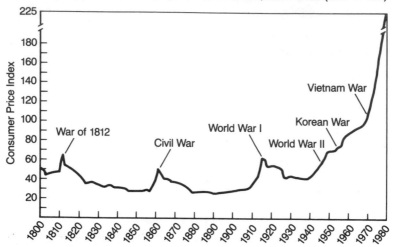

Source: U.S. Department of Labor, *Handbook of Labor Statistics, 1971*, p. 253, and *Economic Report of the President, 1980*, p. 259.

foundation for the industrial structure that has characterized most of American industry in the twentieth century.[18]

A second wave of merger activity from 1925 to 1930 firmly established most of the giant national corporations of today and the basic contours of today's industrial market structure. By the end of that period three or four firms had established a dominant position in several areas, including automobiles, oil, steel, and tires.[19] The new businesses served a national market, sold several products, established a complex administrative apparatus, and sold stocks to the public.[20] Profit was, as always, the key to survival, but barriers to entry, especially sheer size, greatly reduced the risk of being undersold. Market control over the behavior of these firms was thus reduced.[21]

As shown in Figure 5-4, the third great merger movement peaked in the late 1960s and early 1970s. From 1965 to 1971, 10,835 total mergers were recorded, compared to 2,864 mergers in the seven-year turn-of-the-century movement and 4,682 during the six years 1925–1930.[22] Between 1948 and 1968 the 200 largest manufacturing corporations acquired 3,684 firms worth about $50 billion. Whereas in 1909 the 100 largest industrial firms owned 17.7 percent of all manufacturing assets, by 1968 they owned 48.8 percent.

Figure 5-4 Merger Activity in Manufacturing and Mining

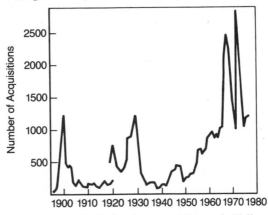

Source: William G. Shepherd, *Market Power and Economic Welfare* (New York: Random House, 1970), p. 71. Broken line represents a use of data sources that are not entirely comparable. Recent data are from Bureau of Economics, Federal Trade Commission, *Statistical Report on Mergers and Acquisitions,* various years.

The largest 272 firms, each with assets of over $250 million, made 69 percent of all manufacturing profits in the first quarter of 1968.[23] Summarizing the growth of the 500 largest industrial corporations over the 1954–1974 period, *Fortune* magazine noted the following.

> In general, the 500's share of the industrial economy has been rising over the years. Their share of total industrial sales rose from around half in 1954 to around two thirds last year. Their share of earnings, which fell last year, is nevertheless up from two thirds to three quarters over the two decades. And while the 500's share of industry has risen in this period, the manufacturing and mining shares of total GNP have also been rising a bit in real terms (to a little over one quarter). There is no doubt, then, that the 500 largest industrials are a substantially greater chunk of the U.S. economy than they were when *Fortune* began compiling these lists [in 1954].[24]

By 1974 four firms or less accounted for 50 percent or more of total sales in nearly two thirds of all manufacturing.[25]

In purely competitive markets the output of each firm is such a small fraction of the total output that no single firm can affect market prices. In monopolistic markets the sales of a single firm are large enough to affect market supply and price. Since, in this setting, the action of each firm affects the profitability of all firms in the industry, monopolistic firms develop group pricing strategies. Conscious of their interdependence, monopolistic firms behave more as price makers than as price takers. Although direct evidence is understandably sparse on the pricing strategies of corporations, it is quite clear that independent firms follow price markup strategies: prices are set high enough to cover average industry costs plus a margin for profits. Any cost rises that are general to the industry, such as higher wages, energy, material, interest or tax payments, or higher unit costs caused by reduced production levels, will be passed on to consumers as higher prices.

It is also evident that prices rarely drop in monopolistic industries, even under conditions of slack demand; for all firms know that if one firm were to reduce prices, a price war might develop in which all firms would lose. Instead, products are withheld from the market. When demand is slack, monopoly firms would rather withhold some products to maintain a high price. Thus monopolistic firms characteristically maintain a margin of unused or excess productive capacity. The *planned* margin protects their market share if demand suddenly spurts up. The *unplanned* margin is generated by the vicissitudes of the business cycle.

According to this reasoning we should expect to find very different pricing responses to declining demand in monopolistic and competitive industries. Several recent empirical studies have corroborated this claim. One economist, studying the behavior of sixteen pairs of products, one of each in an oligopolistic and the other in a competitive industry, found a notable difference in the price responses to slack demand. During the two recessions of the 1950s, the price indices of every competitive industry fell, whereas in thirteen of sixteen of the concentrated industries the price index rose.[27] Another study found that in the September 1973 to September 1974 period of plummeting sales (excess capacity increased 25 percent, unemployment 23 percent) wholesale prices in "concentration dominated industries" *rose* 27 percent. In "competition dominated industries" the price rise was less than 5 percent.[28] Thus the increased concentration of American industry helps to explain the trend toward rising prices maintained since World War II, for during this era, initial periods of price inflation were not followed by periods of price deflation.

Notice the limited extent of our claim. The power of the monopolistic firm to administer prices does not give it sufficient power to set profit margins in all situations, nor is this new power alone the cause of economic instability. The capacity of monopolistic firms to raise prices in concert does not oblige consumers to purchase at the higher prices. Consumers may discontinue purchase of the product or, especially since the postwar reconstruction of the economies of Western Europe and Japan, purchase foreign products. Higher prices can reduce sales enough to reduce profits and thereby drive up unit costs.[29] As shown in Figure 5-5, recent history suggests a strong positive correlation between profits and variations in capacity utilization.[30]

Monopolistic pricing, then, has two effects: first, monopolistic firms introduce an upward bias in prices even during periods of slack demand. The upward pressure is accentuated by increased production costs, which, we argue later, have been rising because of the form assumed by corporate-state expansion in the post-World War II period.

Second, monopolistic price setting contributes to instability by hampering both market and government adjustments to changes in the conditions of supply and demand. When demand is slack

Figure 5-5 Profits and Capacity Utilization

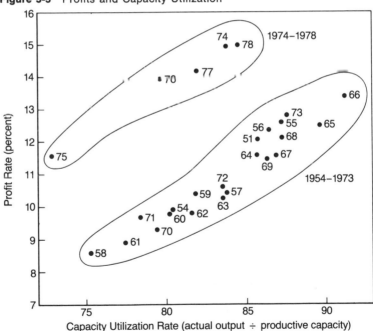

Source: Economic Report of the President, 1980, pp. 251 and 301.

and prices do not adjust downward (as they would under competitive conditions), this inflexibility can in fact intensify the downturn. For example, if the response of business to a slackening in demand is to build up inventories and lay off workers (instead of to reduce prices and thereby stimulate demand), then the downturn would be intensified by a reduction in spending power. Monopolistic price setting can also reduce the effectiveness of government deflationary policies. When the government reduces expenditures, imposes higher taxes, or increases interest rates, the monopolistic firm does not necessarily reduce prices. In fact, Arthur Okun estimated that when the government squeezes the economy into deep recession, "90 percent of the effect is lost output and jobs and only 10 percent is diminished inflation." [31] Under these conditions the anti-inflation measures of the New Economics can be counterproductive.

The monopolistic firm creates a climate in which prices do not fall when demand slackens and in which a gap between sales and productive capacity is maintained. However, if this were the whole story, inflation could be remedied simply by government price controls. The issue we must now turn to is, what has caused *costs* to rise?

■ Product Priorities and the Cost of Living

The evolution of American capitalism has not only increased the price-setting power of corporations. The economy has been politicized in other ways: corporations have become more strategic in establishing product priorities; government spending and regulation have increased; collective bargaining has modified the labor system; and the expansion of corporate debt has restricted government monetary and fiscal policy.

While the increased politicization did reduce the cyclical character of the competitive-market system, it created new irrationalities in each of the preceding areas as well. Inflation is one of the most important symptoms of these developments.

First, a rational production arrangement satisfies consumption needs while minimizing resource depletion. Second, it fulfills worker needs for tasks that are challenging and productive of useful goods. Third, it supports those social, cultural, and recreational relations that give meaning to life. Conflicts among these goals will always exist. For example, the consumption needs of two groups can be in conflict with each other or with the work needs of a third group. But some systems of production, investment, and consumption extend these conflicts, while other minimize them.

The political economy of corporate capitalism proliferates a mélange of goods and services, but such a system does not fare well in meeting the criteria of rational production. Irrationalities lodged inside the order drive up costs faced by individuals, firms, and the state, and these rising costs in turn expand the size of wage demands and tax bills. Since the participants are spending more and enjoying it less, they resist efforts to curtail consumption. They act privately and publicly to exacerbate inflation. The behavior that induces the inflationary spiral is not primarily the result of greed, irresponsibility, or irrationality on the part of individual citizens; it is rather the result of irrational imperatives within the economy. Four of these areas will be explored in terms of the relationships among:

1. private product priorities, increased costs of living, and inflation

2. warfare costs, increased taxes, and inflation

3. worker alienation, the decline in productivity, and inflation

4. increased debt, higher interest costs, and inflation

The first relationship is the focus of this section. The others are treated in each of the following three sections.

Under competitive capitalism, market pressures forced individual firms to reduce production costs. In the process, costs to capitalists in general were driven down as, for example, in the case of wheat. Between 1859 and 1884, wheat production increased from 173 to 468 million bushels; the price of a bushel of wheat was $1.24 in 1871, but by 1894 it sold for 49 cents.[32] By driving down the price of a crucial commodity, the firm drove down the wage level required by all workers. Automobiles provide a similar example in their early development. When the Model T was introduced in 1908, it sold for $1,000; by 1924 it cost $300.

In the politicized economy of today, corporations cannot simply force a product on consumers; a successful corporate strategy, however, can channel consumption toward the most privately profitable product. And the product that best serves corporate profitability might also be the one that produces the most indirect increases in total consumption costs. In Chapter 3 we examined product priorities in terms of environmental compatibility. Here we will consider the inflationary effects of these priorities.

In the 1970s and 1980s the system of production for private profit, bolstered by state priming and subsidies, has tied itself in knots. The central problem is no longer the size of investment but rather the irrationality of investment priorities. The system has channeled enormous amounts of labor, capital equipment, and scarce resources into irrational product forms in energy, transportation, military, and health, which together account for roughly 40 percent of the national product. As the social costs of a broad spectrum of irrational products accumulate, the investable surplus declines; upward pressure on prices and a slowdown in the growth of new productive capacity are generated. Today society is a prisoner of past investments; little is left over after the resource and capital equipment requirements of these corporate complexes are met.

Neither the free-market perspective nor the mixed-economy perspective addresses the issue of product irrationality.[34] Individual consumer dollar votes are assumed to guide, via the price mechanism, corporate allocation of labor, capital goods, and resources into the product lines that are collectively rational. Even where market failures are recognized, they are treated as exceptions that can be corrected by government taxes and subsidies to the *existing* product line. We are claiming that the structural roots of inflation are grounded as much in products and product irrationality as in prices and price-setting capacity. Consider three areas in which irrational product forms simultaneously enhance the pursuit of individual corporate profit making and inflate the cost of living.

Depletable resources and economic rents. When market demand increases, possible reactions are that: output will expand, prices will rise, or both. The market works best when output expands in response to increases in demand. Excess profits are then an ephemeral phenomenon—and the pursuit of private self-interest by capitalists leads, as if by an invisible hand, to the public interest in low prices and large output.[35] If, however, resources or goods are limited in supply, the output adjustment process becomes retarded. Output remains constant, and prices rise to curtail *effective* demand. Under such conditions the invisible hand no longer ensures a coincidence of the private and the public interest. Following Adam Smith, classical economists David Ricardo and Thomas Malthus worried, for instance, that the growing demand for food would not induce a proportionate expansion in supply because land was a finite resource. Instead, food prices would expand unearned income in the form of rent to landowners. With every increase in food demand, the proportion of national income going to the idle class of landowners would rise, squeezing both profits and wages.[36] Assuming that landlords spent much of their wealth on unproductive consumption, the economy would be starved of investment funds. It would stagnate.

For a century and a half, developments unanticipated by classical theorists kept these dire predictions from being realized. A combination of food production on foreign continents and technological developments in transportation and agriculture led to an expansion of food output. The tendency of land rents to rise was thereby contained. Unfortunately, the failure of this *particular* prediction to come true encouraged later generations of economists to ignore the development of processes similar to that articulated by Malthus and Ricardo. The problem of limited resources was ignored.

But concern over the distributional effects of depletable resources is returning with a vengeance in the case of oil. Many Western economists had faith that the energy price rises inspired by OPEC would be short-lived as substitute energy sources expanded energy supplies and pushed prices downward once again. Instead, as discussed in Chapter 3, oil is being rapidly depleted on a world scale. Oil has assumed the role that land played in classical economic theory. The share of the national income going to direct energy consumption has doubled to roughly 10 percent in the 1970s, and it will continue to rise in the future.[37]

To understand inflation, we must return to the classical problem of diminishing returns to finite resources. Once the highest-yield oil wells, for example, are pumped dry, it will take additional labor and machinery inputs to get the same output. Thus diminishing returns to finite resources increase the cost per unit of output. But, as shown in Figure 5-6, production costs are less than the market price on all but the most costly oil wells in production. The difference between the market price and the cost of producing a barrel of oil is an economic rent that accrues to the owners of the finite resource and is independent of productive effort. As resources are depleted and prices rise, a larger share of national income is thereby transferred to resource owners. Inflation results if either workers or capitalists attempt to push up wages or profits to maintain a constant share of national income in the face of the rising economic rents.

Unfortunately, it is not only oil that is in finite supply. World

Figure 5-6 Resource Depletion and Economic Rent

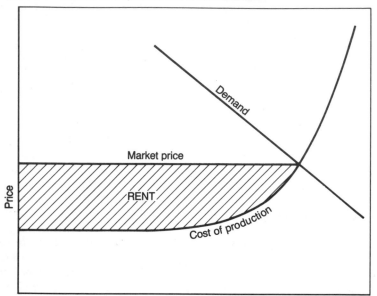

Barrels of Oil

wood production peaked in the mid-1960s, and this meant rising fuel costs to that one-third of humanity that relies on wood. The tripling of lumber costs in the United States since 1967 was a major factor in the 1970s explosion in house prices from an average of $30,000 to an average of nearly $70,000. Furthermore, there is mounting evidence that fish, beef, and cereal production all peaked in the 1960s and 1970s, and that diminishing returns are forcing up costs in these areas as well.[38] Finally, as we pointed out in Chapter 3, while oil-derivative petrochemicals earlier increased agricultural production, the current energy crisis has resulted not only in increased costs for farm inputs but in the conversion of farmland into production sites for the manufacture of alcohol to power automobiles. As shown in Table 5-3, an intensification of the worldwide food problem might result: a typical U.S. car would consume as much cropland and grain as nearly forty people living on a subsistence diet.

Each example illustrates our theme: the rising costs of depleted resources help support worldwide inflation. But resource pressures are themselves linked to institutional configurations. Capitalism, for example, requires growth: without growth, profits

TABLE 5-3   *Fuel versus Food*

	Grain (pounds)	Cropland (acres)
Subsistence diet	400	0.2
Affluent diet	1,600	0.9
Typical U.S. automobile* (10,000 miles/per year at 15 miles per gallon)	14,600	7.8

Source: Lester R. Brown, "Food or Fuel: New Competition for the World's Cropland" (Washington, D.C.: Worldwatch Institute, March 1980), p. 27. © Worldwatch Institute, 1980.

* Fuel use converted at 380 liters of alcohol per metric ton of grain.

decline, investments shrink, demand slackens, and stagnation deepens. Capitalism without growth is like a human without a heart. It stops breathing.

While the inflationary impact of depleted resources has been neglected by modern economics, it is less likely that corporate management has ignored the potential profitability of such resources. Corporate leadership can be expected to try to channel consumption to those depletable resources that bring the greatest promise of high corporate profits. In the 1950s and 1960s, energy industries, for example, were not interested in solar energy. The fact that solar energy can be renewed indefinitely and generated locally made it an unpromising resource for corporate control. But an entire economy organized around the use of a limited supply of oil was perfect for companies in control of this resource because of the higher prices that could be imposed on consumers.

Exclusive goods and market bias. A second form of market failure that leads to product irrationality and a rising cost of living is the bias of the market in favor of exclusive goods and against inclusive goods. Exclusive goods provide their highest value as long as they are reserved for a few. They diminish in value as consumption is made available to all. The automobile-based transportation system examined in Chapter 3 centers around an exclusive good. As long as cars were restricted to the middle class, the users could enjoy their benefits. But as cars became accessible to the working class, congestion, pollution, fuel scarcity, road construction and maintenance expenses, and urban sprawl have increased the costs to both consumers and the state. Technical education, designer clothing, private resorts, and suburban living all possess the characteristics of exclusive goods. Their private and social costs tend to increase as they are extended to more people, while their utility and aesthetic value to the earliest users decline.

An economy centering around the illusory goal of universalizing exclusive goods has built-in inflationary pressures, for the extension of *these* goods to more and more people increases both the costs of individual consumption and the expenditures imposed on the state. As the social infrastructure of consumption matures around the production of exclusive goods, the income needed to make ends meet constantly increases.

Inclusive goods, on the other hand, can be extended to all participants without decreasing utility or increasing costs for anyone. An electric rail-based transportation system approaches an inclusive transportation system. A health care system organized not around curative medicine and fees set by private physicians but rather around preventive health care and a salaried medical staff would convert health care from an exclusive to an inclusive good. It would reduce medical costs for all consumers and provide health care to all.

Exclusive goods, when broadly extended, increase consumption costs and generate demands for income increases that outstrip productivity gains. A rational anti-inflationary program would convert our transportation, energy, health care, and housing systems into forms that are more inclusive. It would emphasize durability over obsolescence, and resource conservation over resource waste. Emphasizing community goods and services, it would not only reduce inflationary pressures by curtailing private consumption *needs* but also promote the preconditions of democratic politics by bringing all citizens up to the level of economic well-being needed for participation with dignity in public life.

Commercialization of social relations. The conversion of barter exchange into market exchange greatly expanded the opportunities for mutually beneficial trade in goods and services. Whereas the standard barter relation was confined to two people, each holding goods desired by the other, monetary exchange in the market enlarged the range of participants to the whole community and beyond. A market price was established by a multitude of buyers and sellers, independently of the will of any single trader. The market price could be denoted in a standardized, tradable unit of account, such as money or labor.

But while the market relation has enhanced the exchange of goods and services, its extension into friendship, marriage, child rearing, and politics has impaired the quality of these relationships. These social relations are constituted by shared norms, such as respect, integrity, trust, dignity, duty, and obligation. The norms dissipate once these relations are incorporated into the market. The quality of human life itself deteriorates, and people begin to look for meaning in new areas.

To the extent that social relations have become commercialized, individuals must turn to the market to provide recreation, "homes" for the aged, hired services for the friendless, counseling for the troubled, child care for the young, and custodial service for the eccentric.

The commercialization of social relations thus increases consumption needs. Ironically, however, it can erode the social preconditions of market exchange relations as well. This erosion contributes to inflation by reducing the efficiency with which market transactions satisfy needs.

Consider, for example, the provision of health care. Providing health care involves a complex social interaction between patient and doctor that differs from the trading of material objects between a buyer and a seller. Trust is involved in both relationships. But sympathy and concern along with trust are essential ingredients for a healthy medical relationship. The patient feels cheated or manipulated if the relationship turns out to be purely commercial. This resentment is quite reasonable. Not only does the commercial relation encourage the doctor to lose sight of the whole patient, it seems that a return to health often is caused by the body's own curative mechanisms; and these mechanisms are often triggered by mind/body interactions in which the quality of the doctor/patient relationship is critical.[40] The commercialization of the market relation increases the costs of medical care and encourages litigation on the part of the resentful patient.

"It used to be that a doctor was a family friend," says an attorney. "But now doctors are more like businessmen, so they get treated like businessmen."[41] Since the market is a set of rules and regulations that are inherently open-ended and subject to dispute, it provides ample room for the expansion of litigation.

Change in the doctor/patient relation merely exemplifies a much more pervasive process. As relations between teacher and student, politician and citizen, employer and employee, and husband and wife have been increasingly commercialized, the United States has witnessed an unprecedented expansion in litigious activity. The number of attorneys jumped from 285,933 in 1960 to almost 460,000 in 1978—an increase from 1.6 to 2.1 lawyers per thousand citizens. Between 1963 and 1977 legal fees leaped from $2.1 billion to $9.3 billion.[42] The commercialization of social relations increases the costs of living by converting more and more aspects of social life into "services" that must be bought. And more often than not, the increase in price is matched by a decline in the value of the service performed.

Another service that has expanded in this way is auto repair and maintenance, which has climbed from $6.1 billion to $25.9 billion between 1963 and 1977.[43] And in 1979 a government study reported that over 50 percent of consumer dollars spent on car repair were for unneeded or falsified repairs. Here, too, to the extent that honesty is drained from the market, the costs to consumers can be expected to expand. The commercialization of social relations increases living expenses. It generates other effects as well that we shall examine later.

Putting the three forms of product irrationality together, we can see that the American economy is today being choked by the expansion of consumption imperatives. Consumers look more and more to the economic system for a habitat free from industrial noise and waste, to health services for relief from the ill effects of the unhealthy urban environment, and to education for the means to compete in modern labor markets. In addition, they must buy the clean air, bright sunlight, pure water, and open space that were free goods in an earlier era. Much consumption is involuntary. Those who are exposed to dangerous gases, chemicals, dust, and criminal assaults at work and play must compensate, however imperfectly, through increased expenditures for insurance, health care, environmental clean-up, and police protection. Each new consumer or public need in areas previously met by nature or by community life generates increased expenses without improving the real welfare of the recipients. It follows, then, that workers' wage demands are not tied simply to greed; *higher wages are needed to compensate for a deteriorating natural and social environment.*

In summary, products have two sides: a *use* value to the society and a *profit* value to the seller. The two values can diverge: public parks have a high use value and a low profit value; adulterated meats have a low use value and a high profit value. We have also noted a third side to each product: the profit value to *all firms,* which can diverge from the profit value for *one firm.*

That is, any single company takes into account the profitability of a particular product to that firm alone; it does not consider either the product's use value to society or the profitability to all firms taken together. We contend that our political economy has widened the gap between use values and profit values. Corporate owners, of course, do not see the roots of the problem. What they see is a growing wage and tax bill, squeezing profits. What they do in response is to raise prices. They think the source of the problem is the greediness of labor and the inefficiency of government. But they fail to understand that their own desire for profit feeds the very wage, tax, and cost pressures they must later respond to. And, unfortunately for monopolistic capital, the market adjustment mechanism that once drove down the price of wages by generating ever cheaper consumer products no longer operates effectively. It was a victim of the transition to the politicized economy.

Three implications follow. First, the intensification of worker demands for higher wages is less a greedy drive for affluence than a response to the structurally constrained context in which people must meet their needs for food, shelter, clothing, recreation, and education.

Second, profits are being squeezed, but the squeeze is not induced by falling prices in response to rising supply as predicted by the free-market perspective but by rising costs emanating from the irrationality of established product priorities.

A third implication is crucial for state policy: the split between production for profit and social needs that prevails in the 1980s is less responsive to government stabilization measures than the imbalance between production and consumption of the 1930s. The source of capital accumulation (profits from existing investments) is separated from the uses required for socially productive investment (products that satisfy social needs). In other words, *although the state can expand profits by stabilization policies, there is no assurance that the profits generated by stimulating the wasteful industrial complexes of the past will be transferred to the new socially productive areas.* For example, the state could increase profits in the automobile industry by stimulating demand; but if the profits were then transferred to investments in mass transit, it is likely that the capital used to produce cars would substantially depreciate. Hence, left to the market, it is unlikely that increased profits will solve the accumulation problems of the 1980s. The corporate system of production for profit must be displaced by a publicly controlled system of production for use.

■ Warfare Costs and Inflation

One form of government expenditure stands out as a powerful agent of inflation. In 1980 the world spent $450 billion on armaments, of which over half was spent by the Soviet Union and the United States. This sum exceeds the total income received by the poorest half of humanity. For comparison, development aid from rich to poor nations is about $20 billion. Reduction of militarism could free massive amounts of labor, resources, and capital equipment for the satisfaction of basic human needs.[46] Two powerful forces propelled militarism along in post-World War II America.

First, the United States emerged from the war as the leading power on one side of a world divided in struggle. No world power has ever existed that did not have a military to protect its foreign sources of raw materials, investments, and markets. The United States was no exception. In the 1920s, U.S. armed forces were stationed in only three countries abroad. During World War II the number grew to thirty-nine. By the mid-1960s the United States had over 2,900 military bases spread out over sixty-four countries. [45]

Second, domestic pressures were also important. The success of the New Economics in the post-World War II period rested heavily on armament expenditures. Government military spending provided markets for corporations and spurred economic growth without placing government enterprises in competition with private companies (socialized production) or flooding the market with consumer goods and thereby reducing prices. Furthermore, the military establishment protects the country abroad and helps to dampen opposition to corporate autonomy at home.

Out of the total federal purchases of $1.5 trillion between 1946 and 1971, $1.1 trillion was defense-related spending (including debt payments for previous wars, veteran benefits, space exploration, and the Atomic Energy Commission).[46] Without this spending (or equivalent spending in some other area that does not compete with corporate sales), unemployment rates in the postwar period would approximate those of the Great Depression. Thus in 1970 there were 2.9 million members of the armed forces, 1.2 million civilian employees in the Defense Department, and 3 million employees in defense industries. This total, over 7 million, includes only those directly dependent on military spending. If one assumes a multiplier effect of 1, a conservative estimate, another 7 million are indirectly dependent on military spending.[47]

If to these first two categories of military-dependent employees we add the 7.9 million unemployed in 1970, the total comes to 22.2 million workers, or about 26 percent of the labor force, a figure slightly higher than the highest level of unemployment during the Great Depression. Without extensive military expenditures, then, it is not clear that Keynesian policies would have dissolved the unemployment of the Great Depression or even maintained tolerable levels of employment in the 1960s.

The limits of militarism in international politics are illustrated by the Vietnam War, in which an estimated 1 million people died, and later by the collapse of the Shah of Iran, who had purchased U.S. armaments to build up the most expensive military establishment in the Mideast. Nevertheless, the buildup goes on. President Carter's defense blueprint called for spending $1.27 trillion over the 1981–1986 period. President Reagan is upping this total dramatically.[48]

A centerpiece of the new buildup is the MX system, the largest single construction project in human history, with an estimated cost running between $33 and $100 billion. The $1.5 billion research and development budget alone is more than the combined budgets of the U.S. Department of Labor, Department of Transportation, Environmental Protection Agency, and Food and Drug Administration.[49] If this money were used instead for increasing the training and productivity of laborers, for rapid transportation, for environmental improvement, or for improving human diets, it would reduce people's market needs and ease inflationary pressures.

The military-industrial complex is a peculiar industry in that it feeds off its foreign competitors. In both the United States and the Soviet Union, the industry has benefited from an interactive, dynamic process that has generated revenues to its corporate beneficiaries on a scale matched only by the energy and transportation industries. The fact that the United States has 1,000 strategic nuclear weapons, or enough to destroy several times over the 200 Soviet cities with a population of over 150,000, has not deterred the arms race. By 1979 the United States had 13,000 strategic nuclear weapons and more on the way. But the costs are also skyrocketing. A recent U.S. Government Accounting Office report captures both the magnitude of the costs to the taxpayers and the benefits to defense contractors.

> The cost problem facing the U.S. military is growing worse, and no relief is in sight. The so-called "bow wave" of future procurement

costs is growing beyond the point of reasonableness. Current procurement programs are estimated to total about $725 billion. If these costs are spread over the next ten years (a conservative projection) the annual average of $72.5 billion will be more than twice the current levels.[50]

Market economists focus on the inflationary effects of government budget deficits as if the *composition* of government expenditure were irrelevant. This focus obscures the inflationary aspects of military spending, the public spending item that is most exempt from the budget cuts of the defenders of the free market.

■ Work Organization, Productivity, and Wage Costs

A large part of the worsening of inflation last year . . . stemmed from poor productivity. Over the past decade or more, the rate of growth in our productivity has been slowing. In late 1977 and throughout 1978, the slowdown in productivity growth reached serious proportions.

President Jimmy Carter
January 1979

Table 5-4 compares the post-World War II growth rates of labor productivity (output per worker hour) with wages for the private business sector of the U.S. economy. While productivity data are notoriously imprecise,[51] these data illustrate the issue of concern expressed by President Carter: since the mid-1960s the rate of increase of labor productivity has dropped steadily, while wage rates have increased at an accelerated rate.

In 1979 productivity per worker actually declined by 2 percent.

TABLE 5-4   *Annual Increases in Productivity, Wages, and Per-Unit Labor Costs*

| | Average Annual Rates of Increase in: | | |
	(1) Productivity	(2) Wages	(3) = (2) − (1) Labor Costs per Unit of Output
1950–1954	3.6	6.6	2.9
1955–1959	2.8	4.8	2.0
1960–1964	3.4	4.3	0.9
1965–1969	2.5	6.1	3.6
1970–1974	1.3	7.5	6.2
1975–1979	1.2	8.9	7.5

Source: Economic Report of the President, 1980, p. 247.

In other words, a worker who had produced, say, 100 baseball bats in 1978 produced only 98 in 1979. If, in this example, prices stayed the same, the bat company revenues would also drop by 2 percent. But wage costs to the company did not decline; therefore, to cover the higher wage costs per bat, the company would have to accept lower profits or raise prices. If, for example, wages were 100 percent of costs, then the company would have to raise prices by 2 percent to cover costs.[52] In fact, wages in 1979 increased by over 9 percent, which meant that companies had to increase prices to cover both less output per worker hour and higher wages per worker hour.[53] Conversely, to the extent that productivity grows, companies can increase wages without increasing prices. For example, if the worker in the preceding example had produced 4 more bats in 1979, then the company could have transferred up to 4 percent in added sales revenue to the worker without any decline in profit margin.

Figure 5-7 shows the diverging movement of productivity and wages in the mid-1960s. This gap indicates the upward pressures on costs facing corporations. Since the monopoly corporation is able to pass these new costs along to the consumer in the form of higher prices, and since the government commonly validates these decisions by inflationary policies, this gap is an indicator of inflationary pressure transmitted from the workplace to the consumer.

Economists within a variety of theoretical traditions agree that much of recent inflation has been cost-push—the push coming to a large degree from worker wage demands. By their own admission, what they have not been able to explain is the secular downturn in labor productivity. As President Carter put it, "The reasons . . . are complex and not fully understood." It is not that labor productivity has gone uninvestigated. A series of recent studies has sought links between declining productivity and research funding and between increased government regulation and declining private investment. They have failed to account for the dramatic drop.[54]

Why, then, have worker demands been so great during this period? And why has productivity grown so slowly? A large part of the answer to the first question has already been given in terms of the structural imperatives of consumption. We think that two other factors are of critical importance.

First, as we saw in Chapter 4, workers are increasingly dissatisfied with the dangerous, unhealthy, uninteresting, authoritarian, repetitive conditions of work to which they are subjected.

Figure 5-7 Changes in Output per Worker and Wages in Private Business Sector, 1948–1979

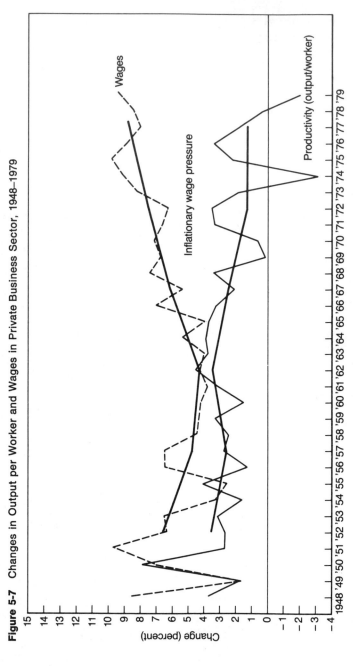

Source: Economic Report of the President, 1980, p. 247; the −2.0 productivity figure for 1979 was revised from the published −1.0 as originally reported.

This disaffection, not easily converted into effective pressure for work reform in our system of political economy, may be translated into other areas where the worker can apply some leverage. It is no doubt translated, first, into higher rates of absenteeism and turnover, wildcat strikes, product sabotage, declining quality controls, and malingering on the job. Second, it intensifies demands for higher wages, the worker trying to make up during leisure time for the drudgery of work time. These two pressures together contribute to lower productivity and higher wages, enhancing inflationary tendencies. Corporate elites would rather acquiesce in these inflationary pressures—which they can then blame on government—than in the need for work reform itself. To accept meaningful reform in the structure of work would weaken owner control over workers and the work process, creating leverage for more basic incursions into corporate prerogatives at a later date. Until the organization of work and the social utility of its products are public issues of paramount importance, it is likely that worker resentment will vent itself in higher wage demands and reduced work effort. Once again, the priorities of corporate capitalism generate grievances for workers (and consumers and citizens) while channeling their demands into public areas that protect corporate dominance, deepen inflationary pressures, and eventually weaken public support for liberal government policies.

A second contributor to the decrease in productivity per worker is hidden from the mainstream view as well: the proliferation of workers not engaged in the actual production of goods. The modern army requires a backup staff of approximately ten persons to each individual on the battlefield, and the modern capitalist enterprise supports an army of staff workers who surround every production worker. Harry Braverman describes the proliferation of nonproduction tasks:

> Sales, previously handled chiefly by the owner himself, perhaps assisted by a clerk who doubled as traveler, became the function of a marketing division, subdivided into sections to handle sales traveling, correspondence with customers, salesmen, and manufacturers, order processing, commissions, sales analyses, advertising, promotion, publicity. A separate financial office takes care of financial statements, borrowing, extending credit, ensuring collections, assessing and regulating cashflow, etc. And so on for other office divisions, among which the most important is an administration office where corporate policy is made and enforced upon all divisions.[55]

Braverman also emphasizes the link between, on the one hand, the erosion of skills and trust in the workplace, and, on the other, the development of large surveillance staffs to prevent employee malingering, waste and pilferage of materials, misuse of machinery, and sabotage of quality.

Parallel to the proliferation of nonproduction tasks within the modern corporation has been the explosion of service tasks in private enterprises, such as insurance, finance, real estate, and wholesale and retail trade operations. Productivity gains are notoriously difficult to attain in these areas. As shown in Table 5-5, between 1950 and 1979 employment in goods-producing industry expanded only 5.3 million and dropped nearly 20 percentiles in total employment, while employment in private services expanded to 25.5 million, or nearly five times as much.

Evidently fewer and fewer people engaged in goods production are supplying the needs of more and more people. We can now interpret Figure 5-7 in a different light. Declining productivity of labor is partly a measure of increasing worker alienation and partly a measure of a shift in the predominant kind of employment from manufacturing to surveillance, sales, clerical, and other service-oriented fields. Clearly, these two factors do not exhaust the source of declining productivity, although they do illuminate inflationary tendencies in the politicized economy obscured by other analyses. Furthermore, they point to a strategy to reduce these inflationary pressures, based on a reallocation of labor—first, toward intrinsically rewarding work and away from deskilled, monotonous tasks; second, toward the production of useful goods

TABLE 5-5 *Employment by Sector*

	Total	Goods-Producing Industries [a]	Service Industries [b]	Government [c]
1950	52,357	29,700 (56.7)	16,631 (31.8)	6,026 (11.5)
1960	59,647	29,896 (50.1)	21,398 (35.9)	8,385 (14.1)
1970	74,342	31,555 (42.4)	30,233 (40.7)	12,554 (16.9)
1979	92,794	35,030 (37.8)	42,151 (45.4)	15,613 (16.8)

Source: Economic Report of the President, 1980, pp. 234 and 242.

[a] Includes manufacturing, mining, construction, transportation, public utilities, and all employment in agriculture.

[b] Includes wholesale and retail trade, finance, insurance, real estate, and other private services.

[c] Includes federal, state, and local governments.

and away from socially unnecessary services such as those provided by monitoring, advertising, and private insurance agencies. The latter areas cannot be eliminated, of course, but their rate of growth could be curtailed in an economy that speaks more fully to the employment and consumption needs of its citizens.

■ From the Financial Cycle to the Debt Economy

Corporations finance investments through profits and loans. Historically, one factor that has limited economic growth has been the tendency of corporate debt expansion to raise the price of credit. Debt is driven down again in the ensuing recession as weak firms go bankrupt or merge with stronger competitors.

The Great Depression and the postwar boom were not exceptions to this historic pattern. As shown in Table 5-6, between 1933 and 1939 total private debt dropped from 229.2 percent of GNP to 136.9 percent; in the heavily regulated wartime economy, it dropped to 65.9 percent. As a consequence, by the mid-1940s the financial markets were literally bulging with loaning capacity, providing an ideal condition for a new expansionary boom.

TABLE 5-6   *Debt and the Business Cycle, 1929–1979*

	Corporate Debt ÷ Nonfinancial Corporate Product (percent)	Consumer Debt ÷ Disposable Personal Income (percent)	Residential Mortgage ÷ Disposable Personal Income (percent)	Total Private Debt ÷ Gross National Product (percent)	Total Government Debt ÷ Gross National Product (percent)
1929	177.4	8.6	37.9	156.5	29.1
1933	315.5	8.6	57.9	229.2	72.8
1939	168.2	10.3	31.3	136.9	65.0
1945	89.5	3.8	16.3	65.9	125.2
1950	93.5	12.5	26.9	86.1	83.8
1955	97.5	16.6	37.5	98.2	68.5
1960	109.2	18.6	46.5	111.9	61.3
1965	115.9	21.6	54.6	127.7	54.3
1970	142.2	20.9	52.2	142.2	49.3
1975	147.2	20.6	54.4	149.2	48.9
1979	132.5	23.1	58.0	145.3	51.9

Source: Various tables and issues from *Economic Report of the President, 1980.*

The postwar boom was fueled, in part, by a doubling in private debt in the following twenty years. As shown in Figures 5-8 and 5-9, corporate debt and residential mortgage debt led the way, while government debt declined steadily as a proportion of both total debt and GNP.

According to the pattern of previous cycles, a downturn should have occurred after such a sustained economic expansion. The resulting downturn would serve a restorative function, preparing the economy for a new period of growth by driving down private debt and interest rates and restoring the liquidity of financial markets.

Figure 5-8 Composition of Debt, 1945–1979

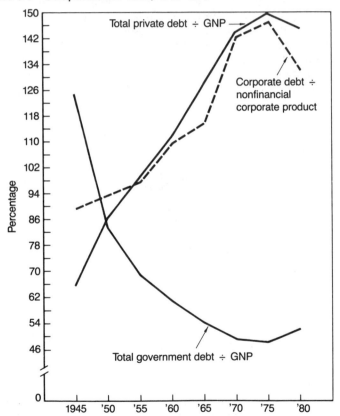

Source: Table 5-6.

But the period of 1965 to 1970 did not follow this pattern. Not only did corporations continue to borrow heavily, extending corporate debt from 116 to 142 percent of nonfinancial corporate product, but the same financial markets were also called on to help finance a war too unpopular to be paid for by higher taxes.

Between 1968 and 1973, borrowers went to the financial markets to expand overall debt at an annual rate of $133.5 billion (corrected for inflation), which was twice the annual rate during the preceding fifteen-year period.

The debt spending sustained an economic boom until financial markets were once again extended to the limit. When economic

Figure 5-9 Private Debt as Percent of Disposable Income, 1945–1979

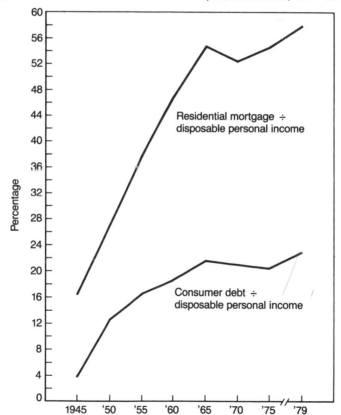

Source: Table 5-6.

growth did slacken between 1969 and 1971, corporations found themselves in a squeeze between declining profits (see Figure 5-10) and the costs of financing a bloated debt structure. At the same time, interest charges were at a historic high level. Hard times struck fast and cut deeply.

The money squeeze of 1969–1970 found many firms hard pressed to cover their debt costs. In the words of Tilford Gaines, vice-president and economist of the Manufacturers Hanover Trust Company, "Short-term liabilities of business have sky-rocketed in recent years while quick cash assets have been steady to declining"; and in a disturbingly large number of companies across a band of industries, "survival questions have arisen." Months later Arthur Burns, chairman of the Federal Reserve Board, stated, "In permitting such a drastic decline in liquidity, many of our corporations openly courted trouble." Reviewing the period, the report of the Joint Economic Committee on the *Economic Report of the President, 1972,* notes, "The liquidity bind ... in 1970 brought many to the edge of bankruptcy." [56] But the commentary of *Business Week* expressed the most urgent tone over the emerging "debt economy": "The Fed and the White House, petrified by both inflation and recession, seem unable to avoid swinging first this way and then that way; the dangers are greater than in the 1930s. ... Never had the Debt Economy seemed so vulnerable." [57]

An old contradiction was reasserting itself: capitalism needs healthy financial markets in order to grow, yet capitalist growth tends to undermine healthy financial markets. The traditional remedy—recession-induced bankruptcy and reorganization of the financially weak—could not be afforded. It would threaten the survival of corporations that had come to dominate the American economy, and the collapse of those units would throw the entire economy into a depression.

The options facing the government were severely restricted.

TABLE 5-7 *Average Annual Additions to Debt in 1972 Prices (Billions of Dollars)*

1952–1967	65.5
1968–1973	133.5
1974–1979	193.3

Source: Monthly Review, November 1979. Copyright © 1979 by Monthly Review Inc. Reprinted by permission of Monthly Review Press.

Figure 5-10 Estimated Post-Tax Profit Rates for All Nonfinancial Corporations, 1947–1979

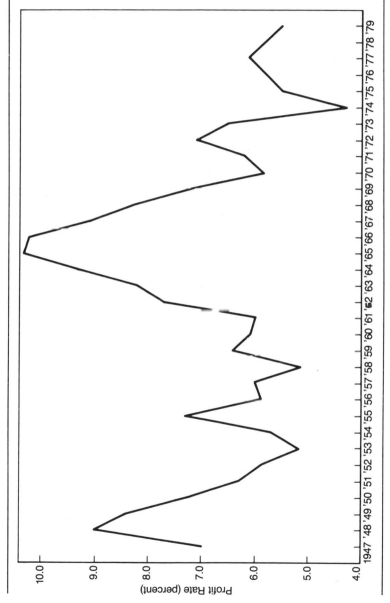

Profit Rate (percent)

1947 '48 '49 '50 '51 '52 '53 '54 '55 '56 '57 '58 '59 '60 '61 '62 '63 '64 '65 '66 '67 '68 '69 '70 '71 '72 '73 '74 '75 '76 '77 '78 '79

Source: Years 1947–1978 are from Daniel M. Holland and Stewart C. Myers, "Profitability and Capital Costs for Manufacturing Corporations and All Nonfinancial Corporations," *American Economic Review,* May 1980, p. 321. Year 1979 is from *Business Week,* August 15, 1980.

Faced with the possible bankruptcy of large firms that were crucial to the performance of the entire economy, the government had to increase their liquidity by expanding available credit. As *Business Week* (January 27, 1975) put it: "The huge U.S. corporations have become such important centers of jobs and incomes that it [the government] dare not let one of them shut down or go out of business. It is compelled, therefore, to shape national policy in terms of protecting the great corporations instead of letting the economy make deflationary adjustments."

The following quote from Arthur Burns describes the Fed's reactions to the major bankruptcy that did occur, that of Penn Central:

> By Monday, June 22 [1970]—the first business day following announcement of the bankruptcy petition—the Federal Reserve had already taken the virtually unprecedented step of advising the larger banks across the country that the discount window would be available to help the banks meet unusual borrowing requirements of firms that could not roll over the maturing commercial paper. . . . As a result of these prompt actions, a sigh of relief passed through the financial and business communities, . . . the financial community was assured that the Federal Reserve understood the seriousness of the situation and that it would stand ready to use its intellectual and financial resources, as well as its instruments of monetary policy; to assist the financial markets through any period of stress.[58]

Thus, to avert a deepening liquidity crisis, the "Fed" moved in to replenish the supply of money in the financial markets. The corporate liquidity crisis was relieved by pumping up the money supply, but the response created the conditions for a new round of inflationary expansion. And in the ensuing boom, corporate price increases, validated by the supply of new money, jumped upward to double-digit rates.

Surging inflation ushered in a sudden reversal of government policy. In the early 1970s antiinflationary policies (increasing the rate of unemployment to reduce demand) were enacted to guide the economy downward. Not only did the liquidity problems quickly reappear, but this time they were worse. The precarious financial situation had by now spread to the banking system. As profits dropped (see Figure 5-10) and the stock market declined, corporations extended their borrowings from the banking system. The banks met the demands, but in the process the liquidity position of the large commercial banks nose-dived; liquid assets divided by deposits, which had been 54.0 percent in 1950, dropped from 22.3 percent in 1965 to 13.6 percent in 1974.[59] The Fed poured over $1 billion into an unsuccessful effort to save the fourteenth largest bank in the country, Franklin National.[60] Obviously, the struggle against inflation was here forced to yield to more fundamental purposes of the government: to finance the Southeast Asian war and to maintain the viability of giant corporations caught in a liquidity squeeze.

While the 1974–1975 downturn was the sharpest since the Great Depression, it did not restore the financial markets as sustained downturns had in the past. The Fed did reassure the financial community by playing the role of the lender of last resort. But it also created the conditions for yet a new round of debt expansion. This time, not only did corporate debt continue to grow, but consumer, residential mortgage, and government debt all took off. During the 1973–1978 period, average annual borrowings, in constant dollars, climbed to $193.5 billion, roughly three times the 1952–1967 rate (see Table 5-7). The prime rate of interest was driven to 20 percent, the highest level in American history.

In the new debt economy, debt and prices are intertwined. Even when consumers are hopelessly strapped in debt, they keep on spending for fear that prices will be even higher in the future. As interest charges mount on corporate debt, they are forwarded to the consumer in higher prices that in turn elicit new rounds of higher interest rates. In this way, debt, interest costs, and prices tend to chase each other upward. While estimates of the actual increase in debt-carrying costs are not available for the corporate sector, interest costs of the federal debt, which is between a third and a half of corporate debt, increased sixfold between 1965 and 1980, from $10.4 billion or 1.5 percent of GNP to $63.3 billion or 2.7 percent of GNP.[61]

Furthermore, the high level of interest rates to which corporations are committed is itself a barrier to policies that reduce inflation. Corporate investors have in effect become speculators in currency, and they are counting on the value of the dollar to continue dropping. If it does not, they will be saddled with a debt load that will greatly increase their real borrowing costs.

Government policymakers are now walking a tightrope. If they do succeed in breaking the inflationary cycle, they run the risk of bankrupting key business enterprises; if they do not succeed, they risk a further debt buildup. To avoid either depression or hyperinflation, the government has been forced to intervene. In recent years it has guaranteed loans to Lockheed and Chrysler and protected the investors who otherwise would have lost after the bankruptcy of the Penn Central. Because the options of the government are so narrow and its public responsibilities so broad, it becomes a handy scapegoat for those who would explain our economic malaise. William Simon, the secretary of the treasury under presidents Nixon and Ford, reflects this tendency:

> There have been many causes for inflation, but, in my opinion, the biggest single factor has been a prolonged period of large government deficits, including the off-budget landing and the loan guarantee programs.[62]

While we agree that the government has contributed to inflation, Figures 5-8 and 5-9 make clear that until 1975 government debt was steadily declining as a percentage of GNP, while private debt was growing sharply. To imply that inflation can be stopped merely by ending government deficits is to misrepresent the events of recent history; worse, it is to express a willingness to force those stuck at the bottom of the system to pay the price for correcting irrationalities lodged in the systems of production, consumption, work, and investment prevailing in modern America.

■ The Closing Cycle

Underlying the shift from an unemployment-inflation cycle to periodic eruptions of stagflation is the fundamental tendency toward instability in the politicized economy. This tendency, though, is not endemic to industrial society as such. A system organized around production for use rather than production for profit would not necessarily oscillate in these ways. It could reduce the *costs of production* and the *social costs flowing from the productive system* by creating a public transportation system that reduces energy use and pollution emissions. It could develop more efficient forms of energy production, improve the ratio of collective goods to private consumer goods, produce durable housing, provide jobs for all citizens willing to work, and control inflation. Addressing the structural sources of instability, it could distribute the burdens and benefits of industrial society more evenly across the population and through time.

The historical tendency toward instability in corporate capitalism is experienced by common people as a recurrent struggle for security. Just as this tendency finds various expressions— first as inflation then as unemployment; once as liquidity squeeze, now as stagflation—the struggle for security itself assumes various modes among different sectors of the population. The young, especially blacks and working-class whites, find themselves frozen out of a production system that does not need their services. Old people, public sector workers, and unorganized workers in the market sector struggle to make ends meet as inflation outruns income gains. Mothers in working-class families seek second jobs at marginal pay, stretching the family income to meet growing food, clothing, utility, and tax bills. Middle-aged white-collar workers, straining to meet skyrocketing expenses in higher education so that their children will have a chance for good jobs, find themselves in conflict with young people who threaten the job security so recently and precariously won. And those on the very margin of society—the sick, the mentally ill, the prisoners, the disabled, the welfare recipients—find public resources shifted away from them and toward corporate needs.

While social tensions simmer, the business cycle, modestly responsive to fiscal and monetary fine tuning during the early 1960s, has acquired a new immunity to the old inoculations. And for good reason. Unattuned to the inner connections among corporate concentration, economic inequality, the irrationality of corporate product priorities, debt accumulation, the deadening structure of work, and the bloated growth of the warfare-welfare state, the New Economists are thereby unprepared as the consequences of these structural tendencies penetrate into the unemployment-inflation cycle itself. They are the last to learn the painful lesson: fine tuning will not fix a machine in need of an overhaul.[68]

NOTES

1. All official unemployment data are from *Economic Report of the President* (Washington, D.C.: Government Printing Office, 1980). Data on the number and lengths of recessions are from Maurice Flamant and Jeanne Singer-Kerel, *Modern Economic Crises and Recessions* (New York: Harper and Row, 1970).

2. Bertram Gross and Stanley Moss estimate that real unemployment for 1971 was 24.6 percent of the labor force. They include 5 million housewives (1 of 7) and 4 million people between the ages of 55 and 64 (1 of 2) who have been "pushed out" of the labor force. See "Real Unemployment Is Much Higher Than They Say," in *Public Service Employment: An Analysis of Its History, Problems and Prospects,* edited by Alan Gartner et al. (New York: Praeger, 1973), pp. 30–36.

3. Harry Magdoff and Paul Sweezy, "Capitalism and Unemployment," *Monthly Review* (June 1975), pp. 1–14. Magdoff and Sweezy add,

"And it should be stressed that the 13.6 percent is still an understatement, due to the conservative nature of assumptions we made."

4. The estimate of three times is based on data in *Manpower Report of the President* (Washington, D.C.: Government Printing Office, 1975), pp. 274–276, cited in Magdoff and Sweezy.

5. Douglas F. Dowd, *The Twisted Dream: Capitalist Development in the United States Since 1776* (Cambridge, Mass.: Winthrop, 1974), p. 161.

6. All the following extracts are from Studs Terkel, *Hard Times: An Oral History of the Great Depression* (Pantheon Books, 1970). Copyright © 1970 by Studs Terkel. Reprinted by permission of Pantheon Books, a division of Random House, Inc., and Penguin Books, Ltd.

7. The effects of a minimum wage imposed by either a labor union or the government are shown in the accompanying diagram. Assume an equilibrium wage and employment situation at W_e and E_e and a minimum wage set (either by a labor union or government) at W_i (wage with intervention). Below W_i the new supply of labor will no longer be determined by the free choice of labor (the original labor supply curve) but will instead run along the minimum wage line until it reaches the original labor supply curve at the minimum wage level. The wage with intervention will be higher but at the expense of a loss of jobs for $E_e - E_i$ workers. In fact, at the prevailing wage, W_i, those willing to work but unable to find a job are indicated by the gap between the demand and original supply of labor at the minimum wage rate, W_i.

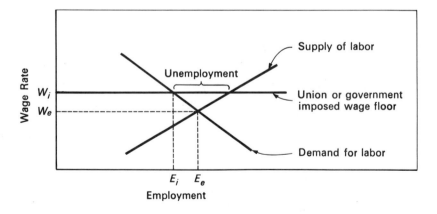

8. *The General Theory of Employment, Interest, and Money* (New York: Harcourt, Brace and World, 1936).

9. Ibid., p. 348.

10. Since income earned from machines is received in future years, it must be discounted by the rate of interest to find the present value. Therefore, a drop in the interest rate increases the present value of future income earned from capital goods.

11. Ibid., p. 348, for the Keynes quote. The dog analogy is by James E. Meade in *Essays on John Maynard Keynes,* edited by Milo Keynes (New York: Cambridge University Press, 1975), cited in a review of same by Robert Lekachman in *Challenge* (September–October 1975), p. 63.

    Put differently, the free-market perspective, based on free choice and price adjustments, stresses a line of causation that begins with personal savings (individual choice to consume in the future rather than the present). For instance, a rise in savings will lead to an equal increase in investment via an interest rate adjustment. The resultant increase in capital will increase the levels of worker productivity and income. The Keynesian perspective, focusing on effective demand and employment adjustments, reverses the line of causation. Investment is the primary force. An expansion in investment operates via a multiplied expansion in employment to expand the level of income until sufficient savings are generated to match the higher level of investment. Thus, whereas in the free-market perspective savings create investment and a lack of savings signifies a higher interest rate and more current consumption, in the Keynesian perspective investment creates savings and a lack of investment leads to unemployment and less consumption.

12. The successful tax cut of 1964, the major achievement of the New Economists, is amply described by two chairmen of the Council of Economic Advisors in the 1960s: Arthur M. Okun, *The Political Economy of Prosperity* (New York: W. W. Norton, 1970), and Walter W. Heller, *New Dimensions of Political Economy* (New York: W. W. Norton, 1967). The data in the text are from Heller, p. 114.

13. Heller, pp. 58 and 105. He goes on to predict a growth rate in GNP of between 4 and 4½ percent for the decade of the 1970s.

14. *Business Week,* February 5, 1966, p. 125. Cited in Heller, p. 3.

15. "What's Right with Economists," *American Economic Review* (March 1975), p. 8.

16. (Princeton, N.J.: Princeton University Press, 1974). Tobin, past president of the American Economics Association and member of the Council of Economic Advisors, remains optimistic about employment and growth: "Active monetary and fiscal policies, dedicated to economic ends and liberated from extraneous taboos, can keep the economy growing within a narrow band of full employment. Not again, I trust, will this hope, along with so many other national aspirations, be betrayed by a Vietnam." But Tobin ducks the inflation issue: "I have certainly not done justice to the subject of inflation in this book. As a consolation, I can only offer my opinion that inflation is greatly exaggerated as a social evil."

17. Milton Friedman, "The Inflationary Fed," *Newsweek,* August 27, 1973, p. 27, and *Congressional Record—Senate,* December 22, 1969, S 17529. Friedman notes a correlation between rising prices and growth in the money supply but fails to prove which comes first or to provide a convincing mechanism by which money supply increase gets converted into higher prices as opposed to expanded output. For a critique of the monetarists, including Friedman, see Tobin, *The New Economics: One Decade Older.*

18. Ralph L. Nelson, *Merger Movements in American Industry, 1895–1956* (Princeton, N.J.: Princeton University Press, 1959). Cited in William N. Leonard, *Business Size, Market Power and Public Policy* (New York: Crowell, 1969).

19. For details about business concentration during this period, see G. Warren Nutter, *The Extent of Enterprise Monopoly in the United States* (Chicago: University of Chicago Press, 1951).

20. The sale of stocks does not mean that ownership is widely diversified. Various estimates conclude that 1–2 percent of the population owns about three-fourths of all corporate stocks and bonds, although the figures are complicated by the emergence of huge bank and insurance trust funds. See Robert J. Lampman, *The Share of Top Wealth-Holders in National Wealth, 1922–1956* (Princeton, N.J.: Princeton University Press, 1962); J. Smith and S. Franklin, "Concentration of Personal Wealth, 1922–69," *American Economic Review* (May 1974), p. 166; and Ch. 3 of this text, "Inequality, the American Way."

21. For an analysis of barriers to entry and other industrial organization topics, see William G. Shepherd, *Market Power and Economic Welfare* (New York: Random House, 1970). In an examination of concentration and pricing power, Willard F. Mueller documents examples of huge price reductions following the breakup of price conspiracies: *A Primer in Monopoly and Competition* (New York: Random House, 1970), especially Ch. 6. A *Business Week* article, "Price-Fixing: Crackdown under Way" (June 2, 1975), suggests that price fixing is widespread and that it pays.

22. Data on mergers are from Mueller.

23. Datum for 1909 is from Mueller, p. 69, and for 1968 from *Studies by the Staff of the Cabinet Committee on Price Stability* (Washington, D.C. Government Printing Office, 1969).

24. Linda Grant Martin, "The 500: A Report on Two Decades," *Fortune* (May 1975), p. 241.

25. Shepherd, Table 7.1, p. 106.

26. Ibid., p. 185.

27. John M. Blair, "Administered Prices—A Phenomenon in Search of a Theory," *American Economic Review* (May 1958), pp. 431–450.

28. Gardner Means, cited in *Consumer Reports* (June 1975), p. 380.

29. In a number of industries prices do not respond to shifts in demand as predicted by conventional economic theory of the firm. Prices

are instead determined by markups over wage and material costs, the amount of the markup and profit being a function of the degree of monopoly that the firm exercises. For example, the prices of autos, steel, aluminum, appliances, and electrical equipment all rose during recessions of the 1950s and 1970s as the enterprises pursued a target rate of return over costs. For a theoretical treatment of pricing behavior under monopoly, see Paulo Sylos-Labini, *Oligopoly and Technical Progress* (Cambridge, Mass.: Harvard University Press, 1962), and Joan Robinson and John Eatwell, *An Introduction to Modern Economics* (New York: McGraw-Hill, 1973). For examples of industries that seek target rates of return as opposed to maximum short-term profits, see Leonard, *Business Size, Market Power and Public Policy*. Leonard estimates that "perhaps . . . one-third of the rise of all consumer prices in the 1950s resulted from price policies of the steel oligopoly." In the 1970s examples of prices rising in the face of declining demand abound. Aluminum sales, for example, dropped by 7 percent in 1974 over 1973, yet profits stayed up as prices rose nearly 33 percent. Furthermore, prices have stayed up in the first quarter of 1975 even though sales dropped 40 percent! Robert Lindsey, "Aluminum Keeps the Price Up," *New York Times,* June 8, 1975, p. 1.

The limits of the connection between the ability to set prices and the ability to set profit margins need more attention. The terms of relation between the corporate sector and the market sector of the economy may be pertinent here, as well as the relations between the state sector and the corporate sector. For example, price increases in the corporate sector may put a squeeze on market firms, thereby placing general economic expansion in peril. And government manipulation of the money supply might aim at expansion sufficient to keep large corporations afloat during a period of liquidity squeeze but insufficient to validate huge price increases. These and other possible connections need to be investigated more thoroughly.

30. For further analysis of the cyclical relations between profits and capacity utilization, see Paul A. Baran and Paul M. Sweezy, *Monopoly Capital* (New York: Monthly Review Press, 1966), Ch. 4.

31. *New York Times,* April 14, 1980, p. D4.

32. Dowd, p. 156. Wheat is not an isolated example. The wholesale price index for all commodities fell from 135 in 1872 to 69 in 1896.

33. Paul M. Sweezy, "Cars and Cities," *Monthly Review* (April 1973), p. 6.

34. The free-market perspective and the mixed-economy perspective sidestep the issue of product irrationality with the presupposition of Adam Smith's invisible hand. Formalized by modern welfare economics, the invisible hand claims that for a *given* distribution of income, free markets will lead to an optimal allocation of resources in that no other allocation is possible where at least one

person would be better off and no one worse off. The vacuousness of this optimality criterion, referred to as *pareto optimality,* is recognized by application-oriented economists who have introduced derivative criteria such as *income*-compensation tests whereby the potential financial gains of beneficiaries of alternative social standing are compared with the potential financial losses to losers. But even here, market failures are recognized as exceptions to the optimum allocatory characteristics of markets, and the issue of product rationality remains a nonissue.

35. For a discussion of the invisible hand, see Samuelson, *Economics,* Ch. 3.

36. Employing additional laborers to increasingly less productive lands leads to declining labor productivity, as illustrated by the declining curve in the accompanying diagram. At point Q_1, for example, profits would be a sizable proportion of national income. But as land of decreasing productivity was cultivated, the rental price would be driven up on all the intramarginal units. And assuming, as the classical economists did, that wages were fixed at subsistence, then profits would be squeezed as less and less productive land was brought into cultivation, until eventually, at point Q_2, profits would be zero and all the surplus over wages would be going to landlords. See Samuelson, *Economics,* Ch. 27, for an analysis of the theory behind this diagram.

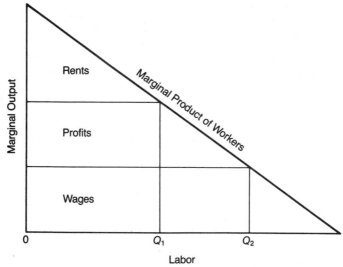

37. Including indirect energy consumption brings the total to 9.9 percent of before-tax income. See Lester Thurow, *The Zero-Sum Society* (New York: Basic Books, 1980), p. 30.

38. For data on resource depletion, see Robert Fuller, "Inflation: The

Rising Cost of Living on a Small Planet," Worldwatch Institute, Washington, D.C.; Task Force on Global Resources and the Environment, U.S. State Department and Council on Environmental Quality (Washington, D.C.: Government Printing Office, 1980); and Barnet, *The Lean Years.*

39. Alexander Cockburn and James Ridgeway, "Who Runs the Economy?" *Rolling Stone,* May 15, 1980, p. 40, and Howard S. Berliner, "Emerging Ideologies in Medicine," *The Review of Radical Political Economics* (Spring 1977), p. 121.

40. For a survey of two recent studies of the links between the doctor/patient relation and the natural power of the organism to control disease, see David Sobel, "Placebo Studies Are Not Just 'All in Your Mind,' " *New York Times,* January 6, 1980. See also Norman Cousins, *Anatomy of an Illness* (New York: W. W. Norton, 1979).

41. Cited in Roger Smith, "Service Costs Spiral, Alter Life-Style in U.S.," *Boston Globe,* December 20, 1978, p. 16.

42. Ibid., p. 16.

43. Ibid.

44. Data on spending for armaments and development aid are from *North-South: A Programme for Survival,* Report of the Independent Commission on International Development Issues under the Chairmanship of Willy Brandt (London: Pan Books, 1980), p. 117.

45. Harry Magdoff, *The Age of Imperialism* (New York: Monthly Review, 1969), p. 42.

46. Dowd, p. 105, and James L. Clayton, *The Economic Impact of the Cold War* (New York: Harcourt, Brace and World, 1970), pp. 51–54. Purchases do not include benefit payments to individuals or grants to state and local governments, since such spending does not directly use up resources by government agencies.

47. Data and multiplier estimate from Magdoff and Sweezy, pp. 1–14.

48. James Chace, "Insolvent America," *New York Review of Books,* April 2, 1981, p. 23.

49. Emma Rothschild, "The American Arms Boom," in E. P. Thompson and Dan Smith, eds., *Protest and Survive* (London: Penguin Books, 1980), p. 171.

50. *Impediments to Reducing the Costs of Weapons Systems,* Report to the Congress of the United States by the Comptroller General, PSAD–80–6, November 1980.

51. *Economic Report of the President* (Washington, D.C.: Government Printing Office, 1979), p. 6.

52. For a discussion as to why, see Paul Sweezy and Harry Magdoff, "The Uses and Abuses of Measuring Productivity," *Monthly Review* (June 1980).

53. If wages were 50 percent of costs and all other costs stayed constant, the company would still have to raise prices by 1 percent to cover a drop in productivity of 2 percent. In this case the decline in output would also cut material costs by 1 percent.

54. For one such study, see Edward F. Denison, "The Puzzling Drop in Productivity," *The Brookings Bulletin* (Fall, 1978), pp. 10–12.
55. *Labor and Monopoly Capital* (New York: Monthly Review Press, 1974), pp. 299–300.
56. Gaines quote from *New York Times,* May 3, 1970; Burns quote from *New York Times,* December 8, 1970.
57. *Business Week,* January 27, 1975, p. 123.
58. *New York Times,* December 8, 1970.
59. Harry Magdoff and Paul M. Sweezy, "Banks Skating on Thin Ice," *Monthly Review* (February 1975), p. 12.
60. "Are the Banks Overextended?" *Business Week* (September 21, 1974), p. 54. See also Hyman Minsky, "Financial Resources in a Fragile Financial Environment," *Challenge* (July–August 1975), for an analysis of why banks have become increasingly fragile and for connections between debt and prices that are similar to those in our analysis.
61. *Economic Report of the President* (Washington, D.C.: Government Printing Office, 1972 and 1980), pp. 270 and 285, respectively.
62. Statement before the House Ways and Means Committee, Washington, D.C., January 22, 1975, cited in *Department of Treasury News,* WS-200, p. 5.
63. We do not, of course, think that the analogy between an economic system and a machine is perfect. It traps the mind into a quest for simple, discrete variables, each with an independent, quantifiable effect. But the term *fine tuning* was introduced by the New Economists themselves, implying a machine that is basically in good repair.

THE CRISIS OF THE STATE

■ The Symptoms and the Illness

A state and a government are not the same thing.[1] Two countries could have the same form of government (for instance, a presidential system or parliamentary system, a democracy or republic) but differ in the form of the state. England and the United States, for instance, both have democratic governments in the narrow sense that the public officials in each are selected through competitive elections, but England has a more developed welfare state. To speak of government is to refer to the institutions through which public decisions are made, the rules that govern the decision makers, the way officials are selected and replaced, and so on. The state includes the government, but it also refers to the range of institutions and practices that are incorporated into public life. The sphere of the state is the sphere of public authority and power.

A public university is not part of the government in the United States, but it is part of the state. In some societies religion is part of the state, whereas in others, such as the United States, religious life remains in the private sphere. Most important for our purposes, some states fully incorporate economic institutions while others primarily enforce contracts, leaving most other aspects of the economy to the private sector.

States differ in the areas brought under public control and in the ways the areas are incorporated. A *laissez-faire* state minimizes the public role in economic transactions and maximizes the private. Economic transactions are left in the hands of private proprietors; the state merely enforces contracts, apprehends and punishes criminals, controls the legitimate means of military and police violence, and perhaps guarantees the protection of certain civil liberties. The *positive* (or *welfare*) *state* expands the public role in economic transactions. While leaving the ownership of productive enterprises primarily in the private sphere, it assumes some responsibility for promoting broad economic objectives such as full employment and low inflation; supports capitalist production by public expenditures for highways, military, airports, research, education of technicians and the like; tries (with varying degrees of seriousness) to meet social needs unmet by the system of private production through programs such as health insurance, public housing, job training, social security, unemployment insurance, and relief payments; and sometimes acquires ownership of economic units (such as railroads or utilities) that are essential to the economic system but not (or no longer) profitable to private owners. The *socialist state* owns the crucial productive enterprises, and as we use the term, it also places high priority on reducing economic inequality among its citizens and on promoting public, collective products and services (mass-transit systems, public education, parks, health-care units) over the private, individualized products more typical of private enterprise. Democratic socialism, as we construe it, is a socialist state in which, first, the major public institutions, including government and corporations, are subject to public participation and accountability and, second, in which the sharp distinctions between people who do mental and executive work and others who do only mindless work are significantly narrowed. It is fair to say that while only a few welfare states approximate the ideals embodied in their justifying rhetorics (for instance, Sweden, but not the United States), no contemporary socialist state approximates the ideal of democratic socialism. With respect to the welfare state and the socialist state, we can ask, can the stated ideals of each be promoted adequately, given the *legitimate means* available to the state in each system? Are the ideals themselves justified? Having answered the second question earlier with respect to corporate capitalism through our exploration of work life and inequality, we will now pay special attention to the first. Our primary attention will be focused on the welfare state in the United States, which given its crucial military and economic role in the "free world" and the distinctive way in which it has developed the institution of corporate capitalism, is not completely comparable to welfare states in other capitalist societies.[2] It is only if these questions are answered negatively with respect to the welfare state that the corollary questions about democratic socialism assume a similar importance.

The positive state, or the welfare state, as we will call it in accordance with conventional usage in the United States, can be understood only within the larger context of corporate capitalism. Given the *public responsibilities* assumed by the welfare state and the narrow range of *ideological debate* prevailing in the United States between liberals and business conservatives, the structural defects and dislocations of corporate capitalism are widely if misleadingly interpreted as defects in the welfare state itself. The legitimacy of the welfare state is indeed being questioned, because of many recent crises, but the crises are not wholly of its own making. It suffers from the fact that it is publicly accountable for the performance of the economy while its resources for coping with that performance are severely limited. Corporate owners, meanwhile, pursue policies that affect the life chances of citizens without being held publicly accountable for the outcomes. Behind the symptoms of welfare state malaise lies the illness of corporate capitalism; the medicine used to treat the symptoms exacerbates the illness and further undermines public support for the welfare state.

The politics of the welfare state, which is a politics of *interest protection* for owners and privileged beneficiaries of the means of production, is, in many ways, a politics of *interest displacement* for the working class and the underclass.

Since production and profit taking are concentrated in the private sphere and public problem solving and accountability in the state, the public issues that are defined do not squarely address the injuries that are done. This is the politics of displacement. The welfare state responds to these displaced pressures within the limits legitimately available to it. Thus, especially during good times, it deflates the pressures through public programs that give private owners incentive to invest while introducing marginal forms of security (social security, unemployment insurance, jobs in the military) for those not included in the expansionary drive. Or, especially during hard times, drawing on repressive elements like the police, the prisons, and the military, it intimidates, isolates, and controls those with grievances while cutting back or stabilizing public welfare programs in the name of fiscal responsibility. Both responses swell the size of the public sector in nonproductive areas, thereby limiting the future options of the welfare state when the next wave of displaced pressures emerge. The welfare state in this way contributes to its own loss of legitimacy. Behind the ineffectiveness of government programs, worker resentment of welfare recipients, heightened racial tensions, declining constituency support for the liberal ideology of the New Deal and the Great Society, and the crisis of legitimacy for the welfare state itself lie fundamental irrationalities in the relation between the economy and the state required by the political economy of corporate capitalism.

If the symptoms continue to be construed widely as the illness itself, an authoritarian reaction to the binds of corporate capitalism may emerge. Those teetering on the edge of insecurity will support repressive control against those already pushed over the edge in the hope that they can thus avoid the plunge themselves. But if the deeper dimensions of contemporary dislocations and malaise receive a wider airing, one preliminary condition for the transition from the welfare state to the democratic socialist state will be secured. That, in summary form, is our thesis. Its underpinnings will now be elaborated.

■ The Paralyzed Economy

A *structural constraint* occurs when of two desirable outcomes, *X* and *Y,* neither can be promoted without limiting the attainment of the other. Sometimes it is possible, as Keynesians showed in the early 1960s with respect to high employment and low inflation, to promote through public policy a tradeoff situation so that each is promoted to some degree but neither so completely that it undermines attainment of the other. A *structural contradiction* occurs when different aspects of established practices collide in such a way that both *X* and *Y* suffer, sometimes so thoroughly that actions designed to promote one undermine both. A *bind* occurs when people in their roles as citizens, consumers, and workers are trapped by constraints and contradictions beyond their control. They can find no viable way out. A bind is the human dimension of structural constraints and contradictions. Often the pleas and demands that binds generate lead to policies that exacerbate the underlying dislocations. But sometimes, if more rarely, emerging awareness of the structural source of troubles generates support for needed institutional changes. The American political economy is beset by structural constraints, some of which increasingly approach the level of contradictions. Its citizens, but especially members of its subordinate classes, are increasingly trapped in binds. These pressures fuel the crisis of the welfare state.

1. The business cycle, once assuming the form of a structural constraint in which the government could choose either low inflation or low unemployment but not both, has acquired new dimensions. Capitalism needs healthy financial markets to grow, but capitalist growth undermines healthy financial markets. Capitalism needs profits to grow, but capitalist growth squeezes profits. It is necessary for government to maintain the liquidity of large corporations even when their debt is overextended and their profit margins are squeezed, but the deflationary tools formerly available to it in times of inflation (for instance, slowdown in the expansion of money, an increase in interest rates) cannot now be so freely used. These deflationary tools would further undermine corporate liquidity. This, combined with other factors discussed in Chapter 5, contributes to a merging of inflation and high unemployment in corporate capitalism and to a progressive weakening of government tools. From the vantage point of the breadwinner, the struggle for security is now fought on several fronts at once: inflation, increased federal, state, and local taxes, and increased job insecurity.

2. The private transportation complex—made up of automobile, oil, trucking, highway construction, steel, tire, and glass companies—provided much of the momentum for corporate expansion and economic growth from the 1920s to the early part of the 1960s. But today the glutted market for cars can no longer grow substantially; the energy waste, air pollution, and urban deterioration flowing from widespread dependence on cars, trucks, and highways has dampened public enthusiasm for the established transportation system. But the private corporations involved, with massive investments in the old system, cannot easily afford to convert to bus and mass-transit production. That would require

a lot of new investment without the assurance of the former huge markets. It would even threaten to undermine what is left of the old market. The established production system, built on rapid product turnover, indefinitely expanding markets, and yearly style changes, retains too large a contemporary market to justify its dismantling, too small a market to promote the earlier rates of economic growth. The automobile-industrial complex, controlled by the imperatives of private profit, is caught in a bind: it can neither retool nor flourish in its present form. Its new circumstances, reminiscent of the situation facing the British steel industry at the turn of the century, symbolize some of the differences between a developing corporate economy in the first decades of the twentieth century and the mature corporate economy of the 1970s. But more than mere symbolism is involved. Since the automobile-industrial complex employs such a large portion of the labor force, its moribund status contributes decisively to the malaise of the whole economy. In the present system one fears that expanded military production is the easiest way to take up the slack.

3. The corporate system of production (expanding as it must) has steadily undermined the family as a *unit of production,* because *household* provision of clothing, equipment repair, gardening for food, care of the elderly, health care, recreation, and child care has given way increasingly to *corporate* production of those goods and services. The family costs of plugging into the established social system have therefore escalated. Corporate services, originally introduced to serve the needs of an affluent minority, tend eventually to become necessities for all citizens. The result is a decline in the family's ability to provide security and other social needs, an increase in wage demands, and an expansion of subsidies from the state. These in turn increase corporate costs of production in labor and taxes, and the corporation with a multinational capacity is encouraged to invest funds or move operations abroad to escape these cost pressures. The final result may be to increase the threat of unemployment for many at the same time that consumption needs have expanded and private protections against insecurity have contracted.[3]

4. Individual mobility, idealized through the myth of equal opportunity, is essential to the political economy of corporate capitalism. Since the unplanned economic system develops unevenly—allowing some geographic areas to flourish while others languish, expanding the need for some occupations and skills while rendering others economically useless—it must have a labor

force ready and willing ("free") to move when and where the system dictates. But the high rate of mobility, and its historical flow from the countryside to the city, undermines the integrity of extended kinship ties, neighborhoods, and large communities. The family, no longer a *productive unit* and now also less viable as a *social unit,* becomes primarily a *child-rearing* unit. The social ties that bind the individual to larger collectives are weakened. Women, isolated in the home, move into the labor market, accentuating the tendencies toward unemployment already present in the system. Women join blacks in the competition for scarce jobs, sometimes deepening class conflict as some middle-class white families have two breadwinners while some lower-class black families have none. Within the established context, the rational and liberal thing to press for would be state policies that encourage growth and expand job opportunities available in the corporate sector. The uneven development of employment opportunities further contribute to the breakdown of established social units without creating functional alternatives.[4]

5. A reduction in economic inequality, which is an important precondition for resolving collective problems generated by corporate capitalism, cannot proceed very far as long as corporate capitalism itself prevails. Capitalist growth depends on the rich to provide the savings necessary for capital accumulation. Moreover, the system needs the threat of unemployment for workers in the most menial jobs and the incentive of relatively high pay for those in jobs of greater responsibility. Inequality is necessary to keep people at work in the unfulfilling jobs available in corporate capitalism; it contributes to the control of the work force. The absence of opportunities to reduce inequality shifts political pressure to the faulty ideal of equal *opportunity* in a system of extensive inequality of *result.* Thus not only are urgent collective needs such as environmental control rendered less attainable by inequality but displaced pressures for equal opportunity foster social atomization.

6. It is in the *collective interest* of the owners of capital to reduce environmental degradation. Otherwise the natural support systems necessary to production will deteriorate, increasing costs of production and making some forms of production impossible. But *individual firms* find it unprofitable to introduce the needed controls unilaterally, while the collective reforms that are workable would require extensive revision of the system of corporate capitalism itself. Corporate capitalism requires economic growth to sustain investment and to fill new consumer needs created by

the side effects of established practices, but a viable environmental policy probably requires a reallocation of resources and a slowing of cumulative growth. Similarly, a favorable setting for environmental reform could be promoted through a reduction in inequality, reform in the structure of work, and policies that encourage the growth of stable communities, but each of these changes is at odds with the established tendencies of corporate capitalism.

7. A reconstitution of work life might help to dampen wage demands in the corporate sector, increase worker productivity, and create one of the conditions for viable democratic participation in other areas of society. Some of these possible effects, indeed, encouraged liberal managers to flirt with modest proposals for work reform in the 1960s. But meaningful work reform would involve workers in decision making, intruding on the private pursuit of profits; it would provide the worker with skills indispensable to the production process, thereby increasing collective worker leverage in labor negotiations and strikes. Work reform, needed to promote some objectives of corporate capitalism, is incompatible with others. Within the framework of this system, then, we must expect a cycle of modest experiments and idealism followed by managerial "realism" and disenchantment with work reform.

8. An increasing number of young people, educated at universities, seek careers consonant with their intellectual development and social needs. But capitalism encourages authoritarian work relations and routinized work processes even at relatively high levels of the occupational system. The supply of aspirants outstrips the supply of good jobs. Since many of these young people know from the experience of their parents that influence is not sufficient to promote the good life, their incentive to compete and work under the prevailing conditions is weakened. The goals of young people are increasingly at odds with the imperatives of the system; and while many "adjust" to these imperatives, the fund of good will and civility that previously tied the middle class to the system is depleted.

9. Though all American citizens require a defense establishment to provide security, we do not all need a warfare state. The warfare state is required to protect the corporate empire abroad and to create demand for corporate products without undermining corporate control of the work force. But world reaction to the warfare state now threatens universal destruction or the return to universal barbarism. The United States sells massive

amounts of military equipment abroad to offset a balance-of-payments problem, increasing the likelihood of war.[5] It exports nuclear technology as part of its policy to reduce the need of other countries for Arab oil and because it is profitable to do so. But a nuclear power plant creates a capacity for nuclear weapons, and the proliferation of nuclear weapons greatly increases the chances for secret attacks against the imperial power itself. The Maginot Line approach to nuclear deterrence becomes increasingly futile, while the size of our deterrent force requires other countries to expand their own. These tendencies, partly rooted in the anarchy of international politics in a changing international economic system, are not the unilateral responsibility of the United States. But because the United States is the leader of the capitalist world, its policies exacerbate the underlying dangers. The warfare state generates new forms of insecurity. The United States cannot long survive with it, but its system of corporate capitalism seems unable to live without it.

10. The United States became a major imperial power early in the twentieth century and the major imperial state in the West after World War II. But its political economy of growth has produced a reversal in that historic course: its *dependence* on essential resources to fuel economic growth has converted it today into a pitiful giant that must deploy massive forces to maintain a steady supply of resources from countries that are increasingly hostile to it and its demands. The dependence on foreign resources flows from the depletion of internal resources and the continuation of the growth imperative. The state must maintain a huge military and intelligence operation to ensure the flow of these resources into the economy today, but its interventionist policies threaten to curtail future supplies. The resource dependence of the political economy of productivity accentuates the likelihood of a nuclear war that will destroy that economy.

As these constraints accumulate, and some come near to being contradictions, the political economy of corporate capitalism approaches a condition of paralysis. Each effort to remedy one problem within the limits allowed by the prevailing system threatens to magnify a dislocation somewhere else. The resulting binds are manifested in the deterioration of the family, the near-collapse of cities, the decay of the natural environment, the continuing struggle by workers for economic security, and the increasing number of citizens classified as welfare recipients. Politically these binds are reflected in the expansion of tax rates, in the decline in utility of state services, in the deadly growth of the warfare-welfare state, in the explosive emotions attaching to symbolic issues such as "law and order," busing, affirmative action, welfare fraud, abortion, and in the general erosion in public support for liberal ideology. The paralyzed economy brings with it doubts about the performance and legitimacy of the welfare state.

■ The Welfare State

The welfare state, as the legitimate agency through which collective problems are supposed to be resolved by public means, is the recipient of pressures generated by the corporate sector. It is held responsible for resolving these problems, but the limited tools legitimately available to it ensure that each attempted solution will be only partly successful in the short run while tending to create new limits to viable state action in the future.

Though the term *welfare state* reflects a liberal commitment to public policies that enhance the material welfare of the working class and underclass by redistributing income from the rich to the poor, in fact the bias of the welfare state moves in a different direction. Its actual priorities fit the following pattern:

1. Because corporate production is social and worldwide in nature, it requires massive support from the state in the form of investments and subsidies to support its activities.
2. Because corporate production is mobilized in the interests of private profit, it generates costly side effects that the state must cope with in some way.
3. Because companies in the market sector are caught in a competitive squeeze and disadvantaged through terms of trade with companies in the corporate sector, the state is also called upon to provide them with subsidies and protection.
4. Workers in the corporate sector, marginal employees in the market sector, and other various outcasts, victimized by social atomization, low supply of jobs, and high costs of living, call upon the state to help them. The public responses to these pleas give the welfare state its name, while accounting for only a small part of its activities.

Spending by all levels of government (see Table 6-1) reflects the impressive expansion of the welfare state during the twentieth century. Total expenditures were $2 billion in 1902 and $680 billion by 1977. They moved from less than 8 percent of GNP in

TABLE 6-1   *Spending by All Levels of Government, 1902–1978*

Year	Billions of Dollars	Percent of GNP
1902	1.7	7.7
1913	3.2	8.2
1922	9.3	12.5
1929	10.3	10.0
1934	12.9	19.8
1939	17.6	19.4
1944	103.0	49.1
1949	59.1	23.0
1955	111.0	29.1
1965	206.0	29.1
1974	478.0	35.1
1977	680.0	38.1

Source: Data for 1902, 1913, and 1922 are from Thomas A. Dye, *Understanding Public Policy* (Englewood Cliffs, N.J.: Prentice-Hall, 1972), p. 186. 1929–1949 data are calculated from tables in *Economic Report of the President,* 1971 and 1975. 1955–1977 statistics are taken from *Statistical Abstract of the United States,* 1979, p. 283.

1902 to over 38 percent by 1977. To understand the *distributional* impact of these state expenditures, we shall move from a consideration of those that primarily and directly benefit corporate owners, professionals, managers, and technical workers to those that primarily and directly distribute the benefits to the disabled, the poor, the unemployed, and dependent children.

Military expenditures promote profits for a range of private corporations. They generate research findings available to corporations, provide civilian jobs for highly trained technicians (a large percentage of engineers, physicists, airplane mechanics, and computer technicians are employed in the defense economy), and offer protection for corporate investments in foreign countries. The expenditures also offer employment for working-class soldiers who otherwise might be unemployed. Expenditures for military and international affairs totaled $105 billion in 1977, constituting 24 percent of the federal budget and 15 percent of all governmental spending.[6] This figure does not include space, energy, and technology expenditures indirectly linked to the military, government interest payments tied to earlier military activities (which primarily benefit the holders of interest-bearing notes), or veterans' benefits.

Expenditures for education composed 16 percent of all governmental expenditures (hereafter called AGE), with 4 percent going to public higher education and 11 percent going to local schools. The expenditures for higher education subsidize the education of children from middle- and upper-income families. Since all workers are taxed to support higher education, and since a significantly smaller proportion of low-income children attend college (see Table 6-2), low-income taxpayers subsidize higher-income taxpayers in this case. The largest proportion of jobs in education is provided to middle- and upper-middle-income professionals.

Government expenditures for highways (3.4 percent AGE), air and water terminals (0.8 percent AGE), retirement of government employees (2.8 percent AGE), interest on government debt (6.6 percent AGE), and capital outlays not otherwise listed (approximately 6 percent AGE), when viewed from the perspective of their distributional consequences, tend to benefit corporate interests and middle- to high-income families more than the marginally employed, the unemployed, the disabled, the mentally ill, or dependent children. The poor and the disabled do not often use interstate highways, airways, and waterways for vacations, business, or recreation; they do not buy interest-bearing notes from the government; they receive neither profits from government capital outlays nor many of the jobs created by them; they are not highly represented in the pool of retired government employees.

Consider farm-subsidy programs. They go primarily to the wealthiest farmers, the richest 20 percent receiving about 60 percent of the benefits and the poorest 60 percent receiving about 10 percent.[7] Or consider expenditures for police activity, up from less than $2 billion in 1960 to nearly $12 billion in 1978 (or 1.7 percent AGE). These expenditures provide the greatest security for middle- and upper-income groups and for corporations, since these constituencies have the most to be protected. They also provide employment for members of the working class, and some degree of protection for the poor.

Even the social security system, while indispensable to many of the elderly, is not very class-redistributive in its effects. Funded out of payments made by those working, it represents a redistribution across generations. The social security system, endangered by the inflationary spirals of the last decade, amounted to $103 billion in 1977, or 15 percent of all governmental expenditures.

Programs that form the core of welfare payments include old-age assistance, aid to families with dependent children, aid to the blind and disabled, food-stamp programs, general-relief payments, and Medicaid. Together they totaled $50 billion in 1977, or only 7.3 percent of all governmental expenditures. Even in this area, a large percentage of the expenditures goes to administrative salaries and overhead rather than to welfare recipients directly. Unemployment compensation adds 2.2 percent to those expenditures that are redistributive in effect. These welfare and unemployment payments are concentrated in the major cities, where approximately one out of every seven or eight residents receives welfare; among blacks, who make up a large proportion of the underclass; and among disabled individuals distributed more broadly throughout the population. The programs are maintained at low enough levels to ensure that little competition will exist between the benefit levels and the lowest-paying jobs available. There is a fair amount of evasion and misrepresentation by recipients, but it is reasonable to suppose that the total cost of this fraudulence to the state is less than the cost in graft, payback schemes, and bribery between corporate contractors and government officials at all levels of government. And certainly the need and resentment of those pushed to the margins of the system of productivity provide a better excuse for such evasions than the greed and ambition of those at the top.

Another way to look at the welfare portion of the welfare state is to consider the proportion of gross national product that goes to public welfare of all sorts. In 1978, as Table 6-2 shows, the United States spent 15.7 percent of its gross *domestic* product (roughly, GNP minus earnings abroad) on public welfare. This figure includes all public expenditures for education, health care, and income maintenance, with social security, unemployment compensation, aid to dependent children, food stamps, and all direct payments for relief and disability included within the latter category. The United States ranked fifteenth among the eighteen states covered in the study, which included all the advanced capitalist states in the world today.

Among the four states that ranked below the United States in this study, one—Japan—has a highly developed welfare and pension program lodged inside its private corporate system. The three others—Australia, Greece, and New Zealand—have a larger proportion of their populations engaged in nonindustrial work.

Whether we consider the *distributional effects* of all public expenditures or the *comparative proportion* of gross domestic prod-

TABLE 6-2   *Public Welfare Expenditure in OECD Area, Mid-Seventies (Percent of GNP in Current Prices)*

	Education	Income Maintenance	Health	Total Welfare
Australia	3.8	4.0	5.0	12.8
Austria	4.0	15.3	3.7	23.0
Belgium	4.9	14.1	4.2	23.2
Canada	6.5	7.3	5.1	18.9
Denmark	7.0	9.9	6.5	23.4
Finland	5.6	9.9	5.5	21.0
France	3.2	12.4	5.3	20.9
Germany	3.0	12.4	5.2	20.6
Greece	2.3	7.1	2.3	11.7
Ireland	4.9	6.4	5.4	16.7
Italy	4.0	10.4	5.2	19.6
Japan	2.6	2.8	3.5	8.9
Netherlands	5.9	19.1	5.1	29.1
New Zealand	4.4	6.5	4.2	15.1
Norway	4.9	9.8	5.3	20.0
Sweden	5.9	9.3	6.7	21.9
United Kingdom	4.4	7.7	4.6	16.7
United States	5.3	7.4	3.0	15.7

Source: *OECD Studies in Resource Allocation: Public Expenditure Trends,* no. 5 (June 1978), p. 25.

uct spent on public welfare, it is clear that the United States does not have a highly developed welfare state. Its distribution of public expenditures is biased toward the higher circles, and its rate of welfare expenditures is comparatively low. And yet the welfare state is today blamed by many for a series of pervasive ills afflicting the country: inflation, the decline in worker motivation, high taxes, the deterioration of the family, low productivity, and urban deterioration. We must ask, why is the American welfare state held responsible for so many ills in the American system of productivity? What share of the responsibility is properly attributed to it?

■ The Bind of the Welfare State

The state, as the legitimate forum of public accountability, is looked to for redress and assistance when people are threatened by inflation, unemployment, toxic wastes, crime, urban decay, isolation in old age, or discriminatory practices. But the parameters within which the state can legitimately act severely impair its ability today to deal effectively with these issues. It cannot respond effectively to the troubles of those most in need of its assistance. As its programs have proliferated, as it has become bloated in size, as its demand for taxes has accelerated, it has become the visible target for grievances and hostilities actually rooted in the priorities and imperatives of the system of private productivity. It is expected to respond effectively to the troubles and grievances of those to whom it is accountable, but its most visible programs seldom reach the end pursued and often create rancor among working Americans asked to pay for them. This situation is fraught with danger for democratic politics: we must examine it more closely.

As the state has come to play an increasingly important role in the economy, subsidizing corporations and providing secondary support to those cast out of the corporate system, the number and variety of public sector employees have increased. James O'Connor, the political economist who has explored most thoroughly the impact of state sector employment on the economy, summarizes these changes.

> The United States federal government employs about 2.5 million civilian workers in eighty departments and agencies and nearly 4 million in the armed forces, and total state and local government employment is roughly 8.5 million... In addition to the 11 million workers employed directly by the state, there are countless wage and salary earners—perhaps as many as 25 to 30 million—who are employed by private capital dependent in whole or in part on state contracts and facilities.[8]

By 1978 the total number of employees directly employed by the state at all levels had increased to over 15 million, and the public payroll had reached $16.5 billion.[9]

As James O'Connor has shown, however, the very size and composition of the public sector set limits to state policy options. While public sector employees strive to match the income levels of workers with similar training and responsibilities in the corporate sector, the nature of social work, teaching, policework, research, and regulatory activities makes it much more difficult to achieve equivalent productivity gains in these areas. Thus the continual expansion of public sector salaries contributes to inflation, while the refusal to match private sector salary levels would drain the public sector of competent workers.[10]

The logic of our political economy promotes this uneven development between the private and public sectors. Activities that are profitable and amenable to productivity increases are kept in the private sector. Those that are not themselves profitable but that are needed either to promote the preconditions of profit creation or to alleviate its adverse social effects or to support people closed out of the system of private productivity are shifted to the public sector. The state, now the recipient of the assignments the private sector cannot or will not handle, naturally looks inefficient, bloated, and incompetent in carrying those assignments out. The logic of this assignment distribution sets the state up to be the scapegoat for high inflation, high taxes, low rates of productivity, high levels of welfare, and the expansion of the state bureaucratic apparatus. The *visible* source of these evils is the state, while the *invisible* source is the political process that shifts the social costs and burdens of the system of productivity to the state and then limits its ability to respond to them effectively.

The modern welfare state is thus perfectly situated to be the object of public resentment and disaffection. It is large, ineffective, and expensive, and, most important, it is the one institution that is accountable to the public through elections. The public accountability of the state and the lack of accountability of the corporate sector combine to encourage public belief that failure in state policies *must* be responsible for the country's ills. If the state were not thought to be responsible, if it were not thought the election of more competent officials could turn things around, then the electorate would have to conclude that it does not live in a democratic society. The wish to view the state as responsible thus reflects the wish to construe ourselves as free citizens in a free state. And the state can be seen as responsible only if its current failures are perceived not as the result of the irrational relation between it and the privately incorporated economy but as the unnecessary product of incompetence in high places. If the latter conclusion is accepted, then the obvious answer is to leave the order intact and to elect more competent officials the next time around. But the wish to shift all the blame to the state in order to preserve the belief in the state's democratic accountability works today to weaken the hold of democratic institutions. It fosters a *politics of displacement* that deepens the burdens and hostilities facing the state.

The politics of displacement emerges to fill the gap between the state's general *accountability* to the electorate and its limited *resources.* Disaffected constituencies redefine grievances until they fall within the orbit of state competence; state responses then increase the size of the welfare state, often without alleviating significantly the burdens that called them into being. Thus victims of spiraling inflation, unable to curb the expensive style changes, shoddy products, manufacturing priorities, and price markups in the corporate sector, demand cuts in school budgets and welfare expenditures to ease those sources of high taxes and inflation that are subject to some degree of voter control. Unemployed workers, unable to hold corporate owners responsible, press the state to subsidize new jobs in the private sector or to expand unemployment compensation. Blacks and whites, men and women, unable to expand the supply of respectable jobs in the corporate sector, collide over symptomatic issues of affirmative action. Commuters, breathing toxic fumes in daily traffic jams, accept the privately profitable but socially destructive system of auto transport while demanding new public highways to ease the worst congestion. In each case, the grievances are redefined until they fall within the range of actions legitimately available to the state in the system of private productivity.

The public orientation to inflation exemplifies this process nicely. The roots of inflation, as we have seen, are the irrational product priorities of the corporate system, the expensive social infrastructure of consumption, the emptiness of established modes of work, the erosion of meaningful community life, and the expansion of state military, regulatory, and welfare expenditures. But the state cannot respond effectively to most of these causes *without reconstituting the organization and priorities of the economic system.* And that would involve a struggle with some of the most powerful interests in America. Most Americans take this background set of practices and priorities for granted and contend that the state could reduce inflation significantly if only it would reduce its expenditures. Thus while a majority of Americans are critical of business greed and corruption, only 15 percent in 1978 held business primarily responsible for the high rates of inflation during the seventies. Twenty percent held labor primarily responsible, and over 50 percent held government policies and high expenditures primarily responsible for inflation.[11] A majority of respondents believe that government spending and environmental policies hold down growth, that government regulation impedes the performance of the economy, that the federal government is too large, and that high taxes are a prime source of economic weakness.[12]

Each of these beliefs allows people to conclude that the economy and democracy would flourish together today if only the state would reduce its role in the economy.

The public commitment to democracy, we have argued, encourages many constituencies to define their grievances to fall within the orbit of policy options available to the state. But as we have argued in this text, social and economic malaise is more deeply anchored in the modes of consumption, work, and profit that prevail in our order. The future of American democracy thus turns not on the state's subordination to corporate desires for high profit margins but on its ability to redefine the priorities of the economy and break out of the bind in which it is caught. To elaborate this alternative understanding more closely, we will examine the "voluntarist" and "structuralist" conceptions of the state, the erosion of liberalism, and the new business proposals to "reindustrialize" America.

■ Voluntarist and Structuralist Theories of the State

Are the binds and limits facing the welfare state generated by inept state policies within a political economy that is otherwise healthy, or do they reflect the crystallization of certain imperatives emerging from the historical pattern of relations between the state and the economy?

The voluntarist thesis fixes the trials of the state in the tendency of state officials to respond too readily to lobbying, bribery, and campaign contributions from a variety of privileged interests. In its leftist version, it implicates corporate domination of state policy—first, through the infiltration of corporate personnel into state positions, and second, through political expenditures to shape state priorities. In its rightist and centrist versions, the voluntarist thesis puts the blame on the excesses of democracy: the state faces a proliferation of demands from an infinite number of constituencies clamoring for more protection, rights, participation, veto power, and benefits.

The structural theory of the state minimizes the importance of lobbying and the social background of public officials. It insists that the state's very location in the economy imposes a set of imperatives on it as the economy matures, and that the state must either meet these imperatives or face an economic collapse.

Nicos Poulantzas, a French Marxist, criticizes voluntarist theories of the state. The capitalist state, he argues, would be responsive to capitalist interests even if the social background of top officials and the rules of lobbying were radically different.

> The relation between the bourgeois class and the state is an objective relation.... Indeed, in the case of the capitalist state, one can go further: It can be said that the capitalist state best serves the interests of the capitalist class only when members of this class do not participate directly in the state apparatus, this is to say, when the *ruling class* is not the politically *governing class*.[13]

Ralph Miliband, whose own study of the state moved Poulantzas to make those criticisms, takes issue with the emphasis in Poulantzas's study:

> What his exclusive stress on "objective relations" suggests is that what the state does is in every particular and at all times wholly determined by these "objective relations": in other words, that the structural constraints of the system are so absolutely compelling as to turn those who run the state into the merest functionaries and executants of policies imposed upon them by "the system".... The state elite is involved in a far more complex relationship with "the system" ... than Poulantzas' scheme allows....[14]

In our view, Poulantzas, if in an exaggerated way, points to tendencies in the relation between the welfare state and corporate capitalism that American liberals and radicals have too often ignored. Two tendencies are at work within corporate capitalism, each moving in a different time frame but combining at strategic junctures to impose powerful constraints on state action.

First, over the longer run, as structural constraints proliferate and some come near to being contradictions, the welfare state must respond within a narrow range of policy options to keep the system afloat. For example, it cannot significantly reduce inequality; it cannot introduce a highly progressive tax system; it must maintain a large military structure; it cannot introduce meaningful work reform; it must, in times of economic difficulty, favor incentives to investors while imposing constraints on marginal workers in the economy; it cannot plan effectively enough to restore the integrity of crumbling urban areas, but it can expand police, surveillance, and prison facilities in an effort to maintain order there; it cannot forestall the erosion of family and community ties, but can only provide marginal material support to the oldest and youngest victims of this erosion. These broad limits apply whether liberals or business conservatives are in office, and whether the ideological pendulum has swung toward or away from "big business."

These long-term constraints on viable state action are set by the fact that the state must support the social and material preconditions of private profit creation if economic growth is to continue and by the fact that economic growth must continue if the state is to maintain the tax base it needs to respond to electoral and interest-group pressure. The welfare state, then, is accountable in two directions: to the public through elections and to the corporate system through its need to maintain a tax base. Its accountability in the second area sets severe constraints to its democratic accountability, and those constraints tighten as the obstacles to profit realization and economic growth become more severe.

Second, within these larger limits, welfare state options fluctuate with the ebb and flow of the business cycle. When the business cycle is at a peak—when investment, production, consumption, and employment are at high levels—*power struggles* between liberals and conservatives in local, state, and national governments exert an important influence over policy outcomes. Liberals typically press to spend a larger portion of revenues on welfare, health, insurance, and education. These are programs benefiting (in order) middle- and lower-income citizens and the working and nonworking poor. Business conservatives press to concentrate public subsidies in areas of more direct benefit to corporate owners, small businesses, and affluent consumers. Federal and individual state legislatures provide the arenas in which these conflicts are resolved; interest-group maneuvering and log-rolling strategies are important determinants of the outcomes.

When the business cycle moves into a contractionary phase, though, and particularly when the contraction includes the stagflation of recent years, the options available to the welfare state are very limited whether its incumbent officers are liberal or conservative in ideology. These limits are most sharply exposed at the level of individual state governments. Thus in the middle 1970s liberal governors such as Dukakis in Massachusetts, Grasso in Connecticut, Carey in New York, and Brown in California were forced to go against their own ideological inclinations. Faced with declining revenues, growing expenditures for welfare, and inflated prices for state services, each gave high priority to welfare cuts while trying to retain other programs favorable to corporate and financial investors. And when increased taxes became necessary, they came mostly out of the pockets of average taxpayers already hit by inflation, high tax rates, and the threat of unemployment.

In a private corporate economy, corporate owners must be given *incentives* to invest, produce, and employ. Otherwise they might reduce investments; they might relocate in another state inside the United States; or they might divert a portion of their investments and plant to another country with a more favorable business climate. The marginal members of society—the unemployed and the underemployed, the old and the indigent, the unorganized workers—can be *coerced* to work for less, to accept higher prices, to pay higher taxes, and to face heightened job insecurity. Liberal governors and legislators may not like the mix of tools available to them, but when the economic crunch is on, they apply the carrot to privileged constituencies and the stick to the marginal clients.

The welfare state operates within a set of structural constraints, sometimes rather loosely defined, sometimes rigidly operative. The crisis in performance and legitimacy of the welfare state reflects its inability to meet the needs of people within those constraints. And the crisis is accentuated by the fact that liberal politicians and publicists have repeatedly made promises in the name of the welfare state that it cannot keep.

■ The Erosion of Liberalism

The crisis of the welfare state does not mean that it will collapse of its own weight. Rather, several possibilities remain open:

1. The state might muddle through for an indefinite period, holding the system together by repression for some, the promise of escape and advancement for others, and protection for the most privileged. But lost in the muddle would be the poor, the needs of cities, the environment, the inflation squeeze on low- and middle-income employees, and the malaise of the workers.

2. An emergent proto-fascist response might protect the welfare state and the corporate system. Those shuffled out of the system, and those who identify with them, would be subject to increasing repression and intimidation, while corporate elites and workers in the corporate system would coalesce in opposition to the outcasts and the critics.

3. As the crisis deepens, and as the United States continues to

depend on foreign markets and resources in an increasingly hostile world, one or more wars might be launched against foreign adversaries. Internal unity against foreign threats would be sought at the risk of nuclear destruction or the return to universal barbarism.

4. The failures and criticisms of the welfare state could generate a viable movement toward a reconstitution of economic priorities. This would be the most rational response, but it is also one full of risks and pitfalls. These risks are anchored partly in the political hostility that socialist movements receive in American society and partly in the insufficient development of socialist theory itself.

What the welfare state of today cannot do is to deliver on the promises of contemporary liberalism. As an ideology supporting the economic and social needs of the working class and the underclass within corporate capitalism, liberalism is increasingly vulnerable. Its vulnerability flows not so much from the widely perceived gap between the rhetoric of liberals seeking office and their actual intentions; rather, the liberal ideology defeats itself in the very process of trying to fulfill its most humane objectives through the welfare state. In the new situation, unless liberals move to the left, they will be forced increasingly by events to slide to the right.[15]

Liberals accept the system of production for private profit while expecting the welfare state to support the corporate structure, to absorb the social costs of production for profit, and to rectify the injustices done to those shuffled out of the production system. Within that framework, liberals pose a range of state programs. We have already criticized liberal programs for management of the business cycle (Keynesianism), reduction in inequality (progressive taxation), ecological restoration (the economics of environmental management), and the marginal reform of work life (reordering trade union priorities). But other implications of these programs, when they are considered as a package, still need to be examined.

First, success in any area is closely connected to success in the others. And a crucial precondition for all the others is persistent success in regulating the business cycle through Keynesian tools while maintaining high rates of economic growth. Without success here, the tax base required for the other programs cannot be created. Without that base neither a reduction in inequality through progressive taxation nor the increased taxes and consumer costs required for environmental management can hope to gain voluntary constituency assent. Without a large social dividend created by an expanded tax base, public programs in health care, transportation, urban restoration, and welfare will not grow substantially. Given the systemic constraints accepted by liberals, then, it is easy to see why liberals in office typically give economic growth the highest priority and often support enthusiastically tax and subsidy incentives to business as the appropriate means to promote that growth. The liberal consistently supports business priorities today in the hope of creating space tomorrow for cherished liberal programs. That is why Walter Heller, a liberal Keynesian economist in the Kennedy administration, was so bullish after that administration had successfully encouraged economic growth through a cut in business taxes. "When the cost of fulfilling a people's aspirations," he said, "can be met out of a growing horn of plenty, ideological roadblocks melt away, and consensus replaces conflict." [16]

But the obverse is also true. When the policies spurring economic growth have adverse "side effects" like inflation, environmental deterioration, overexpansion of debt, an international arms race, unemployment, and withdrawal by the affluent from the urban centers, the state will lack the resources and will to cope with these consequences when the next downturn occurs. When production for profit requires extensive inequality and alienating work, the state will refuse to tamper with these institutions. When the horn of plenty turns into a squeezed accordion as the business cycle slides into its contractional phase, ideological roadblocks will reappear and consensus will be replaced by class conflict and coercion. Liberals, refusing to acknowledge these structural limits to the liberal agenda, repeatedly justify short-run sacrifices by the subordinate classes in the form of unemployment, wage restraints, and welfare cuts while looking ahead to the next boom for a climate more favorable to the expansion of the welfare state. If radicals, as their critics say, continually tilt at the proverbial windmill, liberals remain content to ride its blade round and round.

But the poverty of liberalism assumes other dimensions as well. By making public promises in the name of the welfare state, liberals encourage unemployed workers, victims of inflation, paralyzed urban residents, and welfare recipients to support policies that will not securely promote their needs over the long run. The disappointed constituencies then blame the state for its failure to solve problems that are in fact outside its capability in the prevailing system of political economy. Expanding the size and role of the welfare state, encouraging its movement into unprofitable areas of public need while reserving profitable enterprises for the private sector, liberalism contributes to the fiscal crisis of the state. It thus plays into the hands of business conservatives who claim persistently that the state is inherently unable to produce goods and services efficiently; and it generates public expectations that cannot be met effectively within the established system. Liberalism, in these ways, accentuates a crisis anchored in the irrational relation between the welfare state and the corporate economy while it diverts the affected constituencies from ideological alternatives that might connect their troubles more closely to the irrational relation itself.

It is clear that most Americans today are unwilling to call themselves liberals. For many, the term connotes softness on crime, state policies that destroy the work ethic and the family, high taxes and inflation, and the overregulation of production and consumption by the state. Thus in 1978, only 25 percent of adult Americans labeled themselves liberal; 39 percent called themselves moderate; and 36 percent considered themselves conservative.[17]

The decline in the fortunes of liberalism is closely connected to the decline in the fortunes of the welfare state. Liberals and their major electoral adversaries—business conservatives—agree on one crucial premise: *when things go wrong in the American political economy, the state is primarily responsible.* Thus as the state has expanded and things have continued to go wrong, the liberal doctrine helps to pave the way for the public conclusion that the state alone is at fault. Further, the judgment that the state is at fault paves the way for a series of selective reductions in state regulation and subsidies, so that the privately incorporated economy can flourish once again. In a political setting where all sides endorse the fundamental imperatives and priorities of the civilization of productivity, the decline of welfare-state liberalism means the ascent of business conservatism.

■ The "Reindustrialization" of America

Liberal ideals are impractical today because the programs that express them often weaken the performance of the political economy of private productivity. This is an assumption we share with corporate conservatives; it provides the basis for business acknowledgment of the structural constraints facing the state in the existing order. They then conclude, of course, that the established economic priorities and imperatives must be accepted and that, therefore, the only rational approach is to reconstitute the state's role in the economy so that these ends can be met more efficiently. The business account supports our thesis of a growing incompatibility between the standards of democratic politics and the priorities of the political economy of private productivity, but they then endorse priorities that are the reverse of ours.

A special edition of *Business Week* issued in June 1980 was devoted to a series of proposals designed to "reindustrialize" America—that is, to remove state policies that dampen incentives to growth in the private sector and to institute state programs that promote conditions favorable to rapid economic growth.[18] The reindustrialists endorse a version of economic theory known as supply-side economics. Supply-siders, as the reindustrialists sometimes call themselves, believe that regulations and high levels of taxation imposed by the state have reduced the growth rate by depressing business incentives to invest in new capital or to increase existing levels of production. When the return is too low and the risk of new regulations too great, capital moves to nonproductive areas; when investment falters, unemployment, inflation, and other social evils are bound to follow. To avert these consequences, disincentives on the supply side of the economy must be removed. The theory of reindustrialization incorporates the assumptions and goals of the supply-side economists and applies them to the specific circumstances existing in the United States today. They have assumed that the economy could

> support an ever-rising standard of living; create endless jobs; provide education, medical care, and housing for everyone; abolish poverty; rebuild the cities; restore the environment; satisfy the demands of blacks, Hispanics, women, and other groups.[19]

These new attitudes and demands—which constitute the core of modern liberalism—have weakened the economy's ability to generate capital, productivity, and growth. Underlying these destructive demands is a more basic phenomenon. It is best described as an inflated notion of *citizen entitlement,* "a new definition of equality that called upon government to level economic and social disparities, an adversary stance toward government and business, and changed motivations toward work."[20]

The obvious answer is to reindustrialize America, and that requires a rollback of liberal programs and policies established during the last two decades. Specifically, reindustrialization demands:

1. a shift in emphasis from consumption to savings and investment

2. a transition within investments to a concentration on "the production of capital goods over quality of life improvements" [21]

3. increased state economic subsidies to business, targeted not for firms that are faring poorly but for those that promise to compete well in the international economy

4. a new social contract between employees and owners, in which workers have a larger voice in deciding the conditions of work and in which they give management more help in improving productivity and decreasing the rate of pay increases

5. a shift to the use of coal, which is plentiful in the United States, and a concomitant relaxation of environmental standards for its use

6. significant changes in the tax system to generate capital, including higher depreciation allowances for capital goods, tax write-offs for research, and lower tax rates on the returns on investment

7. a turn toward government deregulation of business—in the areas of environment, health, equal opportunity, and energy efficiency—to reduce the huge costs of administration and compliance

8. an increase in military expenditures

Amitai Etzioni, the sociologist who claims to have coined the concept of reindustrialization, summarizes the general thrust of the proposals and their anticipated consequences succinctly:

> A decade of public and private belt tightening is therefore needed if all the obsolescent elements are to be replaced and others adapted to the current environment. Otherwise, the slow economic growth, decline in productivity, inflationary pressures, and other well-known signs in the strained economy will persist.[22]

There are some similarities between the new business account of "strains" in the economy and the version we have given in this text. Both theories agree that the privately incorporated economy of growth requires a greater mobilization of social and state resources if it is to continue on its present course. Both agree that the future imperatives of growth will require a curtailment of current levels of consumption, a reduction in state benefits to those constituencies closed out of the corporate economy, and a rollback of state protections in the areas of product quality, citizen health, job safety, and environmental quality. *All these features of the welfare state are also impediments to productivity, profit, and economic growth.*

There is another area of partial agreement. We contend that since the costs of plugging in to the social infrastructure of consumption are so high; since the established routines of work are experienced by many workers as empty and deadly; since the existing welfare expenditures are essential to many people closed out of the corporate economy; since the social effects of environmental deterioration are so harmful to health and safety; since the advance of the civilization of productivity tends simultaneously to deplete traditional sources of social meaning and to increase the compensatory need for monetary income; since the burdens of reindustrialization in the present order will inevitably be distributed unevenly and unjustly, those who are asked to bear the heaviest sacrifices in support of reindustrialization will resist with the means at their disposal. The resistance will take a political form for those who have political resources; it will evince itself in an increase in crime, subversion at work, and entry into the underground economy for those who lack effective political resources. Both responses will emerge together, decreasing the state's ability to support economic expansion by democratic means, impairing the reindustrialization effort, and escalating the use of disciplinary mechanisms of control by state and private bureaucracies. *The reindustrialization of the American economy means the de-democratization of America.*

We say that the reindustrialists only partially concede these points because they do not formulate the harshest implications of their own position. They believe that since reindustrialization is the only rational course, reasonable workers should accept a decline in living standards to promote it—even while investors reap greater rewards. And, they believe, if fair-minded people accept the new "social contract," reindustrialization will proceed in harmony with democracy. But the proponents are, finally, doubtful as to the realism of their own assumptions at this point. From their own perspective, the existing state of American politics is the biggest obstacle to reindustrialization. The reindustrialists, therefore, are only one step away from drawing the next conclusion: if some groups refuse to abide by the dictates of "reason" of their own accord, it will be necessary to impose a reasonable course of action on them. To view reindustrialization as the only rational course open to the country is to accept the means necessary to its fulfillment.

The basic difference between our view and the reindustrialization thesis can now be stated. We believe that today the continued pursuit of rapid economic growth is irrational because of the implications it bears for citizen entitlement, the quality of social life, the risk of war, and democratic politics. The only rational course, therefore, is to reconstitute the prevailing practices of profit, investment, work, consumption, and resource deployment so that democratic institutions can flourish. In the collision between democracy and private productivity, the latter must give way.

■ Reconstituting Economic Priorities

Our primary purpose in this text has been to support the case for an exploration of economic arrangements and priorities that differ from those now governing American society. The student of political economy today, we suggest, is in a position somewhat analogous to that of the political economists of the seventeenth century who sensed that the old ways could no longer secure the allegiance of the populace. The seventeenth-century theorists lacked a well-established model of economic life to guide them in developing alternatives, but they explored the possibilities inherent in a market economy nonetheless.

We have good reason today to believe that the existing models of political economy—capitalism and the state socialism represented by the Soviet Union—contain internal imperatives that threaten those aspirations we value most highly. This is a time when exploratory thinking is desperately needed; it must be guided by the desire to break the binds now imposed by the civilization of productivity while protecting the standards of democratic life that civilization sustained during its period of greatest achievement.

Perhaps the best place to launch this exploratory search is in the area of consumption. In the political economy of corporate capitalism, the pressures to expand existing levels of consumption not only contribute to inflation, dependence on foreign resources, and the deterioration of kinship and community relations; they also generate militant opposition to state efforts to impose austerity. A new model of consumption is needed. It will decelerate the production of *exclusive goods* and accelerate the production of *inclusive goods*. Goods whose extension to larger numbers of people decrease their value and impose heavy social costs of pollution or energy depletion will be deemphasized, and goods whose use can be universalized without producing such heavy collective burdens will be emphasized.

We have given some examples of each type of commodity in earlier chapters. But consider another. In 1980 Chrysler Corporation was on the verge of collapse. The political debate revolved around two courses of action. The state could let Chrysler go under and hence eliminate one player in an already cluttered economy, or it could prop Chrysler up to stave off an increase in unemployment and a major recession. The wrong options governed this debate.

The most rational course would have been a state subsidy accompanied by the insistence that Chrysler's product be changed substantially to fit the transportation, ecological, and resource needs of the country. A couple of options could have been explored. Chrysler might have shifted to the production of mass-transit vehicles, supported by a subsidy that would have allowed it to compete favorably during an interim period of retooling. The expansion of mass-transit systems would reduce individual costs of travel, relieve collective dependence on foreign energy, and improve the quality of the air we breathe. Alternatively, perhaps because the existing investment in the highway system is too expensive to replace, Chrysler might have been retooled to produce cars and buses designed to last fifteen to twenty years. Under this plan, the company would have guaranteed that the basic design of core models would not be changed during a ten-year period (saving expenses in changeover costs), that parts would be standardized, and that the firm would charge a fixed yearly fee to maintain each car for a stated number of years. The result would have been an incentive on the producer's part to build a more durable product, a shift in employment away from production and toward maintenance, and the preservation of nonrenewable resources used in production.

This example could be extended to an indefinite number of areas. Health-care programs could employ salaried physicians and charge a fixed fee for health maintenance; the health service then would have a vested interest in preventing expensive illnesses and in eliminating unnecessary surgery. The cost of medical care would be reduced, while its organization and availability would be enhanced. All "durable" goods could be produced according to the new Chrysler model, making them truly durable once again. Public parks and recreational facilities could be expanded to reduce the private costs of recreation and entertainment. New types of housing designed for several families could be developed, providing energy-efficient space for common use as well as private areas. Food processing and distribution could be altered to lessen the collective costs imposed on the environment and the health costs imposed on individuals.

A concerted program to accelerate the production of inclusive goods would diminish the nation's resource dependence, provide socially valuable forms of employment, curtail the expansion of private consumption costs, protect the environment, and reverse the pressures on the state to impose disciplinary controls on its populace. But such a shift in the social infrastructure of consumption would also require a corollary series of shifts in the role of profit, the place of the market, the organization of work, and the structure of community life. The shift in the mode of consumption involves a reconstruction, evolutionary in form, of the political economy.

The vocabulary available for characterization of the sort of political economy that might be constructed from materials residing in the present order is quite crude and limited. If *capitalism* and *socialism* are the only terms available, then the fact that it would enhance public control over investment and production priorities makes *socialism* the correct term to use. This characterization of the model we support is appropriate in one respect and inappropriate in another. It is appropriate in that the traditional aspiration of democratic socialism is to regulate the production of goods to promote equality and the public interest. It is inappropriate in that twentieth-century systems of socialism have mobilized their populations around the pursuit of economic growth and have suppressed democratic aspirations. They have thus shared one of the central priorities governing capitalist systems and have lost sight of the most important virtue that has accompanied capitalism. The presence of these repressive regimes has stifled creative thinking about the distinctive problems and possibilities confronting advanced capitalist states today. The similarities between the two regimes have been treated unreflectively, as if they were features necessary to any advanced civilization.

The priority of growth was necessary to economies in transition from agricultural to industrial society, but it is a priority that advanced industrial societies must today supplant in the interests of sustaining democratic politics. The economic debate in contemporary politics is concerned with how to impose austerity on one segment of the population while giving privileged constituencies new incentives to invest. It should focus on how to reorganize production and the infrastructure of consumption so that *private consumption needs* can be relaxed and so that *collective programs to restructure the economy can be developed by democratic means.*

The hesitancy to consider any version of socialism flows from the fear, well founded in recent history, that socialism must be incompatible with freedom. We close with some preliminary reflections into this issue.

■ Socialism and Freedom

Historical experience with socialism is quite limited. Advanced industrial societies with highly developed constitutional traditions have not yet introduced it, and industrializing and non-industrial systems have experimented with variants under the most adverse circumstances. There is, then, no historical experience closely applicable to the United States as an advanced industrial society. Optimistic or pessimistic extrapolations from the experiences of other countries must therefore be viewed with caution.

Nonetheless, sociologist Frank Parkin's exploration of the promise and problems of socialist countries in the Soviet orbit deserves to be taken seriously. First, the promise. In these systems, says Parkin, since economic burdens and benefits are distributed *transparently* through a political process rather than *opaquely* through a market mechanism, economic inequality is notably diminished (through the reduction of unemployment, the expansion of public over private goods and services, and the narrowing of income differentials):

> Thus, one of the features of a stratification order based primarily on the market is that the allocation of rewards is generally not in the hands of an easily identifiable and political bounded social group. . . . This is especially so with respect to class perceptions of inequality. . . . In a command system, on the other hand, distribution is primarily decided on the basis of direct political agency. . . . In other words, the source of inequality is primarily political, and by this token, more readily controlled by legislative fiat.[23]

But there is another side to state control of production and distribution. The central coordination required to rationalize the system of production and to reduce inequality increases the state's resources and incentive to stifle political dissent. Parkin, writing with socialist aspirations, is blunt about his perceptions and fears in this regard:

Egalitarianism seems to require a political system in which the state is able continually to hold in check those social and occupational groups which by virtue of their skills or education or personal attributes might otherwise attempt to stake claims to a disproportionate share of society's rewards. The most effective way of holding such groups in check is by denying them the right to organize politically . . . to undermine social equality.[24]

Parkin squarely confronts the sorest spots in socialist theory and in established socialist practice. His fears echo the more stark assertion by Milton Friedman noted in Chapter 1—that there is complete, uneliminable antagonism between socialism and freedom. Let us, though, consider various aspects of this issue in an American context.

1. The inability of the welfare state to cope satisfactorily with poverty and racism, to reverse the trend toward urban collapse, to create meaningful careers for new generations, to reduce the hostility of the Third World to the United States—all these failures encourage it to expand police, military, and surveillance forces at home and abroad. If it cannot cope with the causes of crime and terrorism, it does have the resources and public support needed to respond repressively to criminals, terrorists, and their actual or purported sympathizers. The mode of response, in ways that hardly need elaboration to the contemporary newspaper reader, undermines freedom of assembly, privacy, and dissent. The threat to freedom emerges inside the welfare state as well as inside the socialist state.

2. A certain range of freedom—the freedom to invest for private profit, to exploit the labor of others, to secure privileges denied to others—must be reduced or eliminated in any socialist society. But the corollary is true in corporate capitalism as well: the freedom of workers to control the work process, to engage in unalienating work, and to gain the benefits of job security are all structurally limited. There are thus different limits set by the pursuit of different ends in each system, and it would be quite misleading to call one set an infringement upon liberties while avoiding that assertion with respect to the other.

3. The proliferating dislocations of corporate capitalism have already generated, and will increasingly require, *expansion in capitalist planning,* that is in planning to spur economic growth by securing increasing profits for owners. Recent calls for expanded planning by such luminaries as industrialist Henry Ford, the editors of the *New York Times,* John Kenneth Galbraith, the

Nobel Prize economist Wassily Leontief, the *Business Week* proponents of reindustrialization, and Felix G. Rohatyn, the Wall Street financier, all testify to the likely acceleration of this contemporary trend. Rohatyn, for instance, calls for a new Reconstruction Finance Corporation that would spur economic growth by subsidizing corporate investment into crucial areas. He observes:

> There can be no denying that such an organization can be perceived as a first step toward state planning of the economy. Yet the time may have come for a public debate on this subject.... The premise that under [existing] circumstances, the country has to husband its resources more carefully, allocate them more prudently, and match its financial capabilities with its social priorities would appear to be worth considering. What many will call state planning would, to the average family, be no more than prudent budgeting.[25]

Set in this context the problem of freedom is increasingly seen as a problem for industrial society as such. The question is not, should we have planning? but, what sort of planning? Subject to what modes of political accountability? Inspired by what social purposes? Our own judgment is that the ideal of social planning must be combined with public ownership of large corporate enterprises, retention of a modest market sector that includes publishing and journal enterprises, work reform, and enhanced worker participation in industrial decision making. That combination, we suspect, carries the greatest promise for protecting citizen dissent while orienting the production system more closely to the needs of all citizens.

Socialism, as an ideal, is outside the range of established political debate in America. This exclusion partly accounts for the failure of radicals to explore closely the problem of maintaining freedom within a socialist polity. It is imperative now, though, that this deficiency in socialist thought be remedied. There is promise in this respect for that version of socialism that does not give the highest priority to the growth imperative and that is willing to draw insights from the practices of established constitutional democracies.[26] At any rate, only when a credible vision of democratic socialism is developed can the left begin to combine its critical analysis with an affirmative agenda, provide new alternatives to liberals who threaten to slide to the right, and exert effective pressure on those owners and public officials quite willing to assert that any industrial society must impose low wages, job insecurity, authoritarian modes of work, high costs of living, and escalating taxes on vast numbers of its citizens.

There is no heaven on earth. But to dissect the irrationalities of corporate capitalism, the crisis of the welfare state, and the erosion of liberal ideology is to make the exploration of democratic socialism a matter of the highest priority for those committed to a more humane social order.

NOTES

1. By *state* we mean a nation-state rather than a state government such as Massachusetts or Ohio, unless otherwise specified or clear from context.
2. When we speak of structural constraints, we do not usually refer to constraints in *all* capitalist countries but to those operative in the U.S. system of corporate capitalism. There are connections, though. For example, where would the other capitalist countries be without our military shield? Where would many of them be without our economic penetration and our role in redevelopment after World War II? The unique features in our system—features we have developed highly—still affect the world capitalist system, even if other capitalist countries have not found it necessary to incorporate them. They have not, in part at least, because we have. This is a consideration when asked, why doesn't Germany have *X* or Sweden *Y* if those are features of corporate capitalism (not just happenstances) in America?
3. The long-range employment effect of corporate movement abroad is controversial. Some argue that a net loss in jobs is the result; others contend that job opportunities created in United States multinational corporate headquarters and by repatriated profits are greater than job losses. It is certain that the greater freedom of capital to move gives management a powerful lever in labor negotiations. For a survey of recent literature on the subject, see Richard J. Barnet and Ronald E. Muller, *Global Reach: The Power of Multinational Corporations* (New York: Simon and Schuster, 1975), Ch. 11.
4. We are not arguing against women's right to work, just as our critique of welfare does not question the rights of those currently in the status of welfare recipients. The point is that the most effective form the grievances of dissident or oppressed minorities can assume in the established system either contributes to problems for them elsewhere or projects new burdens on other minorities.
5. In 1974 the United States exported $8 billion in arms. Between 1963 and 1973 the United States was responsible for 51 percent and the USSR for 27 percent of world military exports. See *World Arms Trade* (Bureau of Public Affairs, Department of State, July 1975).

6. These figures and those that follow for education, capital outlays, social security, police activity, and so on, are taken from U.S. Bureau of the Census, *Statistical Abstract of the United States, 1979* (Washington, D.C., 1979), pp. 283–285.

7. Branch Taylor, "The Screwing of the Average Man: Who Gets the $63 Billion?" *Washington Monthly* (March 1972), p. 64.

8. James O'Connor, *Corporations and the State* (New York: Harper and Row, 1974), pp. 105–106.

9. *Statistical Abstract of the United States, 1979*, p. 313.

10. See James O'Connor, *The Fiscal Crisis of the State* (New York: St. Martin's Press, 1973).

11. *Public Opinion* (April/May 1980), p. 23.

12. Ibid., p. 23.

13. "The Problem of the Capitalist State," in *Ideology in Social Science*, edited by Robin Blackburn (New York: Vintage Books, 1973), pp. 245, 246.

14. "Reply to Nicos Poulantzas," Ibid., pp. 258–259.

15. We focus on liberal economic programs, not on the liberal commitments to dissent and free assembly. But the latter ideals depend to a great extent on success in promoting the liberal economic agenda within the welfare state.

16. Walter Heller, *New Dimensions of Political Economy* (Cambridge: Harvard University Press, 1967), p. 12.

17. *Public Opinion* (April/May 1980), p. 28.

18. *Business Week*, special issue: "The Reindustrialization of America" (June 1980).

19. Ibid., p. 84.

20. Ibid., p. 84.

21. Ibid., p. 88.

22. *New York Times*, June 29, 1980.

23. Frank Parkin, *Class Inequality and Political Order* (New York: Praeger, 1971), pp. 160–161, 168.

24. Ibid., p. 183.

25. "A New RFC Is Proposed for Business," *New York Times*, December 1, 1974.

26. The problem of making socialist planning consistent with individual freedom is perhaps the crucial issue in socialist thought. An excellent beginning is made by Paul Ricoeur, "The Political Paradox," in *Existential Phenomenology and Political Theory*, edited by Hwa Yol Yung (Chicago: Regnery, 1972), pp. 337–367. For a more recent account of the problem of freedom in socialism and some institutional means for coping with it, see William E. Connolly, "A Note on Freedom under Socialism," *Political Theory* (November 1977): 461–468.

INDEX

Galbraith, John Kenneth
  on concentration, 32–33
  as a perspective, 31–38
  on power, 31, 32, 33, 37
  on the state, 33, 37
  on state planning, 69–70, 231
  on technocrats, 33–34
  on terms of trade, 37
Gauley Bridge disaster, 102, 108
Georgescu-Roegen, Nicholas
  on second law of thermodynamics, 114n
Giddens, Anthony, 47n
Goldthorpe, John
  on class consciousness, 118
Gordon, David M., 46n
Gordon, Glen, 15n, 76n, 145n
Gorz, André, 17, 144n
  on alienation, 38, 43
  on collective needs, 39–40
  on new consumer needs, 38–40
  production relations perspective and, 38–43
  on structural reforms, 42
  on technocrats, 40–41
Gross, Bertram, and Stanley Moss, 191n
Growth. See also Depletable resources; Exclusive goods; Heller, Walter.
  rising social costs and, 205–6
  limits to, 226

Habermas, Jurgen, 147n
Hampshire, Stuart, 112n
Hardin, Garret
  tragedy of the commons and, 112
Harmon, R. G., 86t
Harrington, Michael, 46n
Heffner, Richard D., 145n
Heilbroner, Robert, 112n
Heller, Walter
  on growth, 158, 193n, 233n
HEW Report Work in America, 144n
  worker discontent and, 120
Hirsch, Fred, 15n
Hirschman, Albert, 3, 15n

Hohenemser, Kurt H., 114n
Holland, Daniel M., and Stewart C. Myers, 187t
Hubbert, M. King, 95t
Hunnius, Gerry, G. David Garson, and John Case, 144n

Identity. See also Ideology.
  and social order, 3
Ideology
  consensus and, 61, 63–64
  functionalism of, 70–71, 74
  hidden injuries of class and, 74
  instrumental view of work and, 120
  management science and, 128
  narrow range of debate in, 201
  on welfare state as scapegoat, 214–16
Incentives
  environmental degradation and, 104
  individual and social, 64
  internal and external, 64
  Taylorism and, 123–24
Individualism. See also Alienation; Needs.
  economic man critiqued, 58
  future generations and, 84
  social structures and, 105
Inequality
  absolute and relative, 54
  functionalist theory and, 59–65
  growth and, 157
  intraclass divisions and, 57–58, 65–66, 204–5
  manual versus mental, 127–28
  market power of professions, 63
  measures of, 49–54
  of occupational hierarchy, 52–53, 70
  stratification and, 77n
  in taxes and subsidies, 51, 209–212
  vulgar socialism and, 71–72
  wage labor and, 65–74
  worker motivation and, 64, 205

International
  corporate investment strategy, 72,
    101, 204, 219, 232n
  raw material dependency, 206–7
Irish, Marian D., and James W.
  Prothro, 111n

Jenkins, David, 144n

Kaletsky, Anatole, 89t
Kapp, William K.
  on political economy of ecology,
    80, 81
Keynes, John Maynard, 155
Keynes, Milo, 193n
Kohlmeier, Lawrence, 113n
Kuhn, Thomas A.
  on theoretical disputes, 46–47n

Lampman, Robert J., 194n
Lane, Robert, 118
Lekachman, Robert, 193n
Lenski, Gerhard, 46n
Leonard, William N., 194n, 195n
Leontief, Wassily, 231
Levy, Walter, 115n
Liberal reforms. See also Structural
  reforms.
  divide political constituencies, 58–
    59, 74–75, 85, 110
  ecological restoration and, 85, 109
  production for profit and, 220
  to redistribute income, 71–72
  work life conditions and, 72–73
Lindsey, Robert, 195n
Love Canal, 108–9
Lukes, Steven, 45n, 145n
Lundberg, Ferdinand, 75n

MacCallum, Gerald, 45n
McClellan, David, 145n
McConnell, Grant
  on political economy of ecology,
    80–81
McGovern, George, 72
Madison, James
  on unequal property, 61–62
Magdoff, Harry, 191n, 197n

Malthus, Thomas, 155, 168
Market relations
  defined 7, 8
  farm model, 18–20
Marx, Karl, 3
  on alienation, 126–29
  on vulgar socialism, 71
Meade, James, 193n
Means, Gardner C., 47n, 194n
Method and political economy. See
  Explanation.
Miliband, Ralph
  on elites and the state, 217
Militarism
  arms exports and, 207, 232n
  costs of, 176–78
  employment and, 168–69, 176
Mills, C. Wright, 118
  on white-collar proletarianization,
    133–34
Minsky, Hyman
  on financial markets, 198n
Montesquieu, 3–4
Moody, J. D., 94t
Moore, Wilbert, 60–61, 63
Mueller, Willard F.
  on concentration and prices, 194n
Muller, Ronald E., 232n

Nash, C. A., 88t
Needs. See also Consumption; Incentives.
  collective, 39–40, 205
  exclusive goods and, 171–72
  family production and, 204–205
  inflation and, 172, 175
  natural environment and, 39, 170
  social environment and, 38–40,
    104–8, 174–75
  species and, 126
Nelson, Ralph, 194n
Nutter, G. Warren, 194n

Occupational Safety and Health Act,
  103
O'Connor, James
  on state employment, 213

Steuart, Sir James, 4
Stobaugh, Robert, and Daniel Yergin, 115n
Stone, Katherine
  on labor in steel industry, 76n
Strikes
  in France, 1968, 119
  in Homestead, Ill., 1892, 67
  in Lordstown, Ohio, 119
  in Vauxhall plant, England, 118
Structural constraints and contradictions
  defined, 202
  facing welfare state, 217–18
  illustrated, 203–7
  personal binds and, 202–3
Structural reforms. See also Socialist proposals.
  defined, 42
  versus liberal reforms, 71–72, 74–75
  to reduce inequality, 73–74
Supply side economics, 223ff.
Survey polls
  alternative theories and, 145n
  on causes of inflation, 215
  on confidence in government, 215
  on erosion of liberalism, 222
  on grievances of workers, 130
  on HEW Report, 120
  terms of comparison and, 121
  work satisfaction, 117–18
Sweezy, Paul M., 192n, 197n
Sylos-Labini, Paulo, 195n

Taylor, Branch, 233n
Taylor, Charles
  on neutrality in sciences, 15, 75–76n
Taylor, Frederick W., 121
Taylorism
  as model of work, 121–26
  on separation of work and play, 137
  spread to white-collar work, 134–36

Terkel, Studs
  Depression interviews by, 152–54
  worker interviews by, 136
Thurow, Lester C., 115n, 196n
Tilgher, Adriano, 147n
Tiratsoo, E. N., 92t
Tobin, James
  on future economic stability, 193n
  on Phillips Curve, 158
Toulmin, Stephen
  on method, 46n
Tribe, Lawrence, 112n

Unemployment
  explanation of, 154–56, 191–93n
  measures of, 149–50, 191n
  military spending and, 176
Usury, 2

Welfare state. See also State.
  characteristics, 44, 201, 208
  crisis of legitimacy, 44, 202, 221–22
  cyclical constraints in, 218
  erosion of liberalism, 219–22
  expenditure by type, 208–12
  politics of displacement and, 201–2, 214–15
  priorities of, 208
  structural constraints of, 217–18
  target for resentment, 10, 214–16
Wertheimer, A., 45n
Whyte, William F., 146n
Wolff, Kurt H., 76n
Wolff, Robert Paul, 112n
Work. See also Alienation; Taylorism; Work reform.
  incentives and, 64
  instrumental view of, 117, 123, 127, 140
  issue displacement and, 132
  manual-mental separation and, 124
  mobility and, 6
  obsolescence of skills, 7
  productivity and, 177–82
  sublimated politics and, 131

4 5 6 7 8 9 0